Going on Being in Challenging Times

In this volume, we explore what it is to live through trauma while experiencing huge losses that threaten our well-being. The book demonstrates how clinicians can help patients regain meaning and purpose once again.

The authors in these chapters sensitively annotate their therapeutic journeys with their patients, all of whom grapple with extremely difficult emotional conditions. There is much that can be learned about going-on-being from psychoanalysts, who have always worked in the depth of the unconscious psychic dimension. The authors focus on the psychic processes, the core experiences, and the qualities of selfhood that help to move the human soul through despair on to hope and new beginnings. Rich clinical vignettes illustrate these ideas in a way that is sure to help clinicians and other readers face and work with their own and others' places of pain and challenge.

We have all been shaken by the winds of unsettling social and political change over the past few years; hence this book will appeal to a wide audience. Psychoanalysts, psychologists, psychotherapists, psychiatrists, clinical social workers, counselors, students, and others in the helping professions will find this book essential reading, as will members of the wider public who have experienced challenges in their own or their loved one's "going-on-being".

Michelle Flax, Ph.D. is a Clinical Psychologist and Psychoanalyst in private practice in Toronto, Canada; Supervising Psychoanalyst and Faculty, Toronto Institute for Contemporary Psychoanalysis; and Executive and Faculty at the Advanced Training in Psychoanalytic Psychotherapy Program (ATPPP).

J. Gail White, Ph.D. is a Psychoanalyst in private practice in Toronto; Supervising Psychoanalyst and Faculty, Toronto Institute for Contemporary Psychoanalysis; and Student Progress committee member of the Advanced Program in Psychoanalytic Psychotherapy (ATPPP).

Going on Being in Challenging Times

Psychoanalytic Reflections

Edited by Michelle Flax and J. Gail White

Routledge
Taylor & Francis Group

LONDON AND NEW YORK

Designed cover image: Image by David Gregg (Getty)

First published 2026
by Routledge
4 Park Square, Milton Park, Abingdon, Oxon OX14 4RN

and by Routledge
605 Third Avenue, New York, NY 10158

*Routledge is an imprint of the Taylor & Francis Group, an informa
business*

British Library Cataloguing-in-Publication Data
A catalogue record for this book is available from the British Library

ISBN: 978-1-041-01023-4 (hbk)
ISBN: 978-1-032-99384-3 (pbk)
ISBN: 978-1-003-60712-0 (ebk)

DOI: 10.4324/9781003607120

Typeset in Optima
by Apex CoVantage, LLC

Contents

Acknowledgments   x
List of Contributors   xi

Introduction   1

PART I
Going-on-Being Through Losses   11

1 **Free to Mourn and Mourning to Be Free: Going-on-Being in
   Challenging Times**   13
   ELIZABETH B. SULLIVAN

2 **East of the Awning: Staying the Course and Moving On**   22
   JULIET HEEG

3 **Going-on-Being: Potential Space in the Uncertainty of
   the Pandemic**   31
   ALEXIA CAMFIELD

4 **Going-on-Being: Aging, Agency, and Downsizing**   38
   MICHAEL STERN

PART II
Going-on-Being Through Threats to the Self   47

5 **Living Atop Archaic Agonies: Treating Children Suffering
   from Early Trauma**   49
   BRENT WILLOCK

 6 The Myth of Philoctetes and the Refusal to be "Cured"   63
    IONAS SAPOUNTZIS

 7 I Rage, Therefore I Am   74
    BRENT WILLOCK

 8 Accepting Death: The Role of Psychic Organizers in
    Death Awareness   82
    JOY A. DRYER

PART III
Representation and Going-on-Being   95

 9 Going-on-Being in Challenging Times: Greek Mythology and
    Mythic Approaches to Resilience   97
    RENÉE CHEROW-O'LEARY

10 Going-on-Being in the Body: From the Concrete Use of the
    Body to the Symbolic Use of the Mind   106
    J. GAIL WHITE AND MICHELLE FLAX

11 So Close and Yet So Far Away: Psychoanalytic Treatment and
    Recovery From Psychosis-Inducing Trauma   116
    BURTON NORMAN SEITLER

PART IV
Going-on-Being Through Social-Political Upheaval   125

12 Dehumanization and Going-on-Being After Catastrophic Trauma   127
    JOHN A. SLOANE

13 Striving to Create a Safe Space in an Unsafe World:
    Responding to Students' Needs in the Days After October 7   137
    IONAS SAPOUNTZIS AND AMIRA SIMHA-ALPERN

14 Going-on-Being in Two Cultures: Nepantla – In-Between the
    First and Second Generation of Latinx Immigrant, Higher
    Education, Scholarship Students   146
    HELEN QUIÑONES

15 Beyond Neutrality: The Role of Political Beliefs in the
    Therapeutic Relationship   156
    JOHN O'LEARY

PART V
Going-on-Being in the Countertransference   167

16 **Going-on-Being When the Going Gets Rough: An Impasse in the Negative Transference/Countertransference**   169
HEIDI KNOLL

17 **When There Is No Room to Play**   175
MEHR-AFARIN KOHAN

18 **Going-on-Being as a Couple During Environmental Trauma**   182
ANASTASIA TSAMPARLI

19 **Taking Sides: Managing Strong Countertransference Feelings in Couples Therapy**   190
MELINDA BLITZER

Conclusion   199

Index   *202*

Acknowledgments

The inspiration for this book came out of a conference that was planned to take place in 2020. Owing to the outbreak of the Covid-19 pandemic the proposed conference was called off, and then rescheduled to 2023. The title of the conference, "Going on Being in Challenging Times", ironically presaged the coming of the collective trauma of the global pandemic.

We thank the members of the planning committee of the Joint International Conference for their creative conference proposal and their hard work in bringing the conference to fruition despite the myriad obstacles of the times. We also thank Kate Hawes and her diligent team at Routledge for their excellent guidance and facilitation of this volume. We give thanks to Danielle Flax who provided invaluable help in the preparation of the manuscript.

Every effort has been made to contact copyright holders. The publisher would be grateful to hear from any copyright holder who is not here acknowledged and will rectify any errors and omissions in future editions of the book.

We thank New Directions Publishing Corp for permission to use a quotation from the poem "The Dead Woman" (La Muerta) taken from *The Captain's Verses*, 1972, by Pablo Neruda and translated by David Walsh.

Contributors

Melinda Blitzer, Ph.D. is a Psychologist and Psychoanalyst in private practice in New York and Associate Professor in Psychology and Human Development at Empire State University.

Alexia Camfield MSW, LCSW is a Psychotherapist and Supervisor in private practice in Houston, Texas and a PhD student in psychodynamic theory at the Institute for Clinical Social Work, Chicago.

Renée Cherow-O'Leary, Ph.D. is former faculty at City College, Rutgers University, and Columbia University, and currently Senior Scholar at the UCLA Center for Scholars and Storytellers.

Joy A. Dryer, Ph.D. is a Psychoanalyst in private practice in New York, currently faculty at the PACT Institute.

Michelle Flax, Ph.D. is a Clinical Psychologist and Psychoanalyst in private practice in Toronto, Canada. She is a Supervising Psychoanalyst and faculty at Toronto Institute for Contemporary Psychoanalysis, as well as Executive and Faculty Member at the Advanced Training in Psychoanalytic Psychotherapy Program (ATPPP). She has previously published in *Psychoanalytic Quarterly*, the *Journal of the American Psychoanalytic Association*, *Canadian Journal of Psychoanalysis*, and *Gender and Psychoanalysis*.

Juliet Heeg, LCSW-R is in private practice in New York City and is Emeritus Chair of Psychoanalytic Psychotherapy Study Center (PPSC) Annex. She primarily works with couples and holds an Advanced Certificate in Core Skills Training in Emotionally Focused Therapy.

Heidi Knoll, LICSW is in private practice in New York City and Washington, DC. She is on the faculty of the Westchester Center for the Study of Psychoanalysis and Psychotherapy in White Plains, New York.

Mehr-Afarin Kohan, M.D. is a Toronto-based Psychiatrist and Psychoanalyst and Psychodynamic Psychotherapy Supervisor at the University of Toronto, as well as Interim Academic Director, three-year program, and faculty at the TICP.

John O'Leary, Ph.D. is a Clinical Psychologist and Psychoanalyst in private practice in New York City and faculty and Supervisor at William Alanson White Psychoanalytic Institute.

Helen Quiñones, Ph.D. is a Clinical Psychologist and Psychoanalyst, Supervisor and faculty at William Alanson White Institute, and Clinical Consultant at New York University Postdoctoral Program.

Ionas Sapountzis, Ph.D. is a Psychologist and Psychoanalyst in private practice in Garden City, NY, Associate Professor at the Derner School of Psychology of Adelphi University, and the Director of its School Psychology Program, as well as a faculty member and Supervisor in the Psychoanalytic Psychotherapy and the Child, Adolescent and Family Psychotherapy programs of the Derner School of Psychology.

Burton Norman Seitler, Ph.D. is a Psychoanalyst and Clinical Psychologist in private practice, Supervising Training Analyst, and Current Board of Trustees Chair at the New Jersey Institute for Psychoanalysis and Psychotherapy.

Amira Simha-Alpern, Ph.D. is a Clinical Psychologist and Psychoanalyst in private practice in Smithtown, NY, Director of the Postgraduate Programs in Psychoanalysis and Psychotherapy at the Derner School of Psychology, Adelphi University, and Clinical Assistant Professor of Psychiatry at Stony Brook University.

John A. Sloane, M.D. is a Psychiatrist and Psychoanalyst in private practice in Toronto, Assistant Professor of Psychiatry at the University of Toronto, and Supervising Analyst at the Toronto Institute for Contemporary Psychoanalysis.

Michael Stern, Ph.D. is a Psychologist and Psychoanalyst in private practice in New Jersey, Former President of the Psychoanalytic Society of the NYU Postdoctoral Program for Psychoanalysis and Psychotherapy, and Former Clinical Supervisor at the Institute for Contemporary Psychotherapy.

Elizabeth B. Sullivan, LCSWR is a Clinical Social Worker and Psychoanalyst in private practice in Garden City, NY, President of the Adelphi Society for Psychoanalysis and Psychotherapy, and a Ph.D. Candidate at the Institute for Clinical Social Work.

Anastasia Tsamparli, Ph.D. is a Clinical Psychologist and conducts Psychoanalytic couple and family therapy and is a Professor Emeritus of Clinical Psychology at the University of Aegean, Greece.

J. Gail White, Ph.D. is a Psychoanalyst in private practice in Toronto, Supervising Psychoanalyst and faculty at Toronto Institute for Contemporary Psychoanalysis, Student Progress committee member of the Advanced Program in Psychoanalytic Psychotherapy, a former lecturer at the University of Toronto and York University, and she has multiple publications in previous books of the Joint International Conference and has published in *Gender and Psychoanalysis*.

Brent Willock, Ph.D. is a Clinical Psychologist in private practice in Toronto, Past President of the Toronto Institute for Contemporary Psychoanalysis, a board member of the Canadian Institute for Child & Adolescent Psychoanalytic Psychotherapy, and faculty of the Postgraduate Program in Psychoanalysis and Psychotherapy, Adelphi University, Derner School of Psychology.

Introduction

We live in a period of colliding existential challenges. Recent history has ush-ered in an era of collective trauma on the heels of a global pandemic, numer-ous wars, environmental crises, and corresponding deadly socio-political events. Ours is a time of great apprehension and instability that has threat-ened our very existence and has challenged our ability to go-on-being. Loss, individual and collective trauma, interpersonal conflicts, sudden or chronic illness, and ongoing developmental crises all challenge our ability to main-tain the capacity to make meaning.

Freud (1915, 1916), in thinking and writing about his times of war and death, spoke about his culture's denial of death. This denial of death led to unconscious illusions being "badly shaken in their expectations" (p. 209) when harsh reality burst through secure defensive psychological structures. In order to fully live our lives, he exclaims, we must first come to accept the finality of death as part of life. This ability to mourn our losses in life instead of turning away in denial is instrumental to our well-being.

By 1920, Freud had suffered through the first World War, was in the midst of the ravages of the Spanish Flu pandemic, and was despairing in facing the death of his beloved daughter Sophie. He speaks of his overwhelming challenges where he struggled to go-on-being, and at the same time, to fur-ther develop his work on the importance of accepting hard realities through mourning the individual and collective losses of the times.

With all change and uncertainty, we experience our vulnerability and our unnerving affect. As Britzman (2024) writes, "the challenge of change is cata-strophic and requires disquieting imagination in working through an educa-tion that had already happened" (p. 30). What are the psychic processes, the core experiences, and the qualities of selfhood that move the soul through despair to hope? Where do we find the possibilities that life has to offer for rejuvenation, restoration, and new beginnings? What can be learned about going-on-being from psychoanalysts who have been grappling with these very questions with their patients over many years?

The concept of "going-on-being" was first described by the psycho-analyst Donald Winnicott (1963). The experience of going-on-being for an infant results from the caretaker psychically holding the infant through

DOI: 10.4324/9781003607120-1

empathic attunement to the baby's needs in early life. This allows for the infant's sense of continuity and the formation of the infant's self. The concept of "going-on-being" is very much embedded in the work of Melanie Klein, Donald Winnicott, Wilfred Bion, and others. Thomas Ogden (2019, 2024) astutely points out that psychoanalysis as a therapeutic venture involves two interdependent dimensions: the ontological perspective, which is about being and coming into being, and the epistemological dimension which has to do with understanding and coming to know. The ontological dimension is captured well in the work of Winnicott and Bion, while Freud and Klein embrace the epistemological approach (Ogden, 2019, 2024). Bion and Winnicott were concerned with the conditions that allow the patient to go-on-being, to become more alive to themselves, and to connect to an 'interwoven' other. Their focus is on the experience of the self. Ogden (2024) emphasizes that "understanding is born from experiencing but experiencing is not born from understanding" (2024, p. 14). The core of the ontological perspective is how the self experiences aliveness, realness, coming into oneself, and going-on-being. The focus in this approach is not necessarily on understanding and being as nouns, but as verbs; the emphasis is on action, that is to say, doing, thinking, dreaming, creating, and reflecting as these activities cleave with new understandings and ways of going-on-being.

The authors in this volume 'play' in the realm of both the ontological and epistemological dimensions as they explore the idea of what it is to go-on-being when we are challenged. The emphasis in these chapters is on the changing experience of the self through tribulation, self-reflection, meaning making, and significant interpersonal relationships. The topics include various challenges faced by diverse populations across the lifespan.

Going-on-Being Through Losses

Pablo Neruda poetically described coping with loss: "My feet will want to walk where you are sleeping, but I shall stay alive".[1] Facing and accepting losses is integral to our mental health and our sense of going-on-being. This first section of the book explores and grapples with the theme of loss. The importance of the process of mourning has been a central tenet in the practice of psychoanalysis (Freud, 1917). The ability to mourn allows us, in time, to accept loss and go on living. This painful process renews and affirms life.

Freud (1917) situated the process of mourning at the core of healing. In describing the profundity of the loss of the self in complicated grief reactions, Freud (1917) wrote, "In mourning, the world has become impoverished and empty, during melancholia, it is the ego itself" (p. 246). Freud speaks of mourning as a developmental achievement, fundamental to mental health. In grieving we face and endure the sadness of loss alone or together with others by working it over symbolically in our minds or externalizing our feelings in ritual and ceremony. Jonathan Lear (2022) writes that "in mourning, 'the imaginative playground' is preserved" (p. 63). If we disavow the grieving process, and refuse to acknowledge our losses and our defenselessness, we regress to narcissistic concretized states of being that Freud termed 'melancholia', where we cannot think through emotionally as we do in mourning. Leonoff (2024) relates the individual capacity to mourn to the society's ability to mourn its losses and ideals. If a society cannot begin to mourn their losses, a "social melancholia" emerges which occurs when "a society . . . has foreclosed on mourning and interprets its losses and disillusionments through the lens of conspiracy and betrayal" (p. 61).

Within this collection, Elizabeth B. Sullivan explores how freedom and mourning are related, in that one has to be free to mourn and that one cannot be free to pursue a new path until one has mourned. She poignantly describes a patient who endured a loss (a betrayal by the Catholic Church) so great that she was frozen and unable to grieve, and who defended against her loss through great hostility towards others. At the same time, Sullivan's complicated and incompletely worked-through relationship with her own religious upbringing constricted her freedom to work with this patient's hostility and complicated dynamics. Sullivan uses Freud's concepts of mourning and melancholia to highlight the importance of consciously processing losses to facilitate psychological growth and freedom for both patient and analyst.

The Covid pandemic presaged deep losses for many, sometimes in unexpected ways. Analysts, so used to using all the cues of the in-person setting, had to learn to work remotely on telephone or online. Contributor Juliet Heeg struggled with the loss of her beautifully curated office during the Covid pandemic, an office that both expressed and created a professional identity in her early years of practice. Covid-19 necessitated her move to an online platform, requiring her to slowly psychologically disinvest from her office, her own longstanding holding environment. Over time, she and a patient recognized that they had succeeded in transitioning the office space to the screen. An interpersonal space was created online and there was now "enough of room" in her. She was able to permanently let go of her beloved office set up by a younger professional self and in that process of letting go, something life affirming emerged for her.

In this volume Alexia Camfield interestingly reflects on how the pandemic surprisingly provided an opportunity for creative adaptation and meaningful change for some patients. She notes that clinicians have had to navigate our own catastrophes and at the same time make sense of the potentially destabilizing enactments of patients. Camfield noticed that it was through the disruption of patients' usual living patterns that new meaningful adaptation could begin to take place. She asks, "Does it take a pandemic to make the space and time that we need in our lives?"

Losses occur throughout the life cycle. Having to let go of objects and versions of ourselves in the process of aging or environmental impingement is a topic that all of us face. Contributor Michael Stern reminds us that objects and object ties acquire a significance in that they symbolize our lived experience and our attachments. Downsizing is thus fraught with emotional challenges to our sense of personal agency and continued relevance. And yet, letting go or modifying object ties that have outlived their appropriateness in the present may serve to enhance fulfillment in the new situation, Stern notes. While it may bring some difficult emotions in the transition, balancing what stays and what goes "requires the embrace of the ever-shifting nature of attachments and the inevitability of loss".

Going-on-Being Through Threats to the Self

Related to the theme of loss is the theme of dealing with ongoing threats to the self. Threats to the self may be threats to the ego and superego, may have a transient effect on self-esteem and self-image, or they may deeply threaten and endanger our sense of continuity.

The earliest threat to the self is the threat to the nascent self where there have been unavoidable impingements upon the infant. In this volume Brent Willock illustrates how excessive separation from caretakers in the early months of life leaves the young child cut off from the root of their fledgling sense of self. Willock sensitively describes his work with a prematurely born young child who spent months in the neonatal ICU. He outlines the primitive defenses that are characteristic of this early stage of development and the treatment process in working with such patients. The holding environment Willock provided in his treatment of this young boy facilitated the 'thawing' of various 'frozen' parts of the young boy's self, allowing for his further development within the therapeutic relationship and beyond.

A sense of threat to the core of the self is particularly prevalent in adolescence. It is quite often the case that adolescents do not stay in therapy, refuse treatment, or resist any cure. Contributor Ionas Sapountzis movingly describes Philoctetes, a mythological character, as a metaphor for young male patients who resist treatment because they are ashamed of themselves and what they cannot be. Sapountzis tells us that these young men fear what the 'other' may find in them, and they retreat to illusory safety in 'caves', filled with screens and distractions. An active stance by the therapist and parents is needed to help these patients come out of the empty void.

In a second clinically rich chapter, Brent Willock develops the idea that underlying the intractable rage of some individuals, there is an unconscious fear that they will cease to go-on-being. The rage is seen as a defense against a felt threat to their very existence. The sense of strength through rage can be intensified as needed, albeit in an unsatisfactory compromise between ceasing to exist, and going-on-being.

The primary threat to the self is actual death. In writing about the recent plague, Jacqueline Rose (2023) asks,

> what do you do with death and dying when they can no longer be pushed to the outer limits of your lived experience or dismissed from your

conscious mind? How do you live with death or rather how do you "live death" . . . when death comes too close, pervading the air you breathe?

(p. 4)

Joy A. Dryer asserts that the idea of actual death needs to be brought into the consulting room for discussion. The symbolic aspects of death have been long considered by psychoanalysts. Dryer tells us that it is important for therapists to be able to face the idea of their own and their patients' actual death. She suggests we develop a mortality literacy for our patients and for the culture at large. The chapter arose out of her therapy with a patient with multiple food allergies who was frequently in danger of imminent death, even within the consulting room. Dryer employs various psychic organizers with her patient, forming a joint language around death as loss, death as relational, and death as reality. She aptly reminds us to consider the well-known Latin phrase: *Memento Mori*, which translates to "remember that you die".

Representation and Going-on-Being

The ability to mentalize, think about, and contextualize what we experience is an essential aspect of going-on-being and is pivotal in being able to grieve what is lost. In the absence of such representational processes, experience must be expelled, miniaturized, disavowed, etc. (Ferro, 2011; Levine, 2022). Intense affect can overwhelm the capacity to process experience and trauma can ensue (Fernando, 2022; Levine, 2022).

As a society, we rely on the arts to express communal emotions. Myths, tales, and their expression through theater, literature, and film join with the visual arts to portray the range of human affect. In this volume, Renee Cherow-O'Leary draws on Greek Mythology to illustrate "what it takes to survive internal trauma, external chaos and the 'slings and arrows of outrageous fortune'". She highlights some essential lessons derived from the myths regarding the human capacity to continue to endure. Interestingly, she adds a contemporary mythic process, that of Chat GPT. She reminds us that as a species, we are adaptive animals. We need now to find new ways to adapt to this challenging technological era, even as those new digital tools require us to contain and restrain our human capacity for destruction.

Representation on an intrapsychic level refers to the ability of the individual to present to the mind their bodily sensations enabling these sensations to be put into words and thought through the psyche. In this volume J. Gail White and Michelle Flax grapple with the question of what happens when the mind is overwhelmed by trauma. These authors point out that the body becomes the somatic reservoir for such unresolved difficult experiences. White and Flax point to a continuum on the one end of which symptoms are symbolically encoded in the body. On the other end of the continuum, there is little capacity for mentalization, and drive unbinding can lead to grave illness in the patient. They include their own and their patients' stories of having to work through painful, unarticulated places of pain that were presenting through the body. In a similar vein, Buron Norman Seitler beautifully illustrates the process of working with an adolescent patient. Using drawings with a psychotic, traumatized adolescent, he helped this adolescent move from somatic symptom to delusional symptom, and then through artistic expression to symbol formation.

Going-on-Being Through Social-Political Upheaval

Psychoanalytic concepts have been applied to the understanding of culture since the early 1900s when anthropologists following Freud's ideas about the unconscious carefully investigated the relationship between culture and the psyche. The chapters in this section address the complex intersection between psychoanalysis and the socio-political world. The authors examine what it is to go-on-being through the social and political upheavals of our current zeitgeist.

Leonoff (2024) writes about the importance for societies to mourn their losses: "Societies which foreclose on mourning can regress into social melancholia, while trying to reclaim some illusive lost destiny or ideal" (p. 61). Having discussed the violent social fallout of war and plague, he writes that societies that revolt against mourning refuse to acknowledge their losses and vulnerability and hence "this foments violence against vulnerable groups within the society and malignantly for the world" (p. 62). He declares that the capacity to mourn is "the pathway to social justice" (p. 61).

In this volume, John A. Sloane laments that a common response to the horrors of the last years (crumbling world orders, the pandemic, climate crises) is the tendency to dehumanize the other. Sloane's plaintive plea is: "Is there any way of transforming our all-out infantile destructiveness into viable limit-setting and capacities for truly human relatedness?" Drawing on his online work with traumatized Ukranian analysts and patients, he contends that it is not only what is done to us that destroys us as human beings, but what we find ourselves doing to others. He argues that what erupts from within requires both 'holding' and 'holding responsible'.

Immigration has become a burgeoning polarizing concern for many nations in these past years, given the destabilizing forces of war, plague, and environmental disasters. Helen Quiñones focuses on the challenges faced by immigrating students caught between their two identities. The challenge for these students is how to integrate and maintain diverse aspects of their identity – to hold a connection both with the country of origin and with the adoptive country. In treating these students, Quiñones draws on her own immigrant experience to help bridge past and present. Her premise is that first and second generation bi-cultural individuals need to go-on-being by finding integrative ways to link the two cultures.

John O'Leary's concern in the present volume is how we can go-on-being through the current trend toward political polarization. His contention is that psychoanalysts lean primarily liberal which can disenfranchise those who hold divergent political views. He notes that political designations ('the left' and 'the right') themselves are undergoing some changes since the invasion of Israel in October 2023, and the subsequent war in Gaza. In his view, we are all subjected to great amounts of propaganda and maintaining a 'neutral' or balanced position is impossible. His case studies illustrate the potentially contentious nature of political divergence in the consulting room and how such political divergence can be negotiated so that there can be a strengthening of the alliance.

The polarization of political views has been even more evident since the October 7th attack on Israel and consequential war in the Middle East. In broaching the theme of violence and destructiveness of human beings, Sapountzis and Simha-Alpern write about a brave initiative undertaken by a private university to offer process groups to students and faculty soon after the catastrophic events in Israel and Gaza. Their aim was to provide a place for people to gather, a place of "radical empathy" where attendees could share their feelings and experiences. To their surprise, few members of the university attended, perhaps in fear of the potentially divisive nature of such discussions. Their attempt to bring together individuals who hold completely contrary views regarding the current crisis in the Middle East was prescient, given the polarizing university protests and counter protests set up in more recent times.

Going-on-Being in the Countertransference

Working With Individual Patients

What is it to go on working as a therapist when we too are experiencing the upheaval of these recent challenging times? It is critical to work with our countertransference as we work with unconscious enactments in our clinical spaces. This *is* the work of going-on-being in the therapeutic dyad.

Contributor Heidi Knoll talks poignantly about how her distress over euthanizing her dog collided with the anger and psychodynamics of her patient when she had to cancel a session just moments before it began. In subsequent sessions, the therapist insisted on exploring the patient's affect with regard to the sudden cancellation. Her insistence acted as an intrusion for the patient and replayed a difficult dynamic between the patient and her mother. It was in processing this complicated enactment between them that the patient and therapist found their way through the impasse in their clinical relationship.

Grappling with her own countertransference was also essential for Mehr-Afarin Kohan to resolve an impasse in her work with her patient. Her patient was an Afghan woman who suffered devastating trauma under the regime of the Taliban. Kohan came to recognize that in trying to save her devout, Muslim patient from her currently abusive husband, Kohan had been asking her patient to submit to *her* version of a secular world view.

The analyst recognized that her own experience of religious indoctrination had foreclosed her attunement to her patient. Going-on-being for this pair came when the therapist was able to reclaim her own split off aspects of her religious self to participate from within the patient's discourse.

Working With Couples

The high divorce and separation rate in couples points to the fact that couple relationships face enormous challenges from which many do not recover. There are what Anastasia Tsamparli calls "environmental traumas" that impinge on the psychic life of the couple (for example, a recession, pandemic, or immigration). There are also couple interpersonal traumas such as a betrayal of one member of the couple, or partnership inequities from which the couple are attempting to recover. Couple therapists can be deeply drawn into the intense dynamics of a couple.

Contributor Anastasia Tsamparli points out that certain traumas become a defining force for a couple who are often unable to assimilate the new conditions. The trauma introduces uncertainty into the link and interferes with the fantasy that held the coupledom. These experiences disrupt the participants' sense of identity and alter their perceptions of their partners. In her work with a couple after they faced an unexpected bankruptcy, Tsamparli demonstrates how important it is to metabolize the 'beta' elements that are projected into the analyst, and to be able to retain the ability to stand back in order to hold and transform the unbearable emotions of the couple.

Melinda Blitzer, in the current volume, presents a case she worked with in which she used her countertransference affect to formulate an understanding of the relationship. She recognized that she was caught up in her own wish to change her parents as she worked with this couple. It was only after Blitzer realized that she was over functioning with the couple because of her unconscious equivalence of this couple with her parents that she was able to see dynamics of the couple more clearly. And just as she could not change her own parents, she had to come to terms with her failure to 'fix' this couple. She touchingly concludes that in therapy, just as in life, we have to accept incompleteness and the limits of what we know and can repair.

Concluding Remarks

The chapters in this stimulating volume illustrate the painful, delicate process of 'going-on-being' in the face of inordinate trauma when our ability to represent and contain our experience in language is overwhelmed, and when our mourning is stalled or foreclosed. The psychoanalytic approach allows for an intensely intimate therapeutic encounter with a witnessing, experiencing other allowing for the process of 'working through'. This powerful relationship involves the mediation of raw, frank wordless experience so that there can be an integration of the unruly and overwhelming affect.

This process enables psychological perspective and well-being to emerge. In these pages you will meet the brave, vulnerable patients who, with the help of their therapists, struggle together through the grieving process to find the state of going-on-being once again. This crucial process is vitally important for individuals as well as societies around the world.

Note

1 Excerpt from "The Dead Woman" by Pablo Neruda. From *The Captain's Verses*. Copyright 1972 by Pablo Neruda and David Walsh. Reprinted by permission of New Directions Publishing Corp.

References

Britzman, D. (2024). *When history returns: Psychoanalytic quests for humane learning*. SUNY Press.

Fernando, J. (2022). *A psychoanalytic understanding of trauma: Post-traumatic mental functioning, the zero process, and the construction of reality*. Routledge.

Ferro, A. (2011). *Avoiding emotions, living emotions*. Routledge.

Freud, S. (1915). Thoughts for the times on war and death. *Standard Edition, 14*, 273–300. Hogarth Press.

Freud, S. (1916). On transience. *Standard Edition, 14*, 303–307. Hogarth Press.

Freud, S. (1917). Mourning and melancholia. *Standard Edition, 14*, 237–258. Hogarth Press.

Freud, S. (1920). Beyond the Pleasure Principle. *Standard Edition, 18*, 3–64. Hogarth Press.

Lear, J. (2022). *Imagining the end: Mourning and ethical life*. Belknap Press. An imprint of Harvard University Press.

Leonoff, A. (2024). On mourning melancholia and war. *Canadian Journal of Psychoanalysis, 32*(1).

Levine, H. (2022). *Affect, representation, and language: Between the silence and the cry*. Routledge.

Ogden, T. (2024). Ontological psychoanalysis in clinical practice. *Psychoanalytic Quarterly, 93*, 13–31.

Ogden, T. H. (2019). Ontological psychoanalysis or "what do you want to be when you grow up?". *Psychoanalytic Quarterly, 88*, 661–684.

Rose, J. (2023). *The plague: Living death in our times*. Ferrar, Strauss and Giraux.

Winnicott, D. W. (1963). Dependence in infant care in child care, and in the psycho-analytic setting. *International Journal of Psychoanalysis, (44)*, 339–344.

Part I

Going-on-Being Through Losses

1 Free to Mourn and Mourning to Be Free

Going-on-Being in Challenging Times

Elizabeth B. Sullivan

Introduction

The year 2020 created a profound intersection of freedom and loss. Our ability to go-on-being was greatly compromised. Most of us became all too acutely aware of the freedoms we lost due to the pandemic, the freedoms we could potentially lose as a result of the new political landscape in the United States, and the freedoms that many of us have never experienced as underscored by the Black Lives Matter protests. As Freud (1917) theorized, what is lost, whether it is human, ideal, or institution, must be properly mourned so that we can redirect our energies and go-on-being. Freedom and mourning are, thus, intimately connected. We must feel free to mourn what is lost and we cannot be free to pursue a new path until we have mourned.

During this time, I worked with a patient, "Maggie," who had endured a loss so great that she was unable to consciously grasp the "what" of the loss. As Freud (1917) wrote, the melancholic "knows whom he has lost but not what he has lost in him" (p. 245). As a result, Maggie was unable to mourn and find the freedom to go-on-being. She internally tried to protect this lost object and became stuck in a vortex of anger and hatred towards anyone or anything "other."

In parallel, I lost my own freedom within the realm of the consulting room. Maggie's political and social value system, although aligned with my upbringing, opposed my adult self in almost every way. I constantly felt the tension between who I actually am and who she wanted me to be. I realize now that perhaps my own understanding of what was lost when I disavowed aspects of my childhood value system and culture had been incompletely metabolized and mourned. I believe that this aspect of myself seeped into the intersubjective space between Maggie and myself. In other words, I believe that Maggie was frozen by an inability to mourn her betrayal by the Catholic Church and this fact intersected with my complicated relationship with my own Catholic upbringing. This chapter explores these themes through the lens of psychoanalytic theory, grounds them in a clinical vignette, and illustrates the complex interplay between freedom, mourning, loss, and therapeutic dynamics.

DOI: 10.4324/9781003607120-3

Freedom

As I approach the end of my analytic training, I reflect on the therapeutic values essential for effective psychoanalytic practice and the factors that cause collapse of the therapeutic space. I usually have the curiosity, courage, authenticity, empathy, and faith that is mandatory for the psychoanalytic process. With Maggie, I struggled with freedom, which is also imperative in the consulting room.

For some, freedom may be more of a concept for discussion in the political or philosophical arenas than for clinical psychoanalysis (Rozmarin, 2011). However, it comes to mind that many patients walk into the consulting room for the first time and state that they have come to treatment because they want to be free of their spouse, free of a bad habit, or, perhaps, free of anxiety. In sum, each patient wants to be free of a particular misery (Rozmarin, 2011). In order to attain this freedom, however, both analyst and patient need the freedom to think, to speak, to pause, to reflect, and to be curious. Neville Symington, for example, wrote about freedom as agent of therapeutic change (Symington, 1983).

Rollo May (1981) wrote that "freedom [is] the capacity to pause in the midst of stimuli from all directions, and in this pause to throw our weight toward this response rather than that one" (p. 163). With Maggie, it felt like I was in a bind. I felt that I was not free to say what I had mentally formulated, which I will add, felt much like my experience at the all-girls Catholic school that I attended during childhood.

Maggie was not aggressive toward me, but she was hostile toward anyone she perceived to be "other." I had great difficulty challenging her or even gently asking her to consider alternative points of view. Maggie certainly did not feel the freedom to reflect and throw her weight toward anything other than the unyielding hate and frustration that she felt toward the world. In fact, I believe that she was unaware that such freedom was possible. I also believe that her inability to consciously understand and mourn the loss of the institution that had been her family's bedrock for generations, the Catholic Church, shackled her and held her back from freely moving forward with her life.

Mourning and Melancholia

In his seminal paper, "Mourning and Melancholia," Freud (1917) described two processes that occur in reaction to "the loss of a loved person, or to the loss of some abstraction which has taken the place of one, such as one's country, liberty, an ideal" (p. 243). For Freud, mourning is a "normal condition" (Jones, 1955, p. 367) that is overcome in time, after the libido is gradually withdrawn from its attachments to the lost object. This process is lengthy and requires decathexis from the mental representation of the lost object that exists even after the loved one passes. Memories of the loved one are brought up and examined, detachment of the libido occurs, and the ego is then free to attach to a new object (Freud, 1917).

Melancholia, on the other hand, may also be caused by such a loss, but it is distinguished by "a profoundly painful dejection, cessation of interest in the outside world, loss of capacity to love, inhibition of all activity" (Freud, 1917, p. 244) and a severe decrease of self-regard. Melancholia may result from an ambiguous loss, or a loss that cannot be consciously perceived (Freud, 1917). Further, Freud (1917) writes, "in mourning it is the world that has become poor and empty; in melancholia it is the ego itself" (p. 246). In other words, "there is a poverty of the ego, a sense of personal unworthiness" (Jones, 1955, p. 369).

Thus, we can conceptualize Freud's idea of psychic "grief work" as detaching from the lost object, adjusting to life without it, and attaching to new objects (Hall, 2011). I propose that for Maggie, it was impossible to detach from the Catholic Church and all that it symbolized for her. She became melancholic and, simply put, did not feel free to go-on-being any longer.

I also suggest that perhaps my own work of detaching from, albeit voluntarily, and mourning the loss of the religious culture in which I was raised was incompletely worked through and that, somewhere in this intersubjective space between Maggie and myself, our freedom to throw our weight in any direction was compromised.

Clinical Vignette

At the dawn of 2020, Maggie, an established patient, walked into my consulting room and, seemingly apropos of nothing, said,

> I know I should go to the doctor, but they're all a bunch of Jews who just want your money. They don't really care about you. In any event, they're probably in cahoots with the damned Chinese. You know they've made this virus that's coming so they can take us over.

I believe Maggie's own words, which for her were tame that day, provide a sense of what it was like to sit with her, as I did, twice a week, for several years. Maggie's baseline prejudice and extreme hatred of anyone or anything "other" made her obstinate and unwilling to consider any viewpoint which veered even slightly away from her own.

Maggie entered treatment, her first experience of psychotherapy, after it had come to light that one of her adult sons had been repeatedly sexually abused in early adolescence by Catholic clergy. Maggie was shocked and horrified to discover what had happened to him, under her nose, while she volunteered at the parish. She had never understood his acting out, which had begun around that time and continued for decades. The diocese offered to pay for therapy and so Maggie chose me based on my Irish surname and because from my photo she just knew that I was a good practicing Catholic who would never miss Sunday Mass. She was also convinced that I shared her disdain for those who attended Mass wearing sweatshirts. "Can you believe it?" she ranted, "Those Italians and damn liberals who only worship on Christmas and Easter show up like they've just come out of the ghetto. I bet you and your husband dress your children respectfully every Sunday for Mass." With this, we began our relationship. Maggie was prickly to say the least. She filled each session with her rants. It felt like I could barely get a word in. There was no real holding, there was no real movement.

She was opinionated, racist, and intolerant. Her internal world was swimming in bad objects. I was able to latch on to the loneliness she must have felt inhabiting such a world. There are some bad objects in my internal world too, and I know loneliness. Still, I was jammed.

I also thought about her anger. I would be beyond angry if one of my children were abused. Although I know my anger would look very different, this imagination did allow me to feel some empathy, enough to be able to sit in the room with her and her despicable intolerance of anyone "other." I understood that her seemingly unending retreat into the paranoid-schizoid position was defending against any guilt or responsibility she may have been feeling about her son's abuse.

During the session in which she directed her wrath towards doctors, I cringed inside at her verbiage but outwardly tried, as usual, to focus on her anger. I said that I could understand why she was so angry at everyone in the world. I asked why she was thinking about doctors. She replied,

> There's a little bump in my stomach. They want me to have another test. It's fine. I need to eat better, but with all this stress, nothing appeals and anyway, my favorite bakery is now owned by Blacks and I can't get any good bread for my ham sandwiches.

It was news to me that she had been going to the doctor for her stomach aches. I tried to discuss her health further, but she effectively shut down the conversation by replying with a single angry grunt, and I did not mention it further. Here again, I lost my therapeutic freedom in her hostile presence and struggled to connect with her.

We did, however, find a bit of connection when it came to gardening. I spoke often with her about what to plant when, and which plants needed more, or less, sun, water, and attention. Never mind that she felt that the "stupid Asians and Indians" in her neighborhood did not know what they were doing when it came to their gardens, she was certain that both she and I knew exactly how to make our gardens thrive.

The pandemic then arrived in full force, and since Maggie "didn't do" technology, we switched to phone sessions. It felt like more of the same. She was heavily defended with her anger and with the torrent of hate that she unleashed during every session. I knew that she was fragile underneath all of it, so I continued to be careful. Here again, I could not find the freedom to suggest another way to look at the world, which perhaps could have allowed her to make some peace with all that had happened. I procrastinated with the mental excuse that I had time and needed to build a more solid foundation before I gently challenged her.

Many months later, she called me in-between sessions for the very first time. She was distraught. Her oldest son, the son who had been abused, and his cousin had been out partying all night. Her son was driving and plowed into a wall. He died instantly. "How could this happen?" she repeated over and over. "After all that had happened to him and, as a result, to my family . . . there are no words." "No," I replied, "there are no words."

She was finally silent and we sat, together, in that silence.

In another session, she returned to her health. "There's still that growth in my uterus that I never got biopsied," she said casually. "What growth in your uterus?" I asked, "I thought you had a sour stomach." "No, it's actually my uterus and there's a growth in it," she continued. "That's very serious," I said, "you need to follow up with your doctor."

She started to cry, "when it's my time, it's my time. I just want to be with my son." I said, "I can't imagine what you are going through, Maggie. All those years of not knowing what was going on with him and now you have lost him." I asked her for more about her statement "when it's my time, it's my time," and if she meant she wanted to take her own life. "No," she replied, "I would never do that. God would never forgive me."

"You really need to get to the doctor, Maggie," I said, and she replied, "I know. I know. I will. I will." Internally, I knew she was only yes-ing me and I was afraid. I can't think when I am afraid, and I freeze. I think that I was feeling the fear and paralysis that Maggie felt. We were both afraid. One cannot feel free to act when one is so afraid. She was afraid to live, but she was also afraid to die. She became paralyzed with this fright. She couldn't live with herself, but she also could not actively take her own life. The world was paralyzed by the pandemic at this point, and in parallel, Maggie and I were paralyzed, the treatment was paralyzed. So much loss was not being put into words and not being properly mourned.

In late summer, Maggie told me she wanted to give me some cuttings from her garden because I was the only one who would appreciate them and, further, she knew I would not let them die. I thought about whether or not to accept this gift and decided that it was important to say yes. She asked me what time I would leave the office the following day because she wanted to give them to me as I was on my way home. "They need to go straight into the ground," she added.

I gave her a time and expected to see her in my office parking lot. The next day, however, it was her husband who awaited me with the plants. I was disappointed. I had not laid eyes on her in months, and I told her how I felt the next time we spoke. Her kindness had freed me in that moment, and I was genuine. She brushed me off, as she was unable to engage with my warmhearted feelings. I would like to think that what she could not put into words she put into the beautiful bundle of cuttings, which was packaged as carefully as a new mother might swaddle her infant. She also enclosed a note in her perfect handwriting that read, "Elizabeth, keep in shade until planting. When you plant, water them in. Sprinkle each day, because the heat will wilt them. – Maggie."

Now, I cannot help but notice that her note referred to living and dying, burial, blessing and rebirth, and, perhaps, an avoidance of mourning. I believe she knew at that point what would set her free. Like the good Catholic school-girl daughter she wanted me to be, I planted her offering, and as summer passed on to fall and then turned into winter, the cuttings went underground. I wondered if I had taken care of them properly and if they would survive the winter. Attached to that thought was another thought that wondered whether or not Maggie would survive the winter herself and if I would ever see her again. In the present, I wonder if when she gave me the plants, she knew she was not long for this earth and trusted me to keep a little piece of her alive.

I remember the last time we spoke. She cut the session short saying in a weak voice, "Elizabeth, my stomach is just rolling today, it's just rolling. I can't stay on the phone."

"Ok," I replied, "I'll call you again on Thursday." That Thursday, she did not pick up, nor did she in the weeks that I kept calling at our regularly scheduled times. I left her voicemails each time that I called and I did this for a long time. Much like Maggie, I couldn't easily free myself and although I did not actually know that she was dying, I did.

Finally, and to no response, I sent her a termination letter. This was during the winter, and I remember hoping that I had not killed her cuttings and that they would emerge from my garden in the spring. I again wondered if she would still be walking this earth when spring arrived. Some time after the fact, however, a family member called and told me she was gone. She never had followed up with the doctor and eventually she withered away, filled with cancer. She found freedom in the only way that she could.

Discussion

I wonder if it was in the moment when Maggie made me into a practicing Catholic that I began to lose my therapeutic freedom. She held me tightly in this vise-like grip as she needed me so desperately to be her good conservative Catholic daughter. She needed me to share her background and world view in order to believe I could understand the magnitude of what had happened. Consciously, she wanted to process the horrific abuse her son had endured, later his death, and how this had affected her family. Unconsciously, and more importantly, she needed me to comprehend the way that the spiritual foundation, the Catholic Church, the bedrock of her family's existence for generations, had betrayed her. It was this loss that she primarily needed to mourn. As Freud (1917) noted, some of the most difficult losses to mourn are those that are unconscious. Furthermore, my own unconscious losses related to my Catholic upbringing are most likely germane as "the unconscious of one human being can react upon that of another without passing through the conscious" (Freud, 1915, p. 194).

Instead of moving through the mourning process and gradually letting go of the Catholic Church and all that it meant to her, Maggie became melancholic. She could not process this loss so that she could invest in something new. Further, the Catholic Church had been so thoroughly internalized as a life-sustaining good object for Maggie that she could not tolerate its bad parts and had to split them off and project them into all that is "other." When we cannot clearly and accurately see what is lost, we lose our ability to mourn it. Maggie made "every conceivable effort to retain the absent . . . ideal and to keep it alive in the shelter of the ego" (Eng & Han, 2018, p. 37). She did this at a cost, however, and the psychic damage was great. Maggie preserved her relationship to this lost object but "only as a type of haunted, ghostly identification" (Eng & Han, 2018, p. 37). The Catholic Church was so beloved that Maggie was willing to preserve it within, even though its toxicity cost her her life.

For my part, in the face of the transference, I lost my therapeutic freedom. I felt the pressure to go along with her despite the contradiction with my own experience. Perhaps this was due to my incomplete mourning process or understanding of what I have lost during my own decathexis from the Catholic Church. After all, it is in coming to consciously know what we do not know about ourselves that impasses may be resolved (Sapountzis, 2009). In retrospect, I realize I also needed to own my true self, the divorced, re-partnered, agnostic, liberal me that is able to think and speak freely, in order to help her. Now that I can think freely, I wonder why I did not gently question her. I could have respected the anger she felt towards the world but also pointed out that maybe there was another, more tolerant way for her to look at things. I lost the freedom within myself to wonder, with her, if there was another way of looking at the world and the people within it.

Now that I am no longer in Maggie's presence, I think freely. I wish that I had challenged her more and presented myself as less of the part-object she imagined and more as my actual whole self. I still believe that she would not have been able to tolerate all of who I am, such as the part of me that despises all things MAGA, the MSNBC watching part of me, and the part of me who from a very young age never really bought into religion at all.

However, she may have been able to tolerate some gentler differences that I could have pointed out and showed her that, despite some of our different views, perhaps she could still like me, and that it all did not have to be in such black and white terms. Perhaps there was a part of the Catholic Church that she could still like and hold onto. The loss of freedom to think and to speak with Maggie about these things is a regret. I know I am speaking with hindsight. I cannot help but have the fantasy that maybe if I had felt free to do something, anything, differently, I could have saved her. Unlike the patient who one day wakes up and jumps in front of a train, Maggie gave me so much time to react and try to keep her alive. However, in her ongoing state of melancholia, Maggie overcame "the instinct which compels every living thing to cling to life" (Freud, 1917, p. 246).

Conclusion

In 2020, I, like many others, lost the freedom to go-on-being as I usually do. I lost the ability to move about the world as I please due to the pandemic, and I lost the feeling of political safety. In parallel, with Maggie, I also lost the ability to freely think, speak, and be myself in the consulting room. It was difficult for me to retain my sense of self in the face of Maggie's negation of my subjectivity and this constricted me. Even when I am used in the transference, I am still a subject and I need to hold on to the thoughts and feelings that make up my own subjectivity. The ability to hold on to myself is necessary to maintain my therapeutic stance. The ability to hold onto my subjectivity is what I lost during my time with Maggie, and this occurred, in part, perhaps, because, like Maggie, I had not completely decathected from my complicated relationship with Catholicism. It takes freedom to think from the core of who we really are. As Symington (1983) writes, it also takes an inner certainty to have this freedom. It is difficult to have this inner certainty while holding onto unmourned aspects of the past.

Maggie, too, had lost a sense of freedom. For her, it was the perceived freedom to live a 1950s-style, white-centric life with her family intact, and the Catholic Church standing nobly behind her. She knew no other way, and this loss was too great to be mourned, or even fully understood. Her ego had become "poor and empty" (Freud, 1917, p. 246), so she found freedom by taking herself to the heaven that she believed in. I wish I had been able to show her another way of being on this earth. Maggie, ultimately, lost the ability to go-on-being in this world.

However, the cuttings she gifted me did end up surviving her final winter. They came up from the warm earth in my garden the following spring and bloomed. The Black Eyed Susans were particularly beautiful and given the fact that Maggie had so passionately professed such a hatred of the black-eyed people of this planet, I was amused to no end. That summer, in my mind's eye, I also had the vision of her shaking her finger at me from her heaven and yelling at me for giving the flowers too much or too little water. This vision, too, made me smile as I felt the freedom to try to make the plants thrive however I wished to. This feeling suggests that I am doing the work of mourning.

I do the best that I can in my garden and the results are usually, but not always, good. I am going to have to accept the fact that I did the best I could with Maggie, but like with all living beings, so many things are out of our control, and all jungles are not meant to be tamed. I think about Maggie's cuttings, and I wonder if they represent the part of Maggie that wanted to thrive or if they are more symbolic of my own wish to keep her alive.

Either way, I will do what I can to keep them growing, and if one spring, they no longer emerge and thrive, I hope I can make peace with that. In the meantime, they will always remind me of the tall, elegant, but very angry woman who walked into my consulting room some years ago. I am free to grieve, and I grieve for her freely.

References

Eng, D. L., & Han, S. (2018). *Racial melancholia, racial dissociation: On the social and psychic lives of Asian Americans*. Duke University Press.

Freud, S. (1915). The unconscious. In *The standard edition of the complete psychological works of Sigmund Freud, Vol. XIV: (1914–1916): On the history of the psycho-analytic movement, papers on metapsychology and other works*, 159–215.

Freud, S. (1917). Mourning and melancholia. In *The standard edition of the complete psychological works of Sigmund Freud, Vol. XIV: (1914–1916): On the history of the psycho-analytic movement, papers on metapsychology and other works*, 237–258.

Hall, C. D. (2011, December). *Beyond Kübler-Ross: Recent developments in our understanding of grief and bereavement*. Australian Psychological Society. https://psychology.org.au/for-members/publications/inpsych/2011/dec/beyond-kubler-ross-recent-developments-in-our-und

Jones, E. (1955). *The life and work of Sigmund Freud* (Vol. 2). Basic Books.

May, R. (1981). *Freedom and destiny*. Delta.

Rozmarin, E. (2011). To be is to betray: On the place of collective history and freedom in psychoanalysis. *Psychoanalytic Dialogues, 21*(3), 320–345.

Sapountzis, I. (2009). Revisiting Searles's paper "the patient as a therapist to the therapist": The analyst's personal in the interpersonal. *Psychoanalytic Review, 96*, 665–684.

Symington, N. (1983). The analyst's act of freedom as agent of therapeutic change. *International Review of Psychoanalysis, 10*, 283–291.

2 East of the Awning

Staying the Course and Moving On

Juliet Heeg

This chapter is a journeying through a pre- and post-Covid office land-scape: to divest or to re-nest? We are all trying to figure it out – even today. To riff off the book by psychoanalyst, Robert Akeret (1996), *Tales From a Traveling Couch* (where the author goes on the road to have a wrap-up session with various patients) during the pandemic many of us experienced "The Traveling Office" going from a room to a Zoom – and then, by now, maybe somewhere in between. In this chapter, I explore who I am in relation to my clinical space (and self) of then – and now. How has my return to the physical office space been shaped by my online experience – and who have I become along the way? What do we make of what Bachelard (1964, 2014) might call our office nest, "a hiding place for winged creatures," (p. 114) – a primitive refuge as well as a reminder of the danger outside of us. On our return to certain spaces, i.e. rooms, Gaston Bachelard (1964, 2014) writes:

> Not only do we come back to it, but we dream of coming back to it, the way a bird comes back to its nest or a lamb to the fold. The sign of return marks an infinite number of daydreams, for the reason that human returning takes place in the great rhythm of human life . . . the intimacy of the room becomes our intimacy . . . it is very deeply our room, it is in us.
>
> (pp. 118, 240–241)

And, yet, I wonder, if the room is so "in us," so internalized, do we really need to physically return to this office/nest with our patients? Is the "room in us" so much a part of us that it doesn't matter where we are? The office and all of the things in it – the clinical space where we sit with our patients – can be described as embodying a "temporal continuity of past, present, and future . . . both merged and emergent" (Hershberg, 2023, p. 399). So maybe we can just fly the coop . . . move on, zoom on, fly elsewhere – leave it behind. Is therapeutic work in an actual physical office space, in fact, so much more dimensional and richer that the therapist/patient dyad

DOI: 10.4324/9781003607120-4

really loses something special if we don't physically share the same room together – especially when this interior design reflects something of our own interior? I recall coming across two books – *Fifty Shrinks* (2014) by Sebastian Zimmermann and *In the Shadow of Freud's Couch: Portraits of Psychoanalysts in Their Offices* (2020) by Mark Gerald – that showcased the relationship between analysts and their offices in refreshingly expressive ways. The veil of anonymity was discarded in these compelling portraits – such a sigh of relief. In my earlier years, I, too, wanted to make a statement, feathering my "shrink-nest" was an essential expression of my emerging professional identity.

East of the Awning: 410 East 57th

Traveling back well over a decade ago, I return to the memory of my pre-Covid office. My first "real" office – one I had invested in, separate from my apartment office where I had initially seen patients while I was still working in advertising. This move to a professional office suite was motivated by my fear that I would be evicted by the landlord of my then rent-stabilized apartment. It also coincided with losing my advertising job – so a challenging time financially – but what better time to "establish" oneself! One rainy day, I saw an ad for an office space pinned on a bulletin board at the New York Psychoanalytic Society & Institute (NYPSI). I promptly called the lightly penciled phone number on a slip of paper and on that very afternoon, I secured a lease for a full-time office in Sutton Place. I was nervous but somehow reassured by the low-key grandeur of the neighborhood and by some not-yet imagined decorating plan to turn this small, rather uninteresting space into something that challenged my sense of the somber "neutrality" of many an analytic space. I was trying to strike that balance of fitting in and standing out – and this new Sutton Place locale seemed like just the spot. I felt a quiet sense of belonging there. On the outside, I liked the faded grace of the neighborhood, the wide, well-appointed sidewalks, the doormen who lined the lobby entrances. The way it almost hummed to the sound of long-ago denizens such as Bobby Short and Noel Coward. This parade of time – somehow outside of time – was marked by spry widows and cheerful dogs. I felt appreciably younger than most folks, but not *too* young.

I especially liked to tell prospective clients where I was, exactly where I was. In my telephone voice I would give specific directions to my office:

Yes, it's 410 East 57th Street, between First Avenue and Sutton. (No . . . Sutton, not Second). You will see a green awning with 410 on it. Walk towards the river and there's a pane-glassed door, *just east of the awning*; enter the alcove and I am the top buzzer on the left. Ring that and I will buzz you into the waiting room. *If you get turned around, you can just ask the doorman.*

Location, Location and Transference

"If you get turned around you can just ask the doorman." For me, just say-ing those words helped me to feel less lost as I navigated this transition to a second career. Already, I could imagine my patient assigning a role to me. Transferentially, the message might be:

> Ahh, you've come to the right place. However, turned around you may be; whatever losses bring you here: a deceased spouse, a lost custody battle; a general sense of who you are in the world: I will – no "we" – will find the way back.

My counter-transferential wish might have been some kind of magical twin-ship, whereby I lead the way but with gentle authority.

But did I know how this transference was *really* developing? Were my directions heard as being anxious, overly concerned, too solicitous . . . or responsible, perceptive, thoughtful? My speaking of even "having a doorman" may have signaled a certain status to my patient – a monied feeling of safety which may be welcoming – or not. But I never really knew and maybe I really didn't want to know . . . at least not then.

Gilbert Cole (2015) spoke to the notion of how he used to wonder how we locate transference and then realized it is there from the very beginning. From the website to the telephone call to the well-appointed sidewalks of Sutton Place to the turning of the doorknob to my very first office, the trans-ference begins. If it sounds like a bit of theater, that's because it is. From my imagining the patient's experiencing a sense of safety in the neighborhood to the unexpected "pop" of my non-traditional, bolder, office space, the stage is being set. The juxtaposition of the outer environment of my neigh-borhood with the less traditional inner decor seemed to strike the right bal-ance: creating a sense of relative safety for a deeper interior journey where newer, more enlivened self-representations and relationships are possible. Or so I imagined. I like to think that the bolder, moodier interior design of my office facilitated a feeling of being "safe but not too safe . . . a safe surprise" (Bromberg, 2008, p. 333). I saw my clinical space as a stage to freeing dialogue, enhancing intimacy and spontaneity within the analytic dyad. Cole (2015), a psychoanalyst and trained actor, speaks to the impro-visational aspect of psychoanalysis. He notes that the improvisational is not just a momentary encounter in a session, it is a continuous process without beginning and end. He references American theater practitioner Sanford Meisner who developed a two-person acting technique wherein "people are most free, most like themselves, when their attention can be diverted away from themselves" (p. 743). Meisner's acting technique "maintains each actor's attention on the other actor, while simultaneously, implicitly experiencing oneself" (p. 744).

Designing Minds: Setting the Stage

So bearing the "freeing power of diversion" in mind, I would like to think that I had created an environment where two people – analyst and analysand – could be more fully themselves and float in the ethereal atmosphere of the office, engaged in conversation, and arrive at newer, more alive place within. Indulge me in detailing what this space looked like and what I had in mind for it to express. In designing this small 8 by 10 foot office space with a painter friend of mine, I went for a deep dark brown which was supposed to create a more spacious feeling. I juxtaposed the deep earth color of the walls with a tomato red analytic chair and an oval-shaped patient couch. Above it was a vivid blue ceiling with spotlights as well as lights in back of the chair and couch. A large, silvery circular mirror hung on the wall, a few feet from an artificial plant so alive looking that one patient remarked how much it had grown over the year.

Hiding in Plain Sight

I thought of my office interior and exterior as a means to ground as well as to inspire the analytic encounter. But perhaps with all this designing and curating going on, I also wanted to hide. Like many analysts there is an ambivalence about being known. I liked being cloaked in the reassuring air of authority in the Sutton Place neighborhood and the well-articulated design scheme of my office. An exterior and interior to hide some of the lostness and newness of being a burgeoning analyst in this somewhat august locale. As the surrealist painter Magritte, notes, "A thing that is visible, is hidden by what it reveals" (Gablik, 1970, p. 11). As Schoen (2023) writes, "Surfaces are scary. These are the parts of ourselves we simply can't hide" (p. 244). Aron (1991) notes: "Our ambivalence about being known is one way of understanding our fraught relationships both to the protections and constraints offered by the ideal of the anonymous analyst and to the demands and potentials of a relational ideal underscoring the value of our patients coming to know us as distinct, particular people" (p. 43). At the beginning of my practice, experiencing more vulnerability in my newer professional identity, I was not so receptive to my patients "probing" or of allowing more "object usage" of my decor and by extension of myself to create a certain "relational freedom" (Stern, 2015) within the dyad.

Finding Our Way Back . . . and Beyond

For a few patients, the loss of my "homier" office environment to this hipper new space was a rupture. I even lost a patient over it. It summoned returning feelings of disconnection, which might take the form of critical comments about the waiting room and the environment's overall less personal feeling. A couple of patients experienced the brown wall color as "depressing" instead of "expansive"; for another patient the over-sized silver mirror with spiraling concentric circles was "dizzying" and puzzling in its hyper-chicness: "what kind of a space is this?" Implied was: Who are you? Where did you go? What are you doing? That combined with the introduction of a non-exclusive waiting room for the suite where the furniture was not particularly comfortable and for some led to a feeling of not belonging. Decorating our office is a kind of "doing" that influences how we are "being" with our patients. I regretfully resisted more exploration of the irritation of some patients as it bumped up against what I wanted them to feel and see: an inviting decor, staged for more psychic expansion and enlivened inquiry. I was definitely more curious exploring the comments that aligned with the positive notion of the office as a "freeing" experience. One patient saw it as a "nightclub"; another as "a womb-like portal"; another as a "very different kind of cool space." Harder to take were the comments that found the new decor a little "too much" or the responses that seemed to suggest that something "more neutral" would have done just fine. I was sometimes distressed that my decor choices/colors/space had impinged upon certain patients which challenged my counter-transferential wishes to be seen as having created a positive, breakthrough space – a platform with greater possibilities for growth. After all, it wasn't just all about me . . . or was it? As with Hershberg (2023), I had outgrown my former office and felt that my "Space Odyssey" would generate more psychic vitality and exploration. It challenged the analytic dyad, as more explicit expressions of my subjectivity were on full view. We had abandoned the safer more familiar "nestlike space." Hopefully, all of my patients – new and old – would find a way to be at home-enough here.

Neutrality Is Not a Color, It's a Process

It was my hope that the notion of "analytic neutrality" whereby neutrality was understood as encouraging openness could be inspired by this bolder looking office. That the evocative colors of red, brown, silver and blue could elicit a space of more openness, freedom and acceptance between analyst and patient. I am thinking of neutrality as a means of giving and taking of space. And within that space, making room for the colour of emotions. As Gerson (1996) considered "in each moment of neutrality a degree of mutual recognition and trust is established and becomes an available haven" (p, 360). Or what Stern (1992) would describe as the embeddedness of transference/counter-transference is broken and "the analyst or patient comes upon a new way of seeing the other or himself that opens new possibilities of interaction, which themselves need to be described" (p. 359). My wish for what I would call a "robust neutrality" is in contrast to the more Freudian one-person psychology which espouses a notion of neutrality as abstinence involved in not granting so-called hysterical female patients their wishes for seduction (Gerson, 1996). This is a very different notion of neutrality than an anonymous posture designed to encourage a patient's self-expression. That, in fact, analytic anonymity, or what Renik (1995) critiques as:

> The pretense of anonymity is a cloak worn by the analyst when pictured as an authoritatively objective observer able to transcend his or her subjectivity . . . whereas an analyst's effort to be anonymous is supposed to allow the patient greater freedom to free associate, the opposite is the case in my experience.
>
> (p. 482)

A less conventional, more enlivening notion of "neutrality" might be expressed as such:

> neutrality is not an attitude nor a posture, nor a declination of action. It is not abstinence, nor is it anonymity . . . [neutrality] is . . . a state of possibility and, as such the extent of neutrality in an analysis may be known via the range of the patient's free association and the breadth of the analyst's evenly hovering attention.
>
> (Gerson, 1996, p. 630)

A Robust Neutrality: Showing Our Colors in the Room

This chapter has helped me appreciate how much of what I did with my office was really about my fantasy about what it meant to be a psychoanalyst. That to be a good analyst, I did not need to "be beige" – something possibly deadening to me. The important thing was for my patients to show up and share their "true" colors about many things, including the clinical atmosphere. For me to have embraced a zest for what I have termed a "robust neutrality" would have meant for me to have inquired more about the patient's subjectivity as well as sharing a bit more of mine. To have made more room for colors of the patient; the feelings about the decor would have helped to create more of Stern's "relational freedom" – versus less exploration of comments that I felt were more negative and intrusive. I did not want to hide behind some drab decor to adhere to some outmoded idea of "objectivity." But perhaps, with all the expression of color on the walls and ceiling, I was hiding a certain vulnerability of not knowing who and what this analytic role and profession held. I had found the safe, monied associations of Sutton Place with its ever-guarding doormen and feathered this analytic nest with bold colors for myself and other "winged-creatures," as Bachelard would say. Within my shrink-nest were two pieces of art that spoke to me about what the analytic journey, and essentially life, were about.

The Once-in-a-Lifetime Event

One print on my wall was called "Once," and the other was called "Return." "Once" had bands of blue, yellow and gold ribbons intertwining and reaching vertically upwards. The other print was called "Return" with blue, yellow and pink ribbons flowing across horizontally. In life, we experience "Once" and "Return" encounters. There are once in a lifetime events: "Once" events, such as the death of a parent or a loved one; the birth of a child; graduation from college; the loss of a house; a pandemic. And then there is the "Return" which speaks to the repetition of early interpersonal dynamics and their returning themes in life. How we, analysts and patients, speak to those seismic "Once" in a lifetime events and weave them in with the "Return" of narrations, responses, transferences within the treatment room is important as a way of thinking about the analytic process. For many of us pre-Covid, changing offices might not be a "Once" in a lifetime move, but it still can have a dramatic effect on patients. It can mobilize those transferential feelings of "Return" – returning abandonment, not belonging, disconnection etc. Going from my home office to an office suite inspired that rupture for some patients. But for the world, a much greater disruption was to come.

Mass Migration: Abandoning the Nest

In March of 2020, that "Once" occurrence happened . . . the pandemic hit. I, like many, left the physical office space but held out hope of returning. After six months, I gave up my Sutton Place office. Instead of directing my patients in my telephone voice to go *"east of the awning,"* I simply sent a Zoom link in an email. Six months into the pandemic, I had mastered Zoom and was doing more couples therapy than ever. While I missed the richness of seeing people in person, I found that couples having a session in their *own* home could be especially therapeutic as the de-escalation of an argument and more responsive listening skills were happening in *their* space, not on the outside, in *my* office space. The transformation of their physical space to a reparative space which they actually inhabited was a positive experience for many. A sense of mastery for many, that might sound like, "we can make it happen in *our* home; not just in *your* office."

The Dilemma: To Re-Nest, Divest . . . Or?

As time went on, I missed my Sutton Place office less and less. Its well-appointed sidewalks, its jaunty widows; the painstakingly decorated and illuminated decor. Instead, I embraced the newer freedom of the traveling office. While maintaining some decorum, I cared less about needing everything to reflect my sensibility. As Gaston Bachelard (1964, 2014) mentioned earlier, "the intimacy of the room becomes our intimacy . . . it is very deeply our room, it is in us" (pp. 240–241). At some point, I became the room and this internalized room showed up on our Zoom. On the screen, it was their space, it was my space; it was neither; both, ours – somewhere in between.

The Freedom of It All: But What Are We Missing?

Online, it was just about me and the patient on this frictionless, contactless screen – something pared down, more elemental, less ornamental than my beloved office decor. Almost magically, Zoom brought us together on the screen; then "poof" the session was over. No doorknob comments. No trace of what had happened, kind of like a sudden death. There was the magic. And there was the loss. Author Virginia Heffernan (2016) talks about the texture and stickiness of relating that is lost in the non-physical online world. The ineffable in-betweenness of what it feels like to be conversing in the same room collapses. Yes, patients can see the background decor – a piece of art, a bookshelf, a wall color – on the screen, but it is not as immersive; it does not feel the same as being in the same room together. I could feel the loss of texture and cadence in sessions. But there was something so freeing about the online world. Most everyone (patients and therapists) seemed to like having more time and space to do other stuff. With online work, I found patients' psychic worlds weighed less heavily on me. I felt lighter emotionally. Yet, I had some mixed feelings about *not* feeling the pull to engage in the more physical, intimate space I had been so intent on creating. It was a dilemma: what is best for the work? Is it just too easy to appear and disappear on screen. Are we sacrificing richness, resonance, texture, a more felt-sense of meaning for convenience? How do we discern whether this greater investment of time and money involved in physical office sessions makes for better therapy overall? Or is that thinking outdated or irrelevant given the way our culture is evolving?

The Return

At some point, though, I, like the birds in Gaston Bachelard's words, returned to the nest. But this returning was a different return. By then I had become a different therapist and would be returning to a different kind of nest. While I experienced an instinctual push to return to a physical space – wondering what it would be like to be with my patients again; and how I had missed the contrast of the home and office space; the ritual of walking to it and entering a new space – both physically and emotionally – I also experienced an instinctual pull to stay away, to not overcommit to it, and not because of Covid concerns per se. Rather this reluctance was more that I had seemed to have mostly outgrown the therapeutic nest as I had come to value more of my own time and space. It seemed less important that I would return to space that was so deliberately designed as mine. Letting go of my beloved office – created by a much younger, less-formed self – there was a reminder of the inevitable losses in life: the forever parting with people, places, things and finally ourselves, that life presents us with. So long as we live, we are perpetually in a state of giving up. In our slow growing acceptance of multiple losses, I wonder if, paradoxically, something more life-affirming and essential emerges in the midst of loss. I, like many, had taken flight from this perhaps overly carefully designed space. Maybe over time I had internalized the boldness and security of my office decor. Somehow it was no longer important that I practice in an office that reflected more of my interior. As mentioned, perhaps the therapeutic space, the room, the nest, had taken root within me and that was freeing. But still, something in me wanted to return. . . . Perhaps, I had grown *enough of a room* in me from previous rooms and outgrown a need to reflect a certain personal aesthetic in a physical office space.

In the fall of 2021, I made the decision to return to an office. I started out with a half-day sublet. It was very unlike my "East of the Awning" Sutton Place space. Some might call this newer sublet space more traditionally "neutral" with the comfortable, large furniture, light gray walls, high ceilings and abundant plant life. I had had nothing to do with the office design, which was an oddly liberating feeling. And although I could claim no credit for the thriving greenery, I loved that it was not mine. My name was not even on the buzzer. And if a new patient got turned around getting here, well, there was no doorman to ask. And, yet somehow, we still found our way to each other.

References

Akeret, R. (1996). *Tales from a traveling couch*. W.W. Norton & Co.

Aron, L. (1991). The patient's experience of the analyst's subjectivity. *Psychoanalytic Dialogues, 1*(1), 29–51.

Bachelard, G. (1964). *The poetics of space*. Orion Press.

Bachelard, G. (2014). *Penguin Classics* (New ed.).

Bromberg, P. M. (2008). Shrinking the tsunami: Affect regulation, dissociation, and the shadow of the flood. *Contemporary Psychoanalysis, 44*(3).

Cole, G. W. (2015). The reality of doing: Discussion of Arthur Gray's paper. *Psychoanalytic Dialogues, 25*, 743–750.

Gablik, S. (1970). *Magritte*. Thames and Hudson Inc.

Gerald, M. (2020). *In the shadow of Freud's couch: Portraits of psychoanalysts in their offices*. Routledge Press.

Gerson, S. (1996). Neutrality, resistance, and self-disclosure in an intersubjective psychoanalysis. *Psychoanalytic Dialogues, 6*, 623–645.

Heffernan, V. (2016). *Magic and loss: The internet as art*. Simon & Schuster.

Hershberg, S. (2023). A space Odyssey: The impact of changing the physical aspects of the analytic setting on the analyst, the patient and their relationship. *Psychoanalytic Inquiry, 43*(6), 399–409.

Renik, O. (1995). The ideal of the anonymous analyst and the problem of self disclosure. *Psychoanalytic Quarterly, 64*, 466–495.

Schoen, S. (2023). The patient's experience of the analyst's physicality: It's what's on the outside that counts. *Psychoanalytic Dialogues, 33*(2), 244–255.

Stern, D. (1992). Commentary on constructivism in clinical psychoanalysis. *Psychoanalytic Dialogues, 2*, 331–363.

Stern, D. (2015). *Relational freedom: Emergent properties of the interpersonal field*. Routledge Press.

Zimmermann, S. (2014). *Fifty shrinks*. Sebastian Zimmermann.

3 Going-on-Being

Potential Space in the Uncertainty of the Pandemic

Alexia Camfield

There is a new point of reference in our lives today, before the pandemic and since, and although it is not uncommon in the life of an individual to experience definitive moments, they usually occur in the context of a fairly stable set of ideas about the container at large. The worldwide pandemic was a significant rupture to our individual and collective ways of living and was met initially with great uncertainty and anxiety. The potential space that opened made way for creative and meaningful adaptation, some of which we have carried into our present ways of living. Experiencing this rupture has inadvertently served to increase our capacity for healthy detachment and being in the unknown. I have seen in my work as a clinician during this shared and unprecedented space of uncertainty and confusion the opportunity for deep and intimate work for both myself and my clients in our efforts to continue "going-on-being." Who did we each become during this experience?

There have been millions of deaths as a result of Covid-19 so far (World Health Organization, 2024), and it is unlikely that any one person has not been adversely impacted in one way or another over the past few years. Within the course of this phenomenon, opportunities also unfolded in our shared experience of "going-on-being." In my work as a clinician, I experienced opportunities in my practice within this newfound potential space. The task of the psychodynamic therapist is to survive potentially destabilizing enactments with my clients. When the world began to shut down and the magnitude of the situation at hand was becoming known as a collective threat not only to our physical well-being but to the routines of daily life, I remember thinking, "I have to stay a step ahead of this." I was able to avert my own annihilation anxieties by directing my focus to the work of being "a good enough therapist," quickly assembling a temporary approach for continuing to provide a holding environment for the work with my clients. The physical space of my office was no longer safe for us to continue our working together, but quickly we turned to the phone, Face Time and shortly after Zoom to create a space for creative adaptation. It is hard now to imagine that there was ever a time that we did not have at our disposal the use of these "potential space" makers which often allow greater continuity and new facets of connection.

DOI: 10.4324/9781003607120-5

I was seeing my own therapist at the time that the news of the pandemic hit. I remember paying close attention to how he was handling the "going-on-being" of clinical work. It was not that I had any illusion that he would have a greater knowing of the way to proceed, but it was of comfort to feel "held" and have continuity in my work with him. It served to support my own going-on-being in maintaining my practice and this necessary space for my clients. Texas did not seem to go on alert as fast as some of the other states, but when it became apparent that we too would be shutting down for what I think we all initially expected would be three to four weeks, the Zoom platform was already becoming widely used across the world. My colleagues on the East Coast had already shifted into finding the creativity necessary to continue practicing which was essential not only for our own survival but ensuring the continuity necessary for so many of our clients.

There was an immediate and noticeable shift in the content of therapy sessions. Because the pandemic was something we were all facing collectively, my clients were interested in how I was managing my personal life and my business, as was I in how they were managing the basics of their "going-on-being." Saidipour (2021) in her paper, "The Precedent of Good Enough Therapy During Unprecedented Times," calls for increased flexibility in the therapeutic frame at these times, an idea which has helped me to organize my experience of working *within* the pandemic rather than attempting to work *around* it. In retrospect, integrating how each of us was managing in this time of uncertainty seems to have been necessary to establish the security we needed for our therapy work. My approach at the time was not theoretically driven, rather it was born through attunement to my clients in an effort to make use of this newfound potential space.

I have been working with Anna for over 20 years. When the news of the pandemic hit, she was the first client I contacted, sensing that she more so than any of my other clients would need assurance that we would continue meeting and would be able to do so virtually until we could be safe meeting in person again. Anna relies heavily on our sessions. She did not grow up with a secure holding environment, and our meetings allow a space where she can process the world around her and locate a sense of self. She lives a fairly secluded life, and it has primarily been through our relationship that she experiences her own existence.

What I had initially thought would be a potentially overwhelming impingement for Anna turned out to be an opportunity for safe expression. The outside world now matched more closely the way in which she had been living. In ways, she was better prepared for this transition than I was as it did not impact her way of living to as significant of a degree. It became clear quickly to me that within the unknown and unprecedented space we might each make a discovery and find new possibilities. I saw Anna come alive during this time, and I attributed this to the absence of tension she had felt with the outside world for so long. Anna's capacity for detachment from the external environment allowed her to lean into the experience of the shutdown with comfort and confidence. The impingement of the pandemic was well within Anna's capacity for creative response. I think we both got to know deeper aspects of Anna. In response to a global crisis, Anna was able to locate resilience and a sense of agency that initially surpassed my own adjustment. There was an ease and almost a sense of delight about her that allowed in our sessions the space for Anna to experience herself as strong and capable. In this new experience of Anna, I found myself relaxing my efforts to support her and allowing the space for her to demonstrate her own emergent capacities.

As the world began to reopen and people returned to activities outside the home, surprisingly Anna too began to participate in life outside of her home in ways that surpassed her pre-pandemic experiences and felt more aligned with an authentic, spontaneous, "True Self." Anna regularly visits an Italian coffee shop in her neighborhood and has become friends with the owners and several of the regulars. She has started to fantasize about possible travel to Italy one day. She has joined a hiking group with women in her community and has plans to host a 70th birthday party.

Kelli called me before I could reach out to her. She wanted to make sure that I was okay and had everything I needed for my family and me to stay safe. She had already managed to secure face masks, Lysol and Clorox wipes. Kelli was making plans to distribute care packages to family members and offered to send me a box when I let her know I had not been able to get my hands on any of those supplies yet. I was struck by her resourcefulness and her efforts to support the people around her. In this moment I noticed how good it felt to be considered by Kelli. In my own overwhelm to this massive change and the task of how to go-on-being, Kelli's offer was soothing. I declined this offer, but, in this exchange, I noted my own feelings of vulnerability and a desire to be cared for.

Kelli grew up with a mom and a sister who were both functionally limited. For as long as she could remember Kelli had been taking care of family. She lived three hours away from them with her husband and their two children who both struggled with chronic health disorders. Kelli has learned to combat any fears of annihilation for herself and those that she loves by staying a step ahead of any potential crisis. What I have learned about working with Kelli is that her preparedness is reinforced by its usefulness at the expense of her own sense of being.

When it became clear that the pandemic had no immediate end in sight and Kelli was limited in her capacity to care for her relatives, a new facet of "knowing" Kelli came into being. With no more supplies to be bought and having exhausted all her manic efforts to prepare, I noticed that Kelli started to settle into just being with her family. I too experienced her in a new way. There was a calm about our sessions that allowed me to relax, and the space to explore other aspects of her life seemed to open up. I began to feel a depth of knowing Kelli that had been absent from our sessions before. I realized that her hypervigilance may have been a false self-presentation arising from earlier her efforts to survive within her high-need family. The content of our sessions shifted. Kelli began to reflect on her childhood and her interpersonal relationships, including an abusive relationship with a male relative that until this time she had not considered important to explore. Kelli began to allow me to hold a space for her to do this. In this space we both found out there was more to Kelli beyond being strong, capable and always prepared. There was space for her overwhelm, fear and hurt by not having felt appropriately protected. She allowed me to provide this space for her. While her good nature did not disappear, it now felt somehow deeper and more genuine.

Before the hit of the pandemic, much of Kelli's energy had been focused outside of self. I could now see how the shutting down of the outside world paradoxically allowed for more space in which she could possibly for the first time experience *being* rather than *reacting*. In our work together, Kelli has been better able to see herself and gain insight into how she used helping behaviors to manage her fears. What was remarkable was that in this new space of forced detachment from her manic pursuit of caretaking, she was also able to see how her over-doing was in many ways ineffective and disruptive. She has since begun to learn new ways of responding.

My client Sam might be one of the busiest people I have ever met. He is one of those Wall Street investment banking types who has his driver drop him off at my office because he is always in meetings and his time is scheduled even en route. I have always been impressed with how he never seems to miss any of his children's most important games or performances, flying between cities and commuting between the suburb he lives in and downtown. Sam seems to be able to do it all. He and his wife are a great team, as they run the family like an impressive company and manage to go on vacations and stay in touch with family members all over the world.

I started working with Sam after his second oldest child committed suicide following his first semester at college. The family was devastated, and Sam's therapy sessions became essential to him. He never felt like he got to do enough of the mourning work that was needed before the demands of life resumed. He checked in with me as often as he could, but he often voiced his longing for more regular appointments. When the pandemic shut down his travel life and significantly decreased his work demands, Sam and I finally got to meet regularly. Sam had been reporting intense anxiety on Sunday mornings for some time. I often thought that Sundays might represent the only time that Sam's "true self" was safe to emerge, but only briefly as that self had to be packaged back in to allow his well-established professional self to survive in order to go back out into the world of investment banking. Sam's son had struggled in his own efforts to fit in with his competitive peer group. For both Sam and his son, the inability to live as their truest selves became intolerable.

The space that opened through the pandemic for Sam allowed time to sit with his grief and to begin to work through the complexities of having lost a child. I remember in our work before the pandemic Sam's need from me for reflections and insights. It was not until he was in a space of good enough holding that he could begin to locate himself. For many people including

Sam, the limitations of the pandemic allowed for more personal time. In this he discovered new grief around the awareness that his son's life had ended before he was able to find the potential space he needed for the discovery of his truer self.

Sam and his other children were all sequestered in their home during the pandemic. He began to live in his beautiful house. He started swimming laps, going on walks, making dinners with his family and playing games over Zoom with family members in other parts of the world. Shortly after the world reopened, Sam decided to retire. I don't believe that he ever wants to be fully at peace with the death of his son, but he has found a more meaningful way to go-on-being through the space opened up in the pandemic. It was as if the diminished accessibility to the outside world weaned Sam of a dependency on external engagement and allowed him to integrate the loss of his son.

I have worked with Rose since the death of her mother from a long-time battle with cancer four years ago, when she was 10 years old. Rose had stopped "going-on-being" years before I met her and was "living" in her room and through her screen, no longer engaged with peers or going to school, and withdrawn from her dad and her older sister. Rose is one of the most alone people I had ever met, and I genuinely did not know how I would ever find a crevice into the light of her true self. The first year of working with her was frustrating and discouraging; she went in and out of emergency care facilities, maintaining her position of being disengaged in our sessions. She would sit on my couch and look at the floor, while I made attempts to connect. I tried to fill up the space, and I tried to not fill up the space. Nothing that I did seem to make any difference.

When the pandemic hit and we shifted to Zoom sessions, Rose and I began "meeting" in her bedroom. This 14-year-old girl, who presented with dark alternative provocative attire, lived in a room that was designed for a modern princess. It was beautiful. I had her show me around, and in doing so, we began to talk about her mom who had made great efforts to create a beautiful home for her family. On subsequent visits I met her dog, Murphy, and saw other rooms in her home as invitingly decorated as hers. I began to know Rose and to know her mother through being in their home.

I came to understand that Rose had experienced anxiety about how to return to school following a long absence after her mother had died. Well before the pandemic, her peer relationships had become limited to people online that she had never actually met. The shutdown that the rest of the world was experiencing seemed to normalize what had been Rose's way of being. The pandemic made detachment from the outside world a normative experience, and for many of my clients this also afforded the space for a reset. Rose began to feel less behind or lost from her peer group and started considering a return to school when it became safe.

For many people I think the use of screens and the internet world allows for a type of intermediate experiencing between inner and outer realities. I could see how this transitional world helped Rose ease anxieties through a space of almost connection. We slowly started to incorporate her key relationships into our work together. The screen seemed to create a potential space for working with Rose allowing for material that she was unable to access on the couch in my office. This new space became a starting point for her to reengage with the world. Slowly she reestablished relationships with her father and her sister. When it became safe enough for reentry into the world, she was ready. Rose started working at a bakery and made two new friends. Since then, she has developed a greater sense of herself and has transitioned into her first year of college and no longer relies on the internet for connection and to be seen.

In the work with Rose as well as in the work with Sam, I have come to appreciate the necessity for the process of creative adaptation and the experience of locating authentic self response to profound loss. A True Self experience, I am witnessing, requires transitional space and is often accompanied by transitional objects. For Sam, it had been important to him that his son's room remained untouched. When he was home, he would spend hours just sitting with "him" in that space. For Rose, the safety of a home that had been meticulously curated by a mother who was no longer available to her as an object, provided the necessary holding until she was able to start to let go and participate in the world outside again. The fast pace and demands of life often do not allow adequate time for mourning. For Sam and Rose, the slowing down allowed by the pandemic created a new space for the necessary work of going-on-being.

In the space of the pandemic, we each had to recalibrate our relationship with the environment. Many of us were able to experience facets of ourselves that had otherwise not been available. The rupture presented challenges and in the uncertainty the opportunity to summon creative growth as seen in the variety of innovative ways humans found for connection, working, playing and even in therapy.

I had a new client this past week, a young mother of four children who tearfully discussed how chaotic life had become this past year with her husband returning to a hectic work travel schedule. She felt they were no longer living the family values that had initially inspired them to create such a large family. When I asked her about their time together during the pandemic, she noted how meaningful that time had been and longed for those times of connection. With four kids in sports, this no longer seemed possible. I too can relate to the experience of a world that seems to have moved right back into more demands than time permits, but what I have noticed is that I no longer see this as the only option for myself or my clients.

For the young mother in my office, the anxiety of her children not participating in sports may mask the cries coming from her truest self. Our task together is to provide her enough space to hear herself. What I have found working in the space of the pandemic has been a path of meaningful adaptation. As in the poem by Antonio Machado, "The Pathmaker" (Trueblood, 1988), where there is no path, one makes a path by walking. Does it take a pandemic to make the space and time we need in our lives? There is a new point of reference for each of us to draw from and what I am formulating is that even brief detachment made possible through intention rather than rupture may have meaningful implications to the work of going-on-being.

References

Saidipour, P. (2021). The precedent of good enough therapy during unprecedented times. *Clinical Social Work Journal, 49*, 429–436.

Trueblood, A. (1988). *Antonio Machado: Selected poems*. Harvard University Press.

World Health Organization. (2024). *COVID-19 epidemiological update – 15 July 2024*. https://www.who.int

4 Going-on-Being

Aging, Agency, and Downsizing

Michael Stern

From the very beginning, life is full of complex relationships with objects, both human and inanimate. In psychoanalytic theory, objects are understood as providing bridges between self and the external world. The ability to utilize them for personal development and life enrichment requires a set of conditions that psychoanalysis, from its early days, has tried to identify and define. That objects play a major role over one's lifespan is recognized by all psychoanalytic branches, though the meaning of objects in later phases of life has received considerably less attention than in infancy and childhood.

I wish to address a moment in the relationship with objects that is gaining more prominence as people live longer and can ideally expect to age with greater agency and self-determination. It addresses choices made when awareness of life's trajectory and meaning forces a reconfiguration of what is being held to and preserved and what is discarded or given away. In some way, this moment, generally referred to as downsizing, mirrors the process in which objects were first encountered and selectively integrated in the early stages of life.

How Do Objects Gain Their Meaning?

From the moment of birth, the baby needs to come to terms with the growing realization that the entities she encounters are separate from her. Through interactions with caregivers and her immediate environment she develops a relationship with objects that is highly subjective and individual. In fact, it can be said that she assigns meanings to objects in a manner that is unique to her alone, thus symbolically creating the object (Elkins, 2012). How this creative endeavor proceeds has been understood in the context of a wider recognition of human nature and innate capabilities. It requires progressive cognitive development and the ability to sustain curiosity and interest in objects (Piaget, 1936), as well as a secure environment in which that interest can flourish.

As the original object in his life, the mother introduces the baby to life's possibilities. He depends on her but needs to separate from her, a complex and hazardous figurative dance that was at the heart of Winnicott's (1953) writing. He coined the term "Transitional Object" to describe the mechanism

DOI: 10.4324/9781003607120-6

by which the growing child can not only accommodate the separation but also play, assign meaning to, and invest energy in objects or activities that appeal to him, capabilities that will serve him for the rest of his life in the form of sentimental object attachments. Separation, the main concern of this chapter, is inseparable from attachments. At the same time this mechanism also solidifies the sense of agency and the ability to hold on to or discard objects at will.

In *The Shadow of the Object*, Bollas (1987) addressed the impact of living in an object-filled world on the development of the self. He postulated that objects become transformational by being encountered, managed, modified, or otherwise interacted with. These interactions persist throughout life and contribute to changes in the sense of self over time.

The give-and-take between self and object is what makes attachments possible. It's an ongoing process, suggesting that we are never complete or whole. While the original attachment is to a person the range gradually expands to include other people, possessions, activities, and other forms of engagement. They gain meaning as they come to represent experiences of significance, as well as cultural influences. Appadurai (1986) noted that possessions have social meanings insofar as culture imbues objects with symbolic meaning, making it a social entity. Objects, and particularly the attachment to them, have the function of influencing or being influenced by emotional experiences. This creates a link between object attachment and emotional regulation, affecting all choices, including consumer, social, and interpersonal behavior (Timpano & Port, 2021). Indeed, much self-regulation involves trying to change relationships with objects, such as with food or money.

Echoes of this process reverberate throughout life, even as the self has evolved and matured and separation from mother has hopefully been accomplished. As individuals encounter more and more objects, they invest in some more than in others. Objects may no longer serve as representing the mother; rather, they are considered as sources of security and identity. Especially when it comes to inanimate objects, possessions become emotionally charged as they capture elements of one's life narrative and as such they help define the sense of "me" and by contract "not me". Where they fit on this continuum may depend on their symbolic expression of connection to others, and on their function as markers of individuality. At times the distinction is not clear-cut as when objects serve maladaptive needs, such as hoarding or fetishes that are experienced as disavowed parts of the self, neither "me" nor "not me". Objects that fail to address either affiliation or autonomy needs are relegated to "not me" status and are more easily discarded.

With time our relations with objects change. Acquisition of possessions is an early concern whereas maintenance and regulation become the challenge in later years. At some point the trend toward expansion and acquisitions starts reversing toward divestment and dispossession, most notably in the process of downsizing.

Throughout life we view things through the filters of nostalgia, revisionist history, regrets, and at times loss. In line with Winnicott's observation that we are all a collection of "bits and pieces" (in Cooper, 2024) some objects leave us cold. Stuff. But others are reminders of what was, and what we wish to remain connected to. The point is that it is not a direct link between self and object; an object's significance arises from its contextual place in one's idiosyncratic life story, and from needs that are at times contradictory, making downsizing the ambivalent process that it is. Unlike objects accumulated by hoarders that have no intrinsic meaning at all (Akhtar, 2019), downsizing refers to objects that "tell a story" and were acquired via active pursuit.

The term "downsizing" is currently used almost exclusively in business and management. It is barely mentioned in psychoanalytic literature, where it is tucked away in the more general writings on aging. This is quite puzzling since it is a process of significant and meaningful implications of its own.

To some degree downsizing is an unavoidable aspect of living past middle age. It occurs under a wide range of circumstances but by definition it reflects a contraction, most often related to a changing set of physical, social, familial, and emotional factors, or at least the anticipation of them. It is the most concrete manifestation of contraction, as it usually occurs when environmental impingement shakes what Winnicott (1971) refers to as "continuity of being".

Downsizing, in its most concrete form, refers to the gradual or wholesale discarding of items that have been in one's ownership for years on end. But more significantly it refers to the accompanying re-evaluation of priorities and meanings through reconfiguration of life with possessions.

The struggle with parting with any object that was more than just a practical necessity is familiar to all, not just to hoarders. There are more garages filled with "old stuff" than with parked cars. Deciding on what to discard is not a straightforward process. It is not determined by monetary value or practical usefulness and is not always rationally considered. A significant number of Senior Housing residents where I served as a consultant have expressed grief over having to part with some old furniture pieces that had been stored in the basement for years, and yet the idea of parting with them was intolerable. The mere contemplation of discarding items that once provided solace and stability, when continuity is under persistent threat, when there is a loss of narcissistic investment in children, when the growing awareness of death renews desire to fuse with life, triggers mourning. It is a process of transformation that affects both the inner sense of self and the place of the object in that inner world. It involves not a breaking of an object tie, but the transformation of the attachment into a sustaining memory. The object, by its loss or threat of its loss, gains a symbolic meaning it did not have before.

As external objects are given away, either by necessity or by a re-valuation of the meaning of life (Beit-Halachmi, 2007), a greater reliance on internal objects must develop. Under such circumstances, especially when the integration of internalized objects has not been fully consolidated, one is at risk of impulsive or conflictual decisions, discarding indiscriminately in what is bluntly called "dumbsizing". A process that starts with rearrangement of the physical environment may inadvertently devolve into psychic disorganization and the activation of aggressive and destructive self-states. When too many highly personal items are stripped away, as occurs in a move from a home to an assisted living studio for example, usually under somewhat traumatic circumstances, stabilizing personality supports are shaken. Eigen (2012) pointed out that dispossession, a form of destruction of the object, reflects hate of frustrating reality and the urge to destroy it. The ability to sustain and survive the process depends on early attachments and their role in providing security and emotional integration.

My own feeble attempts at downsizing demonstrate the conflicts, considerations, and fears involved even under benign conditions.

The piano. An upright Yamaha piano, bought by your typical upper Westside, yuppie parents, full of aspirations for their young daughters. In spite of weekly lessons the music career ends at Fur Elyse. The daughters discover other artistic pursuits, yet the piano remains. It accompanies the family to a new home where it fits against one wall but prevents a more coherent arrangement of other furniture. On occasion there is talk of selling or donating it, but it goes nowhere. The conversation focuses on what will take the piano's place, and once a large screen TV is mentioned the conversation is over. It goes without saying that a home with a piano is clearly superior to a home with a 60-inch TV in the living room. What becomes clear is the impact of a deeply ingrained value system and the barely conscious desire to maintain it. The piano is kept as a symbol of sophistication as well as an homage to my European parents' appreciation of the classical. But it is also a reminder of missed opportunities and a still embraced hope for redemption. I more than once entertained reveries of musical wizardry while attending a concert, yet never went beyond playing the lowly recorder myself. It's definitely late for wizardry, but the piano, even in its dormant state, offers an open invitation to pursue frustrated aspirations and creative outlets, as well as anchoring to early personal foundations.

One of my hidden treasures is a large folder holding dozens of letters that were sent to me in the years following my arrival in New York. They are mostly in Hebrew with some German and English in the mix. If ever a review of my emergence as a mature individual were authored, this would be a rich resource. That is paradoxically why I have never opened it since it was figuratively sealed years ago. Many of the letters simply acknowledge a connection, remembered experiences, soft intimacies. Some generously share life events, plans, and hopes. But I suspect, or rather I know, that more than a few portray feelings of being left behind, abandoned, dismissed. Some are angry, puzzled by a change, unable to understand why invitations to return home are experienced as a guilt trip. They address a young man, on his own, pushing ahead, defending against his own loneliness by detaching. Sometimes growing up involves growing apart. Things are being said that are later regretted. The picture reflected may not be as pretty as wished. The correspondence fades in intensity and frequency, like lovers turning away, sadly but inevitably.

Will I ever re-read these letters? Would you? I wonder about it from time to time, always pushing the decision into a remote future. In the end I think it really does not matter. Their significance now lies in their mere existence, in what I need them to be at different life phases. They have served in affirmation of connections but also in self-mirroring and self-reproach. At this stage of my life they are silent connectors to a rich but increasingly distant past. I may not read these letters again but will keep them nevertheless with what I hope is a growing sense of forgiveness and compassion.

Stamp Collection

Like many of my generation I started collecting stamps at a young age. In fact, stamps were my introduction to the English alphabet as well as to the world at large. The somewhat claustrophobic sensation that comes with growing up in a country surrounded by hostile neighbors was palpable even in an otherwise carefree childhood, and stamps offered a window to more hospitable environs. They also offered concrete lessons in history as, for example, when 1932 German stamps, with face value of 20 pfennig, were stamped over with one million pfennig denomination due to out of control inflation, then followed by 1934 stamps featuring Herr Hitler. A history lesson as relevant today as it was then. I felt a special affinity to the Israeli stamps, but the beauty and elegance of stamps were appreciated no matter where they were coming from. I suspect that my love of exploration and travel was greatly enhanced by this early exposure.

There is, however, another element to this attachment. My father, who like many of his generation held to a mostly hands-off approach to parenting, somehow found the time and patience to engage in this pursuit, place stamps in a global context, assist in cataloging them, and essentially share some quality time. Well, nobody collects stamps anymore. Who needs stamps when you have Tik-Tok? But I hold on to the fantasy of sitting with grandchildren, taking them on one-inch magic carpets to exotic destinations. It is the anticipation of such moments, of handing over a unique, almost forgotten key to discovery, the transmission of intergenerational wonder, that gives the collection its current meaning.

Sometimes, even the most prosaic objects gain unintended meanings that complicate their disposal.

My garage served its original purpose for a brief period before becoming a safe haven for the un-needed. For almost its entire length lie a bunch of siding strips, left over from a construction project of some 25 years ago. They are unused, and early lessons of not throwing away perfectly good things prevent their disposal. I also imagine a tree branch damaging the house and the Home Depot guy shaking his head "oh yeah, this was discontinued. They don't make them anymore". So I am prepared, though I know I am very unlikely to climb up a 20 foot ladder and fix the problem. I have no attachment to these strips. Should my downsizing include a move, the strips would be the first to go. Yet saving them now has meaning beyond the practical. It evokes memories of scarcity and reflects an awareness of potential breakdowns and the wisdom of being prepared, thus mirroring not only early parental lessons but also a growing concern over vulnerability and fragility.

My focus up to this point was on tangible possessions, but the same conflicts and ambivalences apply to all forms of downsizing, including in social circles, empty-nesting, travel choices, physical activity, and professional aspirations. Addressing his own stress in adapting to aging as an analyst, Pizer (2019) asked: "And, at what cost this exertion to defy nature? How many of us are, literally, at pains to deny not only death but also the season of living with reduction?" (p. 545). Analysts tend to stay in practice beyond traditional retirement age, presumably because they get engrossed in a difficult, meaningful, but never-ending challenge, and never fully experience their work as merely a job.

I started thinking about cutting back my work hours a few years ago, but it took a pandemic to nudge me into taking concrete steps. Not retirement, mind you, but even trimming around the edges proved more difficult than expected. It is not just the work ethic and the rewards of a busy practice, but also a reflection of how central this work experience is to my identity. On top of that, during the pandemic my patients and members of a professional peer group were the only people I saw regularly besides my immediate family, a connection that anchored me at least as much as I hoped it anchored them. True, it was all on Zoom but bringing work home, concretely and figuratively, and living through a shared crisis that threatened to downsize us all, blurred some of the protective boundaries usually available to us. Work and home have intersected and just as I struggle to legitimize anything that would replace my living room piano, I find myself stubbornly committed to a full workload and its symbolic meaning. Declining to take on a new patient simply because I want my evenings free feels a bit like slacking off. There are no established criteria for when and how and why to decline additions to one's practice. Is having leisurely dinners a good enough reason to turn down a referral? Down time in the afternoon? Yes, I tell myself (as does my wife), though it still feels like a dereliction of duty. What plays a role here is the giving up of omnipotence, mixed in with the anxiety of starting to let go not knowing where the letting go stops. It may not be fear of dying but the threat of diminished productivity and obsolescence is intimidating enough. Levin (2020) described the process of preparing to close a clinical practice as initiating a complex-grief process. Pizer (2019) wondered whether "a frantic clinging to the stage of Generativity at all costs is driven not only by a dread of experiencing decline and existential anxiety, but perhaps by a failure to arrive at loving ourselves as we are, loving our life" (p. 545).

So, what is the right way to downsize? In the absence of specific analytic references, I challenged the ultimate authority, ChatGPT. I keyed in: "What would psychoanalysis advise about age-related downsizing?" What I got was a fairly generic view of downsizing as a normal and healthy progression and an appropriate response to changing life circumstances. It specifically added that "Winnicott might view downsizing as a complex and challenging process, but one that, if approached with playfulness, curiosity, and spontaneity, is ultimately an opportunity for growth and adaptation while maintaining continuity and coherence in life".

So, there is an upside to downsizing when conditions are favorable, allowing for a gradual, voluntary, and disciplined process to occur. When done right it serves to enhance the goal of old age integrity, liberating and allowing the pursuit of life unencumbered by relics of the past or by despair. Ruti (2009) wrote, "Precisely when we are not tied to a predestined blueprint of what we are supposed to become we have a much greater degree of leeway in carving out the contours of our existence".

Downsizing entails a reassessment of what is essential and triggers a search for new venues for narcissistic fulfilment. Eigen (2012) suggested that maybe a recognition in later life that possession, ownership, and domination are destructive elements of the life-force, that they do not lead to a better or longer life as expected when younger. This is especially true in recent years as Csikszentmihal and Rochberg-Halton (1981) noted: "For the first time in history there is growing awareness that the resources of energy that have fueled material expansion are finite and that their desperate pursuit threatens the continuation of life on the planet". For many, the realization of having too many possessions forces a review of priorities. A recent NYTimes piece about changes in generational consumer behaviors put it this way: "Deep down, it's perhaps less about open-plan kitchens and cashmere knitwear than a desire to release a well-earned exhalation and be oneself without apology" (Avins, 2022). It remains to be seen how this change in attitudes toward ownership will affect downsizing behavior down the line.

What we possess is not always in the service of growth and good adjustment. Getting rid of some of what we have is not always a loss. But as it occurs at a stage of life in which dis-integration is threatened and self-reliance increasingly fragile, downsizing inevitably demands attention to the nature and maintenance of one's attachments. As objects and specific attachments are lost, new ones may acquire meaning but are rarely an exact equivalent for what was lost. A different intrapsychic dialogue develops based on current needs. Loss can be debilitating but also a source of inspiration. The ability to move from loss to creativity is the challenge of this phase of life. Ideally new opportunities develop for self-discovery and new connections that may be reminiscent of the past but different enough to allow for new and fresh options.

In the current heightened awareness of environmental footprints and social justice, conscientious downsizing offers a mark of good citizenship and moral correctness. Productive downsizing is facilitated by management of guilt over greed and by the nurturance of benevolence. Kohut (1982) suggested that a firm and coherent self that is capable of empathy, sublimation, and healthy participation in the happiness of the next generation makes necessary personal transitions easier. The transition from gratitude to generosity facilitates a stronger sense of belonging. When objects are seen not only as reflective of one's own past but also as potentially useful to others in the future, the process gains a quality of continuity and affirmation of social engagement. Of course, anyone who has tried to bestow their treasured possessions upon their children learns rather quickly that the need to give far surpasses the wish to receive. Nevertheless, holding on to the wish that by transferring objects to others their invested meaning can be preserved is quite powerful. This, more than the anticipated cash, is what truly motivates people to have garage sales.

One may look at downsizing as a transitional process with the potential to leave one bereft, liberated, or anywhere in between. In that regard it is no different from other developmental challenges. The fact that it occurs on the declining part of the curve makes it more demanding than the upsizing that preceded it. Balancing what stays and what goes, rightsizing, requires the embrace of the ever-shifting nature of attachments and the inevitability of loss. Done right, it is an expression of agency and self-determination, renewal when it is most appreciated.

References

Akhtar, S. (2019). Hoarding: A multifactorial understanding. *International Journal of Applied Psychoanalysis, 16*, 145–159.

Appadurai, A. (1986). *The social life of things: Commodities in cultural perspectives.* Cambridge University Press.

Avins, J. (2022, August 18). Boomers are all the rage. *New York Times Magazine.*

Beit-Halachmi, B. (2007). Triggering metamorphosis: Freud and Siddhartha. *Annals of Psychoanalysis, 35*, 151–163.

Bollas, C. (1987). *The shadow of the object: Psychoanalysis of the unthought known.* Free Association Books.

Cooper, S. H. (2024). Splitting and the use of the object. *Psychoanalytic Dialogues, 34*(2), 142–144.

Csikszentmihal, M., & Rochberg-Halton, E. (1981). *The meaning of things: Domestic symbols and the self.* Cambridge University Press.

Eigen, M. (2012). On Winnicott's clinical innovations in the analysis of adults. *International Jornal of Psychoanalysis, 93*(6), 1449–1459.

Elkins, J. (2012). Revisiting destruction in "the use of the object". *The Psychoanalytic Quarterly, 86*, 109–148.

Kohut, H. (1982). Introspection, empathy, and the semi-circle of mental health. *The International Journal of Psychoanalysis, 63*, 395–407.

Levin, C. B. (2020). Becoming wise. *Psychoanalytic Inquiry, 40*, 207–217.

Piaget, J. (1936). *The origins of intelligence in children.* International Universities Press.

Pizer, S. A. (2019). That time of year thou may'st in me behold: An analyst encounters aging. *Psychoanalytic Dialogues, 29*, 543–547.

Ruti, M. (2009). *A world of Fragile things: Psychoanalysis and the art of living.* State University of New York.

Timpano, K., & Port, J. H. (2021). Object attachment and emotion (dys)regulation across development and populations. *Current Opinions in Psychology, 39*, 109–114.

Winnicott, D. W. (1953). Transitional objects and transitional phenomena. *The International Journal of Psychoanalysis, 34*, 89–97.

Winnicott, D. W. (1971). *Playing and reality.* Basic Books.

Part II

Going-on-Being Through Threats to the Self

5 Living Atop Archaic Agonies
Treating Children Suffering from Early Trauma

Brent Willock

Our greatest catastrophes are so deep inside of us that only their furthest waves touch our surface.

— Rilke (1969, p. 89)

In a baby's mind, the feeling of absent mother's existence lasts for x minutes. Away longer, her image, and the baby's capacity to use it, fades. The infant's distress is repaired if mother returns within x + y minutes. In x + y + z minutes:

> Mother's return does not mend the baby's altered state. Trauma implies that the baby has experienced a break in life's continuity, so that primitive defences now become organized to defend against a repetition of "unthinkable anxiety" or a return of the acute confusional state that belongs to disintegration of nascent ego structure . . . a *break-up* of whatever may exist at the time of a *personal continuity of existence*. After "recovery" from x + y + z deprivation a baby has to start again permanently deprived of the root which could provide *continuity with the personal beginning*.
>
> (Winnicott, 1971, p. 97)

Most mothers protect their babies from this "rupture of the infant's self" (Winnicott, 1965, p. 97). If they cannot, "there is a serious interference with the natural tendency that exists in the infant to become an integrated unit, able to continue to have a self with a past, present, and future" (p. 86).

> The infant whose pattern is one of fragmentation of the line of continuity of being has a developmental task that is, almost from the beginning, loaded in the direction of psychopathology. Thus there may be a very early factor (dating from the first days or hours of life) in the aetiology of restlessness, hyperkinesis, and inattentiveness.
>
> (pp. 59–60)

This contribution investigates one such child's struggle to go-on-being.

DOI: 10.4324/9781003607120-8

Background

> The trauma of birth is the break in the continuity of the infant's going on being, and when this break is significant the details of the way in which the impingements are sensed, and also of the infant's reaction to them, become . . . significant factors adverse to ego development. . . . In some cases this adverse factor is so great that the individual has no chance (apart from rebirth in the course of analysis) of making a natural progress in emotional development.
>
> (Winnicott, 1975, p. 189)

Born prematurely, Ming lived two months in a Neonatal Intensive Care Unit (NICU). His mother contacted me before his sixth birthday. He never spoke as much as other family members. His junior kindergarten teacher thought he might be deaf and should repeat the year. "He only speaks when he thinks you care," Mother said. A speech/language pathologist thought Ming might be gifted.

In senior kindergarten, a behavioral therapist observed Ming. He was deemed normal. When his cousin killed himself and another relative and pet died, Ming feared he'd perish. Wanting to be with deceased family, he considered poison. Perhaps prematurity sensitized him to loss, prompting desires to return to a prior state (womb).

Ming became more disruptive. He pushed a child and resisted transitions (contiguity disruption). He refused "too loud" gym (sensitivity related to prematurity?). He resisted schoolwork. It was too hard or too easy. Asked to do things, he ran, sometimes with scissors. When his teacher, whom he likes, grabs him, he bites, scratches, throws things, breaks pencils. He finds school insufficiently interesting to distract him from death fears. If his nanny, who has been with him since birth, is present (continuity), he feels relaxed at school. His brother upsets him, declaring Mother only likes him.

Beginning

When Father left Ming at a children's party, Ming broke balloons and hit children. "Perhaps to have Father return," Mother reasoned [and/or filling the void with aggression].

"Can a car go off into space?. . . . Can the floor of our house collapse?" Ming asked. Prematurity can exacerbate a fundamental sense of self as ungrounded/unbounded (Willock, 2015). This unattached, plummeting or dissolving self is the autistic-contiguous position's core anxiety (Ogden, 1989), preceding Klein's (1950) paranoid-schizoid position.

Ming drew: "The shapes are in the shelter" [bounded/contained, uterine; Tustin's (1984) autistic shapes]. "There's a nice dragon overhead" [positive paternal transference]. He tried to colour me with marker pens [My self is not uncontainable – I defy boundaries, force restraint, restoring contiguity]. "The shapes are now outside the shelter but like being inside it" [his life story].

"You is Happy." Was he describing him or me? Mother said he sometimes talks of himself in the third person (like some autistic spectrum children).

In the midst of commenting, "It's so much fun," and criticizing my appearance and smell, Ming mentioned: "I'm you and you're me" [Searles' (1970) therapeutic symbiosis]. . . . Why don't you curl your moustache like my educational assistant?" [separation/boundaries].

A bear defecates a rabbit, baby, toys [birth]. They enter dog puppet. Bear pounds them out [countering womb retreat]. "What a mess!" [postnatal]. Ming straightened the room [reassembling self, with assistance].

"Who did you marry?" ("Liz") "For real?" ("Yes. . . . Do you want to marry someone when you're older?") "Can I?" ("If you want.") "Can I marry you?" ("I'll be old when you're marrying age.") "Maybe you'll be one" [denial; maybe we'll be one] "Will I ever be a baby again?" [Is there any hope of redoing my beginning?]

It was hard for Ming to leave his new room/womb. He clung, then ran out, shouting, as if to say: "You're not ejecting/birthing me; I'm launching."

Ming drew characters playing ball. "Their owner is cleaning them. . . . The oval is asleep" [attended to, relaxed]. . . . "Do you press the 2 button?" ("On the elevator to my office?") "Yes." ("I do. Do you?") "No. I live here. Don't tell my parents."

Joining marker pens, Ming built "long legs." They fell apart. He hurled them [I'm not fragmenting; I'm creating chaos]. He poohed his pants.

("5 minutes left.") "What about 'That's All' that you said we should work on?" ("We did discuss managing goodbyes. . . . That's all, folks! 'Til next week.") Ming enjoyed my goodbye song.

> Failures of basic provision. . . . The main point is that these failures are unpredictable. . . . They result in the *annihilation* of the individual whose going-on-being is interrupted.
>
> (Winnicott, 1963, p. 343)

It was crucial to Ming that we predicted and carefully managed disruptions to our going-on-being at each session's end.

Ming insisted my beard was his [symbiosis], therefore he could pull it. I restrained him from throwing pens at me [Winnicott's (1975) holding environment]. "My hands are holding your hands" [The reverse was true; symbiotic mix-up]. Presses his nose/face against mine [contiguity].

"God . . . married his helper who came down to Earth [undoing separation]. . . . Underground rabbits got flooded" [forced out of home/womb]. "Bugs Bunny could have died." Ming's transformer car "shoots power and bombs" [versus self exploding]. "I made it from chemicals" [omnipotence].

"I'll tell you a story. It's a fine day. The square sees thunder, lightning. She wants to go back into the house [womb]. . . . "Next session's story [continuity] will be: The Boy in the Cupcake Factory" [womb/breast/oral gratification – antidote to previous story that might be called The Girl in the Stormy Birth]. Mentions sleeping in my office [cupcake factory]. Climbing on me, Ming resists parting. Engineer father: "Was he focused?" ("Yes.") "I don't think he's a psychopath." ("No.") "It's volitional." ("Different agenda.") "Yes."

Ming bangs my door. A woman leaves. . . . "Why the lady?" . . . Later claims he said "latie." ("Were you angry feeling I'm late?") "You're stupid" [denying/confirming my comment] . . . You don't know anything."

> Sensitive adaptation to an infant's ego-needs only lasts a little while. Soon the infant begins . . . to get something positive out of being angry . . . fusing aggression in with loving.
> (Winnicott, 1965, pp. 86–87)

"My name is Nathan" [lady/latie insult not happening to Ming]. . . . "What if I stayed forever in this cupboard?" . . . Rips cotton surrounding door [separation; misbehavior defends against parting]. . . . "Will you throw me out?" . . . I carry Ming out. ("It's hard to say bye.") Father disagrees there's any such meaning in Ming's misbehavior.

Ming tests my ability to see what is obscured/latent: "Can you find the English letter among the Chinese? . . . Can you see numbers beneath this ink?" [see Willock (1990) on how games like hide-n-seek process separation]. He's amazed whenever I succeed. "It is a joy to be hidden but a disaster not to be found" (Winnicott, 1965, p. 186).

"I'll draw a picture for you to take home tomorrow, I mean next time" [slip reduces separation]. Oppositional parting. Father: "Same shit, different day."

"Did I draw last time?" [Do you hold me in mind?]. Seeks physical contact [contiguity].

Builds ship with red chair for king ["his majesty the baby" (Freud, 1914, p. 91)]. Puts me in its "caboose". . . . Emphasizes controls/mechanisms [growing interest in regulating behavior]. Ship has brakes, except in wavy [challenging] moments. Ming and Father leave hand in hand. Perhaps Ming carries a comforting sense of our connection [caboose].

Discontinuity

After four months, Covid-19 interrupted treatment. After 18 months, Father called: "Ming has tummy aches that worsen in relation to school/social activities. Kids make fun of him. He refuses playdates." (Once Father said Ming calls our sessions "playdates.") I said I now only work via telephone/screen. Father assured me that will work.

Ming did well at home during Covid, Mother said, as long as someone was with him [contiguity]. He no longer needs a "shadow" (assistant) [symbiosis], but one plays with him at recess. School "loves him," but he pleads for home schooling, saying he hates himself and everyone hates him.

It was difficult to engage Ming in discussing these problems. He said children aggressively rush outside at recess [escaping confining classwomb]. He just plays in the snow, digging a hole, deep pathways [womb, containment].

Our dialogues about parent-identified problems felt unalive. Ming talked quickly, barely listening. It seemed progress would more likely come from following his associations, working on separation.

Minecraft: "You die almost from looking at the sword" [precarious going-on-being]. . . . If you die, you spawn to a new world with nothing you built [Birth, the death of intrauterine life, massively disrupts nascent self-structure]. . . . If you find the creator of Minecraft [postnatal parents], they give you things. . . . A black hole sucks you in [doomed]. . . . Lightning [NICU lights?] struck my face [The girl in the storm wants back inside]. . . . I can make anything [omnipotence]. . . . You fall into the void" [omnipotence fails].

After two sessions, Ming's stomach aches settled.

Oral and Anal Worlds

Ming often shares his screen to show me what he does between sessions [continuity], interjecting allusions to archaic experience: "Feather cradle. . . . Little boy creeper mad. . . . Boom. . . . Crater. . . . Explode . . . a black hole pushing. . . . Nighttime sun is in the void. . . . End of the world."

"I showed Brent. Oh, you are Brent" [overcoming discontinuity]. . . . "My mom with teeth bigger" [bad breast; projecting hunger/anger?]. . . . "Want to get a new pizza pie crust in the sender . . . for you and me to eat [He's good breast]. . . . I love you" [Freud's (1912) unobjectionable positive transference]. . . . "Pool of poop" [he could become a poop puddle, like Little Black Sambo's toothy tigers running/dissolving to butter, then eaten in pancakes]. . . . "Poop eats the pizza" [Pooped out at birth, he reconstitutes himself via good breast]. . . . "Mona Lisa is dead. How did they draw her?" [create/resurrect mother]. . . . ("5 minutes.") "I love being with you."

"Every time I draw, I get hungrier. . . . I'll be in the sender [contained]. I'll be a new pizza" [Lewin's (1952) oral triad: eat; be eaten; sleep]. Ming types random letters [filling void]. . . . "Uncreated granite [unborn, potentially rock-solid]. I found it in Minecraft [transitional space/reality blur]. Unpolished granite. Unknown granite [needs recognition]. . . . Heavier than 5 dolphins [intrauterine; burden to self/others]. . . . Only thing that can break it is these sticks [vulnerable]. . . . So much in it [potential]. . . . UFO [his arrival onto Earth]. . . . Killed alien [hostile environment]. . . . Magic [omnipotence]. . . . Nothing in tube – something drops out. Liquid [milk?]. . . . String [umbilical cord/nipple] from rock turns the rock gold [miraculous relational alchemy]. . . . Matricite [mother] is magical" [science fiction mineral created from remains of Population 0 stars – its radiation blocks telepathy (NICU disrupts primal communication)].

"Pictures of inside Mom[!]. . . . Sun [son?] blowing up . . . 200 layers of opacity" [difficult to see/connect with selfobject]. Presents a multiplication test involving gigantic numbers [filling disrupted autistic-contiguity]. . . . "Jesus apple sauce" [supernurturance]. . . . "Your age and your wife's plus mine and my sibling's and my father's = 851 – grandmother's age" [multifamilial support].

Pretends he can't hear me [projecting NICU frustration]. . . . "The one and only Ming! [Birth!]. . . . My brother doesn't live here [maternal preoccupation restored]. . . . Tiny gun becomes real" [transitional space cannot contain]. . . . "Shoots his hand [aggression turned against self]. . . . Missile stuck in holder [anal holding on vs. letting go; can't destroy others]. . . . I don't have a family. I'm alone now [defenses fail to prevent object destruction/loss]. . . . I made a nice big poop yesterday. . . . In my face. I had to go to the hospital because the poop stuck in my mouth [self-birthing (Willock, 2017)]. . . . Dr. Madbrain" [project insanity/discontiguity into me/us].

Cameo Phallus

Teaching me his language, Ming writes in Chinese: "I like Brent." Much mouth movement. 'Plays' guitar. Music really emanates from his computer [technological symbiosis]. . . . "Trouble clef is a weird note" [feminine figure fused with troubling offspring]. Turning guitar keys: "I twisted these notes [nipples?] . . . 5 . . . 8 . . . 109 . . . 500 times. . . . Double trouble note . . . ¼ . . . ½ trouble note." Calls French horn "mouthaphone . . . mouthing a phone." Inserting tube into mouthaphone: "Bonerphone. . . . Take these parts out makes it a tuba" [bonerless female].

"94 times the mass of the sun times the mass of black matter [good/bad breast/void]. . . . Dark matter is like a virus. Most powerful thing. Can consume the world in milliseconds – my arm [castration], a bird, the sun. . . . They'll make defense systems to push dark matter away from the universe [going-on-being]. . . . A supernova exploded. . . . The mass of dark matter compared to the sun is infinite . . . 94 [number that began session restores contiguity] billion years 'til the Earth is consumed. . . . I made a potion . . . drinks a black hole." ("Meaning?") "It just tastes like that . . . Radium [matricite] poisoning racoon [displacement], consumes brain. Could die. I'm terrified of skulls. They're so crazy. . . . Flying rock coming from sky" [bombarding objects].

Ming says he plays lots of video games, makes much money. "A flying cow" [good breast] . . . Earth would be destroyed in 5 days if there were dragons [phallic father]. . . . Can you drink oil? [absent breast]. . . . They broke my eyeballs" [castration].

"Newton's Cradle broke" [suspended metal balls/testicles]. . . . "Neutron star pulls, could rip your arm off, suck your finger in" [bad breast/void/castration].

"Ming is at the hospital. . . . He died. . . . Pooooooooooooooooop" ("Because we don't meet next week?") "No . . . I'm a gigital halker. Space is very cold. . . . Go to space with Richard Branson [togetherness]. . . . They're falling, Brent!!!!" [Balint's (1968) basic fault = 'dropped' by parents]. ("You're mute, invisible"). . . . Plays instrument, looking up frequently to ensure I'm watching.

Pretends he's Mother, messaging me [primary identification defending against longer-than-usual separation]. "Poop! . . . An Ice Age woman was brought back to life" [self/mother/analyst put in cold storage to survive separation].

"If you have to be in Dubai [so far from Ming]. . . . We used to eat and drink on your website [You're absent, but memories nurture me]. . . . I am you soon [symbiosis]. . . . Ping [his pet] is a very smart boy [Yes, Ming is very intelligent.]. . . . Battery lasts 43 minutes. Perfect for our session." Pounds out: 9999999999999999999999999999999x88888888888888888888888888888. "I'm the next Albert Einstein. $\pi \times \pi$. I'll eat all the pie. . . . Ping $\times$ Ping = . . . 31 minutes" . . . ("5 minutes"). . . . "I'm aware I have 5 minutes" [almost doesn't need reminders]. Plays "Ode to Joy" [sustaining happiness despite parting].

"9 minutes, 47 seconds left. . . . Who cuts us off? [external force]. . . . I'll be 4 minutes when . . . 1'51". Writes in Chinese: "Good bye."

Dolls nested in dolls [womb]. . . . "I baked cookies" [good breast]. . . . Card trick [Magic helps survival]. . . . Closes our video connection, doesn't respond, turns video back on, makes ball disappear/reappear ("Like us"). Spits out ball, turns off clock [control time/events].

Ming moves with his phone/camera: "You are going out of my bathroom [living together]. I'm ok if we go out to eat [perinatal]. . . . Our first meeting. . . . Ancient divorce language [natal 'divorce' necessitates external eating]. . . . Extremely difficult to master [trauma]. End London. Vermont. And" ("'End' is like our sessions ending. 'And' is like 'and we meet next week.'") "Good observation. . . . Only 5 people know Pig Latin" [our unusual language].

Preferring Paranoia (Versus Autistic-Discontiguity)

Ming arrives speaking of outer space. "Black hole! Let me get out of it. I hope I don't shove my camera [that connects us] in the black hole. Hope I land back on Earth. Bridge space engine broke". . . . Baby voice, much tongue protruding, lip licking. "Fall. . . . Face plant. Plant with face on it. When you hit the ground hard, it grows a plant. Need hospital [NICU]. . . . Did you know I hit my head with a hammer? [I'm in charge of my traumatization]. . . . I lost an eyeball" [wrecked worldview].

"Fading away [autistic-discontiguity]. . . . Toxic tree covered in thorns up to 17 inches long. . . . Apples [bad/good breast]. . . . When monkeys climb it, they explode [autistic-discontiguity]. . . . Baby pumpkins. Hard shell [protective exoskeleton]. . . . Loud as a gunshot, force of hand grenade" [postnatal cacophony]. Pumpkins explode, hurling "everything inside. The seeds spread and make more trees" [resurrection/rebirth].

"60-pound pine cones" [burdensome offspring/seeds]. . . . If one falls on you, you're done. You might break one with a hammer [earlier hit head with hammer]. . . . Strong as bedrock [body armor]. . . . African trees bear toxic fruit. . . . Can eat insides [bad/good split]. . . . Giant pumpkins weigh up to 6 tons [protective grandiosity]. . . . One of the most dangerous trees. . . . Spreads bad smelling gas. If it gets in your lungs, you can die. Burns for 16 days [splitting defense may fail]. . . . Inside tastes like coconut/strawberries/pineapple [good breast]. . . . Fruit is as long as me" [fits my needs].

"Flame Thrower Tree blows out tiny darts . . . releases neurovenom that blocks your lungs and blood system . . . your kidneys fail, you hallucinate, burn. . . . Stabbed in back with metal key [much goes wrong in NICU]. . . . Big berries like my face [nipples/breasts]. . . . No toxins in the fruit [splitting]. . . . If you get sap in your eyes, you go blind. Burning could lead to no eyeballs. . . . It's not dangerous [denial]. . . . It's a humanity tree [connection to root of being]. . . . Eel tree is toxic" [splitting].

Talking and moving staccato fashion, Ming pretends computer problems [NICU imperfections]. We keyboard messages [find alternatives]. "Type Control Shift qq to unmute." These instructions prove fruitless. . . . "3 minutes left . . . 2 minutes . . . 50 seconds . . . I'm upside down . . . falling" [birth, basic fault].

Discusses upcoming trip, rock collection: "This diamond is one of the world's biggest" [good breast; I'm a gem]. . . . It carries a conduit [milk duct] that shines through despite opacity [The good breast continues to exist even though its absence makes it fade in my mind's eye]. Can find in California. . . . This is a piece of a star the weight of Mount Everest. Even 1 gram of it [*pars pro toto*]. . . . Water makes it lighter as a baby dolphin [entering/leaving water symbolizes birth (Freud, 1900)]. . . . Place water next to it, then you can lift it [With the right knowledge/substances/people, perinatal miracles happen]. . . . A compound creation [2 to tango]. . . . Connects to everyone [self/world unity restored]. . . . Grinds away heavy metal [armor]. . . . Breaks down gold and disonic diathon material heavier than 720 elephants and 20 blue whales. . . . Chuck it in water. Breakdown into particles. . . . If you put a mirror on top, something crazy happens. It casts a light and starts levitating [resurrection]. . . . I'll go find the next thing. Bye until I find it. . . . The first sample from Uranus. First pee from your anus [valuable body substances]. . . . Piece of the sun. A piece of my son [maternal identification]. . . . Dropped it [better than being dropped]. . . . Burned a hole in my ground [I created the fault in my being]. . . . A piece from a black hole [escaped death]. Damaged. . . . Like radium. . . . Burning, biting. . . . First piece from Mars. . . . Found in a comet. . . . Alien skin from a comet [epidermal contiguity]. . . . I look at these every day."

"I'm a superb Minecraft builder. . . . Eating gold apple gives me restoration regeneration [postnatal recovery via the good breast]. . . . Hydrochloric acid is one of the weirdest substances [dangerous versus restorative postnatal fluids]. . . . Erupts if oxidized, like elephant's toothpaste [that I squeeze out of breast]. Burns and breaks through the tube [nipple]. Could break through stone, like nitroglycerin. . . . OMG! We only have 2 minutes. This box is sponsor of of of of of of . . ." [filling void].

"Arriving from space, Ming flies to the Golden Gate" [Paradise]. . . . Baby talk. . . . "Gummy bears. I'm hungry. Order a pizza [much tongue movement]. . . . I can't reach [good object]. . . . I'm dying" [NICU]. Turns himself into different animals [rather than staying in one endangered identity]. "Shark eats deer" [uterine/sea creature devours land being/breast].

Runs back and forth getting food. Disconnects, reconnects. Turns us into other colours = monsters. "That's what's really real" [fantasy versus parental concerns]. Space ship dodges obstacles, crashes [Balint's (1955) philobats rely on skills to navigate 'friendly expanses' between untrustworthy objects]. . . . Nonsense typing [fills void]. . . . Points out two real words in letter heap: "Join. Hello" ["We'll rejoin and say hello next week"].

Refers to a game where you eat to get long [as neonates do]. "Then you can eat long guys [recall fruit his length]. . . . Wrap around my victims. That's the end of the world [incorporating destroys primary object]. . . . Just want to die [womb/tomb]. . . . Change my name to Master of Chaos [vs. victim of chaos]. . . . It's life or death, like Minecraft [approach existence like game]. . . . Lot of droppings. . . . Eating my business [extrude, re-incorporate bad objects]. . . . People farting on everyone [anal/perverse 'solution']. . . . I killed a big dude. . . . He dropped all this stuff. . . . Eating my guts" [provision].

Music in the Air

Increasingly, Ming shared musical instruments. He loves his clarinet that had been Father's [continuity]. . . . ("Time's up") "Ok. Bye." [having established our secure base, he can venture contentedly into the world with Father/music].

"For this song, you're gonna blow here and finger like this." Ming instructs me lots lately on how 'I'll' play clarinet [therapeutic symbiosis]. Moves perfectly to music 'he'/his computer plays [new comfort in his body/world]. ("I like the mellow parts.") "Me, too." Accepts ending, sadly.

Ming wishes he could bring his clarinet to my old office [contiguity]. "How long since we met there?" (2.5 years) . . . What happened to your old office? . . . What countries have you been to? . . . You're lucky I'm Chinese" [We're separate; I'm a gem].

Recalls Father teaching him to play music when Ming was 3. Not hyperactive today. . . . "Do we have to sign off? [intersubjective 'we' loss!]. . . . Ok. Bye."

Ming's music often sounds bad. "This is what you don't want to hear from a child (makes vomiting noises on instrument). . . . This pee sound annoys me. . . . Pooping noises are more irritating. . . . Worse is farting. . . . Diarrhea, farting in pools, tubs. Nobody likes" ("unlike music"). Looks suspiciously as Mother returns from store work: "We're so glad Ming's learning/practicing music again." He: "I want a trumpet. . . ." Recently he referenced vending machines providing things. Now he hopes/expects his wishes may be gratified.

"I can't believe my father bought me new reeds [Winnicott's good mother anticipates wants before baby knows them] . . . 4 years to make them in France . . . 2 years of growth, 2 years of dying [NICU life/death]. . . . Dad and I recorded, with studio help." [In an early session, Ming demonstrated relational play's importance, enjoying taking turns adding features to create a human.]

"This is my first instrument. Since I was a baby" [continuous self]. . . . ("5 minutes left") "Only 2 instruments left [to play for you]. . . . Cost $2,000,000" [I'll have and hold these valuable objects when we separate versus falling into void]. "A friend sent me his music to complement mine. I told him about you. Another friend plays cello" [Ming never mentioned friends before! He's found relational continuity outside versus in my cupboard/womb].

"You're probably dizzy watching me play" [increasing empathy].

Transformation

Ming mixes "18 karat gold" with alcohol and water "to make it purer" [Jungian alchemical concern with self-transformation]. . . . Smashes mixture "to add pressure . . . Saran Wrap keeps the tension of the heat by reflecting it back. . . . Light toasts back the water. . . . This is the ashes of the gold [death/rebirth]. . . . By the time this lesson is over [sense of our analytic session's rhythm]. . . . Spit from my French horn. . . . Dental floss to clean the water. . . . Spin. . . . Melting process tomorrow to purify. . . . Right now it's just puriated" ("Meaning?"). "It's cleaned and ready to go" [like him!].

"My friend showed me a computer game. You mix 4 elements. . . . I never got this far before!" [progress!]. Mother: "Peach tea?" [breast offers before wish expressed]. . . . ("You didn't thank Mom.") Thanks her, returns: "How do you make a person?" [my suggesting people should be acknowledged?] Solo play ['alone' in the presence of the other (Winnicott, 1975)]. . . . "Tornado. Hurricane." ("5 minutes.") "I better speed up [adapt]. . . . My game's called *Little Alchemy*."

"I'm in China" [versus outer space]. . . . Goodbye" (in Chinese). . . . I'm coming home today" [reunion]. . . . Long flight" ("Long time since we've been together because you were at your cottage"]. "I'm Fred, waiting 15 minutes for my teacher" [too long between appointments, therefore 'dissociates']. Ignores me [See how it feels to be treated as if you don't exist].

Next session, he's silent, invisible. Chatroom: "How long is the class? . . . I fixed my microphone" [I break/restore relationships]. . . . ("1 minute") "Oh gosh." Tries to solve a puzzle to beat the clock [I have ways of mastering separation challenges].

A red-lit room. Ming's a terrifying, knife slashing devil [mastering terror by becoming it]. . . . "Bye. . . . Sucked into a tornado! . . . Bye. . . . When do we see each other again?" [Loss no longer eternal]. Devil returns. "I'm 36 [Grownups don't fear]. . . . I don't want to say bye [increasing capacity to verbalize to master]. . . . Brent is awesome."

Biological Transformation

Father emails: "Boys pick on Ming. He's regressing. Won't line up for school; clowns; doesn't request help; avoided class on puberty because if he goes through it, he'll be closer to dying" [development, like birth, brings death anxiety]. Mother encouraged Ming to discuss these problems with me:

Ming: I only talk to Brent about happy things [building secure base].
Mom: You're acting out like you used to when distressed.
Ming: Maybe I need a physiologist.
Mom: Psychologist?
Ming: Yes.
Mom: You see Brent.
Ming: Brent is not a psychologist; he's just Brent.
Mom: Brent's a psychologist.
Ming: Wow! I'm so lucky!

When asked if he'd speak about problems if Brent brings them up, Ming was noncommittal. I raised these issues. Ming: "Growing up is bad. Parents will, too. Then they'll die. . . . Puberty – just learned about it. Disgusting! . . . Homework is hard, so I don't do it. . . . Parents yell at me if I don't know 4 × 4."

Introducing these troubles into our 'happy' space triggered pessimism: "Dear Future, I exploded myself with a gun" [recall suicidal relative]. Ming puts bullets in safe [containment] . . . Explosions [containment challenging]. . . . Computer screen blackens . . . Ming bows, blows kisses, as if all that preceded was mere performance. Containing feelings in letters/theatre suggests authoring his life rather than being victim of overwhelming forces.

Ming disappears repeatedly. He looks sick, dead. Types "futfutkfk . . ." at great length [alluding to: Dear Future/fuck/puberty; filling void autosensuously].

Processing Birth Trauma

"There's a black hole in my ceiling. Just kidding" [differentiating fantasy/reality]. . . . "I like to sleep under stars on my ceiling" [benevolent breasts watch over me, like NICU lights, through nocturnal separation].

"I'll write a book [cultural containment]: "The Mystery of the Missing Controller" [selfobject, ego]. . . . Interrupts sound/video [control]. . . . "Music instruments as high as a house" [protectors]. Game where you try to prevent black holes from destroying you."

"2.5 million years to make a diamond the size of a football [gestation]. . . . 23 generations. Kentucky" [long ago, faraway]. ("I don't see you") "Camera's broken. . . . Game called Don't Press the Button" [don't disconnect]. Obstacles and challenges where you can die. "What time is it? What's half that?" . . . ("4 minutes left") "Ok. . . . How much time left?" Makes instrument from soda can [he's invisible, but 'music' communicates]. ("Sounds like a baby crying") "Being smacked."

"Only 16 people know how to breathe through their ears [preemies often have difficulty breathing]. . . . Pilots ear breathe" [buttressing their philobatic skill]. "Mother sent me a photo of me as a baby. Shows my weenie [autoerotism helps survival]. . . . I'm breathing through my ears . . . . Hear that?" ("Tap, click?") "Baby crying." Screen goes black. ("Hide-n-seek"). . . . Ming's hand blocks the camera.

Father shares Ming's notes: "I fear Dieing. . . . It feels hard to live sometimes. . . . Nothing helps. . . . I don't tell Brent because I can't. . . . I feel like I'm going to end up like Chu (suicide)." Father: he had three meltdowns, panicked he'll die. Withdraws, curls up on floor, looks miserable. . . . Wants me to tell you. . . . May relate to screen time. . . . He's hypochondriacal."

Beginning our session in darkness, Ming suggests these fears began at age 6. "Shows scare me. . . . I look things up. ("Like what?") "If you taste cinnamon in water, it could be poison. . . . I thought a drink tasted like that. . . . After scary TV, I don't sleep. . . . Demons, monsters. . . . Doesn't affect me much, but I can't think if they're real" [difficulty distinguishing fantasies/reality]. "Zoom follows me. It uses human eye sensors" [NICU staff/machines].

Mouth movements. ("I can't hear you.") "I'll try to fix it." ("Still having worries?") "Not as much." ("About?") "My parents are always busy." Blackout. Pig sound. . . . 7000 years ago, I was born. . . . Bye" ("Feels long till we meet again?") "Good riddance" ("And goodbye"). "Good riddance and goodbye" [Ambivalent parting].

("You're topsy turvy today") Turns visual off. "I'm upside down." ("I only hear half your words") Keeps 'fixing' audio. Searches how to reset computer. "The sound will go until I fix it. . . . Sorry for keeping you waiting. . . . How much time left?"

"Here's a fly in amber in stone [doubly preserved/imprisoned/saved from autistic-contiguous disintegration] . . . 1,200,000 years ago" [distancing trauma]. . . . Sucks water bottle. . . . "Mr. Humpty Dumpty [referencing dropable/fragmentable Ping]. . . . Crying, waiting for me to get home [I'm the parent]. . . . Floppy arms, weird texture nose, strange teeth, red eyes when sleeping – that's how you know he's not dead. . . . Life on Mars" [reassembling self; surviving inhospitable milieu].

Dimming/brightening bedroom lights [controlling environment/object]. Playing music through nose [easier than ear breathing]. . . . "Tranquil is fast. Over tranquil is so fast strings break and instrument falls apart [Mania brings at least pseudo tranquility. Infants project death fear into mothers, hoping for containment, but sometimes the container cannot hold (Bion, 1959).]. . . . You have to hold your breath so long. . . . Only 3 have done it [virtually impossible]. . . . My music teacher can [idealization]. . . . Reed explodes" [partial loss versus whole].

Two Steps Forward . . .

Ming proudly announced he's in Grade 6. "Next year we can go off campus for lunch!" Maturation is now positive, not deadly. He's repairing what

Winnicott (1965) called infants' natural tendency to become integrated selves with pasts, presents, and futures.

Concluding Thoughts

Fear of breakdown reflects past dis-integration Winnicott (1974). Ming's death anxieties may reflect similar, archaic agonies. Via his cryptic communications and symptoms:

> A real disaster is being conveyed. A disaster as great as soul or self or world destruction, an apocalypse now, then, ongoing. A forever apocalypse. It is as if the personality dies and comes to life . . . saying over and over . . . something terrible happened to me and keeps happening.
> (Eigen, 2004, p. 65)

Eigen's description fits Ming. Burdened by trauma, as heavy as 720 dolphins/whales/elephants, these children carry on as best they can. They need venues where ancient agonies can be expressed/integrated into a more comprehensible/cohesive personality. Otherwise, they are, at most, dissociatively connected to their ground of being.

Meeting weekly, we made significant progress. The Menninger Psychotherapy Research Project (Wallerstein, 1989) found psychotherapy brought borderline patients surprisingly significant, structural changes. In contrast, they often worsened with more frequent analysis.

Ming resembles children struggling to go-on-being on the neurosis/psychosis border. In scattered words, then increasingly coherent fantasies, his ancient anxieties sought/found therapeutic space. With all we now know about borderline conditions and the impact of prematurity, facilitated by comparative-integrative psychoanalysis (Willock, 2007), Ming may have benefitted from more frequent treatment. Most essential was establishing a secure base (Bowlby, 1988) in treatment/life/psyche, where he could experience/express/discuss/process disruptive matters, creating a more satisfying life, less encumbered by primitive agonies.

Erikson (Homburger, 1935) stressed "the importance of letting children express repeatedly, in conversation and in play, their questions about, and their conceptions of the world. . . . More than half the battle is won when the child succeeds in expressing itself" (p. 62). For the other half, it takes a village. Ming's hamlet included family, teachers, pets, and a psychoanalyst.

References

Balint, M. (1955). Friendly expanses – horrid empty spaces. *International Journal of Psycho-Analysis, 36*, 225–241.

Balint, M. (1968). *The basic fault*. Tavistock.

Bion, W. R. (1959). Attacks on linking. *International Journal of Psychoanalysis, 40*, 308–315.

Bowlby, J. (1988). *A secure base: Parent-child attachment and healthy human development*. Basic Books.

Eigen, M. (2004). *The sensitive self*. Wesleyan University Press.

Freud, S. (1900). The interpretation of dreams. *The Standard Edition of the Complete Psychological Works of Sigmund Freud, 4/5.*

Freud, S. (1912). The dynamics of transference. *The Standard Edition of the Complete Psychological Works of Sigmund Freud, 12*, 97–108.

Freud, S. (1914). On narcissism: An introduction. *The Standard Edition of the Complete Psychological Works of Sigmund Freud, 14*, 67–102.

Homburger, E. (1935). Psychoanalysis and the future of education. *Psychoanalytic Quarterly, 4*, 50–68.

Klein, M. (1950). On the criteria for the termination of a psycho-analysis. *International Journal of Psychoanalysis, 31*, 78–80.

Lewin, B. D. (1952). Phobic symptoms and dream interpretation. *The Psychoanalytic Quarterly, 21*, 295–322.

Ogden, T. H. (1989). On the concept of an autistic-contiguous position. *The International Journal of Psychoanalysis, 70*, 127–140.

Rilke, R. M. (1969). *Letters of Rainer Maria Rilke* (J. B. Greene & M. D. Hester, Trans.). Norton.

Searles, H. F. (1970). Autism and the phase of transition to therapeutic symbiosis. *Contemporary Psychoanalysis, 7*, 1–20.

Tustin, F. (1984). Autistic shapes. *International Review of Psycho-Analysis, 11*, 279–290.

Wallerstein, R. S. (1989). The psychotherapy research project of the menninger foundation: An overview. *Journal of Consulting and Clinical Psychology, 57*(2), 195–205. https://doi.org/10.1037//0022–006x.57.2.195

Willock, B. (1990). From acting out to interactive play. *International Journal of Psycho-Analysis, 71*, 321–334.

Willock, B. (2007). *Comparative-integrative psychoanalysis*. The Analytic Press.

Willock, B. (2015). Psychoanalysis of prematurity. *Psychoanalytic Dialogues, 25*, 34–49.

Willock, B. (2017). Dreams and self rebirthing. *Psychoanalytic Dialogues, 27*(3), 264–277.

Winnicott, D. W. (1963). Dependence in infant care, in child care, and in the psycho-analytic setting. *The International Journal of Psychoanalysis, 44*(3), 339–344.

Winnicott, D. W. (1965). The maturational processes and the facilitating environment. *The International Psycho-Analytical Library, 64*.

Winnicott, D. W. (1971). *Playing and reality*. Basic Books.

Winnicott, D. W. (1974). Fear of breakdown. *International Review of Psycho-Analysis, 1*(1–2), 103–107.

Winnicott, D. W. (1975). *Through paediatrics to psycho-analysis*. Brunner-Routledge.

6 The Myth of Philoctetes and the Refusal to be "Cured"

Ionas Sapountzis

In his paper on the myth of Philoctetes, Gottlieb (2004) makes a connection between the mythical archer who refused the requests of the ancient Greeks to join their army in Troy and clients who are very dismissive of what their therapists offer to them in treatment. Gottlieb presents the case of Mr. A., an educated man from a well-connected family who was in analytic treatment for several years with him and displayed the same refusal to be cured as the famed archer Philoctetes did. Philoctetes could not forgive the Greeks for abandoning him on their way to Troy and leaving him wounded in a cave on an uninhabited island. After a ten-year-long siege during which both Achilles and Hector died, Teiresias, the seer of the Greek expedition, had a vision in which the Gods revealed to him that Troy would not fall without Philoctetes and that Philoctetes' incurable wound would heal once he agreed to join the Greeks in Troy. But when Odysseus and Neoptolemus, the son of Achilles, came to the remote island to ask Philoctetes to join them, Philoctetes angrily dismissed them and told them that his only wish was to have his revenge on the Greeks.

Philoctetes' refusal is understandable in view of the betrayal he had experienced. What is harder to understand, though, is that in his determination to extract revenge for this emotional injury, Philoctetes was denying himself the gratification of becoming a hero, the savior of the entire campaign. More importantly, he was also denying himself the opportunity to be healed of his incurable wound. To Gottlieb, clients who display a similar disregard toward their own well-being and the prospect of being cured have a similar self-destructive desire for revenge, one that is rooted in long-simmering injuries and in having felt, just as Mr. A. had felt, emotionally abandoned from early on.

One can argue that the similarities Gottlieb sees between Philoctetes and the clients who maintain a very negative attitude toward treatment do not extend beyond their refusal to engage with and participate in what is being offered. Unlike clients whose negative reactions are linked to ongoing failures, lack of recognition, deprivation, and envy, Philoctetes' refusal was based on the profound disillusionment he felt due to the betrayal and deceit

DOI: 10.4324/9781003607120-9

of his companions, who sailed away in the middle of the night while he was asleep and left him wounded and unable to fend for himself. Similarly, unlike clients whose negative reactions are closely linked to how marginalized they feel in life, Philoctetes was not an unknown individual but a famed archer who knew that the entire expedition depended on him. That knowledge gave his act of refusal an intoxicating sense of revenge that blinded him from seeing the implications of his refusal: the fact that he was condemning himself to remain wounded on an uninhabited island for the rest of his life.

In addition, unlike the clients who refuse treatment and instead retreat from contact, Philoctetes had an idealized figure to look up to, Hercules, a demigod who recognized and valued his skills and who appeared before Philoctetes to ask him to change his mind. The young clients who angrily complain about everything and find little in what therapists offer them do not have the sense of importance Philoctetes had, nor do they have a mythical hero who holds them in high regard to appear in person to help them. In fact, most of them feel that they have no one to turn to and are very troubled by how others see them and what they think of them.

The challenges such clients present in treatment have been well known to analysts. Freud (1918) hypothesized that individuals who respond very negatively in treatment have an unconscious masochistic wish to limit themselves and to keep their ambitions in check. Keeping one's ambitions in check is related to an unresolved Oedipal conflict but also to the wish to thwart the analyst for the work they are doing. To Klein (1957) and her followers, such as Josephs (1975) and Rosenfeld (1987), the destructive acts of individuals are directly linked to the deprivation they experienced earlier in their lives and the envy they feel as a result. Fairbairn (1941) hypothesized that individuals who withdraw into themselves and display a negative attitude may react this way not because they feel envious but because they find that their love is not reciprocated. Such individuals learn from early on to keep their love "shut in" because they have experienced it as "too dangerous to release" (p. 26) upon others. Kohut (1972) makes a similar point about rageful individuals. According to him, the narcissistic rage individuals display is linked to the deprivation they experienced growing up, specifically to their parents' failure to meet their mirroring and idealization needs. Green's (1999a, 2005) work on the negative adds another perspective to our understanding of individuals who present as oppositional and are resistant to treatment. Unlike the other analysts mentioned earlier, he does not focus as much on earlier experiences of loss and deprivation that may have contributed to the negativity of these individuals as he does on their tendency to negate their experiences and to deny their need for others. Despite the differences in the conceptualization and understanding of the dynamics that contribute to the negative states of these individuals, there is an underlying agreement that their earlier experiences have left them with a sense of something missing as well as an experience of having been neglected (Music, 2009). "Inside every thick skin patient," writes Britton (1998, p. 46), "is a thin skin patient trying not to get out." Although

Britton never states this explicitly, the thick skin client he refers to is similar to the narcissistic clients Kohut and Ornstein describe in their articles, the clients who deep down wish to feel understood and recognized by an Other.

The narcissistic injuries clients with a negative disposition have often experienced in their lives and their tendency to retreat into themselves have led therapists to advocate for a more empathic stance toward them. To resonate with the experiences of patients who are highly resistant to treatment and to find meaning in these experiences, Ornstein (2015) believes that therapists need to maintain their ability to empathically immerse themselves in the patient's inner world. In his view, the negative therapeutic reactions of clients in the course of treatment should not be interpreted exclusively through the prism of pathology and should not be understood as a refusal to be cured. Rather, they should be treated as indications of what has not been effectively addressed in the treatment and of missed opportunities to work through feelings of shame, annihilation, and abandonment.

The Young Philoctetes

The challenge in working with individuals who are easily hurt and are prone to disengage from others and from themselves can be even more daunting when working with adolescents and young adults who are self-destructive and want nothing to do with treatment. The clients described by analysts such as Ornstein (2015), Wurmser and Jarass (2013), Kohut (1972), Freud (1918), Rosenfeld (1987), Josephs (1975), and Gottlieb (2004) are all individuals who have taken the step to seek treatment for themselves, specifically analytic treatment. In doing so, these clients are conveying a willingness to look into themselves. But the adolescents who end treatment after a few sessions and refuse to go on and who exist in similar states of negativity have not sought treatment for themselves. Unlike the clients who initiate treatment, these youngsters are not seeking to develop a better understanding of themselves. They are clients who have been brought into treatment by their parents and feel very uncomfortable at the prospect of reflecting on their experiences and internal states. Despite their considerable emotional distress, they insist that there is nothing wrong with them and are prone to discontinue after a few sessions.

Take the case of a 17-year-old adolescent male with a neurodevelopmental disorder. He was an awkward and overweight youngster who liked the restrictions imposed in the early months of the Covid pandemic because he did not have to be in school and be exposed to the gaze of his peers. He refused to continue with treatment only a few weeks into it after going on a sailing trip with his cousins, all experienced sailors whom he had not seen for years, who had invited him to come and spend a week with them. Although he never expressed it, I suspect that he found the contrast between them and himself so unbearable that his only escape was to retreat into himself and to make himself unreachable.

Another case was a 19-year-old adolescent with severe learning disabilities and a history of aggressive outbursts. He was a star wrestler who took no pride in his athletic accomplishments and opted not to pursue college despite the multiple offers he had received. Instead, he opted to stay at home and spend most of his days in his room. He stopped treatment after a few months following another unpleasant incident at home during which he got very angry at his parents' questioning of his decisions and their urging him to go to college. "What's the use?" he typed in his text message when I urged him to continue, and remained adamant that there was no point whatsoever in continuing with therapy.

Finally, there was the bright PhD candidate in nuclear physics at a top university whose sense of importance had been punctured by several setbacks and by the growing realization that perhaps he was not as exceptional as he had always thought himself to be. Like the 19-year-old wrestler, he liked the sessions but felt the weight of what he could not undo. "What's the point?" he asked in at the beginning of the third session, and stated that he would not continue with the treatment. Unlike the star wrestler, who expressed his opposition to treatment in the form of a question that at least left an opening for a response, the young physicist denied that there was any value in the treatment and stated that he was not interested in seeking to find any answers.

Adolescents, Winnicott (1963) writes, are afraid of being found "before there is anything there to be found" (p. 190). For these youngsters, Winnicott adds, the prospect of being found is more threatening than the prospect of being "eaten by cannibals" (p. 190). Winnicott was referring to the deep anxiety adolescents have that they are not good enough and that they do not have anything worthwhile for others to find. He was also referring, I think, to the anxiety adolescents feel at the prospect of not eliciting an approving gaze from others and of being seen as not good enough. And yet, as Winnicott (1963) pointed out, present in the fear of being found is also the need for privacy, the need to preserve a part of oneself that one does not wish to be known by others. It is the part of oneself that feels too personal, the "non-communicating central self" that belongs to "being alive" (p. 192), that needs to be protected from the intrusive gaze of others.

The three young Philoctetes described earlier, however, were not simply seeking to preserve their privacy and to protect the part of themselves that needed to be kept away from others. Nor did they seek their identity in the "aggregate" (p. 190) as most adolescents do, however much they may have needed or hoped for that. Convinced of their inadequacies and afraid of what others would find about them if they had a chance to know them, their retreat into themselves was not an act of "joy" (Winnicott, 1963, p. 186) that served to preserve a non-communicating part of themselves, but an act of fear of what others would find in them. Unlike Philoctetes, the young men were not seeking revenge but resisting being in treatment because they were ashamed of themselves and embarrassed about who they could not be. Their opposition to treatment may have given them a fleeting sense of potency and identity but little else. Unable to contemplate their experiences and to look into themselves, they went on in life in a state of "negative hallucination" (Green, 2005, p. 218), convinced that they had been wronged and failed by others and believing that they needed and wanted nothing from others or for themselves.

Refusing to Know

The literature is filled with cases of adolescents who feel unloved and unliked and are resistant to treatment. In his insightful paper on such children and adolescents, Willock (1986) pointed out that the strong counterreactions the young clients elicit in others through their angry acts serve to deflect blame and to protect themselves. These counterreactions also confirm for them how they are being seen in the world and how others regard them. But the adolescents I am focusing on in this chapter, who retreat into the illusory safety of their well-furnished caves, spaces that are filled with screens and other devices, have not been unloved, nor do they seek to elicit negative reactions in others. Some may have felt, as Bion (1957/1967, p. 104) put it, "dutifully responded to" and thus may have found their parents' responses to be devoid of the understanding they had been longing for. But many of them have been cared for and attended, and they know that. Their opposition is not rooted in their anger about their parents' preoccupation with other matters, as was the case of Mr. A., but in their shame and their sense of how unlike others they are.

Paradoxically, for all of them, their parents' care and concern have not been enough to sustain them. In fact, their parents' concern and confusion are likely to have added to their shame and anger. The parents' failure to tolerate the destructive acts of their children, writes Winnicott (1971), can leave the children feeling angry at them. It is an experience that confirms their views of themselves as bad and unlikable. Writing about children with an ADHD symptom presentation, Salomonsson (2011) makes a similar point. The parents' "fragile containment" (p. 90), he argued, only confirms the underlying fears and expectations that many of these children have. It confirms their double fear that they are not good enough and that others cannot make sense of them.

I feel sad for the young Philoctetes who cannot go on in treatment even though they seem to have found the experience to be meaningful and supportive, and instead, choose to discontinue. I feel sad for their need to shut themselves in negativity when something begins to feel possible, however fleetingly, and for their compulsion to self-amputate and deny. To Bion (1957/1967), individuals who do not allow the therapist to take in the projective identification and to respond to them are seeking to destroy the link between need and meaning, as well as between the need for containment and the experience of being contained. This is a defensive act, not unlike the one Willock (1986) described, that serves to protect them from the possibility of knowing. But it is also an act that interferes with the ability of these young men to learn from their experiences (Bion, 1962) and leaves them stuck in the negative. Despite never expressing it, two of the three youngsters had been injured by the multiple failures they had experienced that made them feel very unsure of themselves. The brilliant physicist was struggling with a different narcissistic injury, that of not being exceptional enough. Unlike individuals who may seek refuge in a fictional reality to satisfy the need for an "available object" (Green, 1999a, p. 6), or the rageful individuals who project their anger onto others that Kohut (1972), Rosenfeld (1987), Gottlieb (2004), and others describe, the three youngsters who were so troubled by the sense of who they were and who they were convinced they could not be did not escape into a fictional reality, nor did they blame others for what was happening to them. Instead, they shut down and avoided reflecting on what was happening to them.

The retreat of these youngsters left them close to the state of psychic nowhere-ness that Durban (2017) described. Unlike the clients Durban describes whose experiences have been so traumatizing that they had lost their sense of time, place, and agency, the two adolescents and the young physicist, as well as Mr. A., were not in such a state. Even though their awareness was dictated by their negativity and by their sense of who and what they were not, they were all aware of time and place and had a strong sense of themselves. Psychologically, however, they were all nowhere as they were unable to contemplate and tolerate their reality. Their refusal to contemplate their experiences and their tendency to act as if what happened did not matter to them were not mere denials because denial presupposes some level of awareness of what needs to be denied. Rather, their acts were driven by the urge to "insulate" (Winnicott, 1963, p. 190) themselves from experiences that were overwhelming and deeply painful to them. Bion (1962) draws attention to the "enforced splitting" that is "associated with a disturbed relationship with the breast" (p. 10). But enforced splitting can happen when one cannot tolerate one's reality, one's sense of who he or she is, and instead goes on acting as if nothing matters and nothing is needed or remembered.

The Anti-Space and the Void Within

What happens, asks Fromm (2018), when the baby looks into its mother's eyes and does not see itself? Winnicott (1974/1989) argued that the mother's absence or preoccupation with other matters represents a breakdown in continuity and in the capacity to go on. To Fromm, such an experience contributes to the creation of an "enormous gap" (p. 32) between the image that is held by the mother and the child's potential. It is the gap between the desire or longing for an acknowledgement and the absence that is registered. But one can also ask what happens to a child when they look into their mother's eyes and see her disillusionment or disappointment? The answer, I believe, is equally complicated. The three young Philoctetes were haunted not as much by what they did not find in their parents' gaze as by what they saw when they looked into their parents' eyes. They saw a confirmation of what they already knew, namely, that they were coming up short, that they were not good enough, and that they were injuring their parents. Deeply wounded and experiencing their parents as unable to respond to them and contain their own anxieties, they sought to avoid seeing others and letting others see them.

The knowledge that one does not meet expectations and elicits little that is affirming in others can be a very destabilizing experience, argues Winnicott (1974/1989). To clients who have been unable to hold onto themselves and as a result, have never felt as though "they possess themselves and their inner life," Fromm (2018) writes, the therapeutic setting may not be a "space of potential," but an "anti-space" (p. 37). The same, I believe, is the case with clients who feel deeply inadequate and are likely to feel ashamed of or embarrassed by themselves. For these clients, the therapist is also experienced as a menacingly present object that needs to be fended off. The three young individuals experienced our sessions as an anti-space, a place that reminded them of who they could not be. The fear, shame, and even hopelessness they were experiencing made the prospect of being found and the idea of an examined life deeply threatening to them. Individuals in the thrall of such emotions cannot but be reactive and cannot but not be receptive. Yet, in denying the other and their need for contact, these youngsters are in effect denying themselves. Green (1999a) speaks of the psychic reduction that happens when individuals disinvest themselves from others and from relationships. Such acts of emotional disinvestment typically serve to protect one from ongoing disappointments and ever-present paranoid anxieties. But they also add to the void these individuals experience, to the ongoing presence of an absence within, of something lacking inside. It is an internal state that cannot be represented with words and instead remains unreflected and unnamed.

The work of the negative, Green (2005) writes, should seek to restore freedom of movement to the structure of the psyche, specifically movement between the real and the imaginary, the idea and the thought, the feeling and the experience. Writing about a borderline boy who had not yet reached the level of disinvestment from self and others that the adolescents I have described in this chapter displayed, Ekstein (1983) asks how a therapist can reach an angry 10-year-old boy who would only speak about imaginary places and about a superhero who was all alone in space, far away from Mother Earth.

Most of the adolescents I have seen who struggle with themselves and with the sense of who they are in the world have long ceased to imagine themselves as superheroes, and they avoid such escapes into the fictional and imaginary. They have all reached an age where they know the fate of superheroes. To reach these young clients who find themselves stuck in the alternative experiences of feeling threatened by the presence of others and being sustained by their determined isolation, between "impingement and isolation" as Fromm (2018, p. 44) put it, one needs to create an experience of a "potentially useful otherness" (p. 44). This experience is based on an attitude of understanding of their need to negate and deny. To create a "useful otherness" when the therapist's presence can feel so threatening, one needs to be mindful of the void that these clients experience and the absences that keep being created. One needs to also be mindful of the fact that the tendency of these young clients to withdraw into themselves often stems from an earlier break-down (Winnicott, 1974/1989) in the environment, one that in all likelihood has been ongoing, leaving them feeling hopeless (Ogden, 2014) and unable to organize themselves. And one needs to be tolerant, if not sympathetic, of the disjunctive experiences (Palombo, 1993) these clients are prone to create when interacting with others, of the exchanges and reactions that can leave a therapist feeling thwarted and flooded by beta-elements and unable to make sense of what is being communicated.

Despite differences in the language that is being used, analysts seem to agree that one has to speak to the hopelessness that is felt, to the void that is experienced, and to the disjunctive exchanges that just happened. What else can one do? One owes to these clients and to oneself to not let the "nothingness" (Tustin's, 1992, p. 110) that has been projected or created to go on and add to the hopelessness that is being felt. This task is not an easy one with adolescents who cannot tolerate their own gaze and find safety in the emptiness they create, as these young clients are prone to deny their own needs and the need for an Other. Philoctetes had Hercules, who came down from Mount Olympus to convince him to change his mind. Little Fhadi in Durban's (2017) deeply moving paper had his father, who insisted that Durban see him and agreed to his son's being seen several times a week. He had Durban too, who felt the need – or better, the urge – to speak to the boy from within, in his own mother tongue. The otherness I have been able to create over the years with the youngsters who find safety in the "not," in not being and not seeing, has often depended entirely on the space I was able to create with them, the space in spite of the internal anti-space that threatened to derail the treatment. It is a space that becomes possible, I have come to realize, not just by the therapist's creativity and capacity to contain projections and enactments but also by the parents' insistence and faith in the treatment and what could be found.

The youngsters I have seen over the years who gradually allowed themselves to emerge from the state of disconnectedness they had found themselves in all had parents who insisted and persisted and did not give up. They needed that. They needed their presence and their refusal to let the absences that had marked their children's lives go on. The angry athlete had his mother, who made sure that he came back. "Am I crazy?" he asked in his first session back. No, I replied, but the way you are cutting yourself off can make you feel like you are going crazy once the anger you feel inside is less intense. The brilliant physicist had his father, who pleaded with him to not give up. He came for another consultation in his usual demeanor of expecting nothing and ready to make nothing out of anything, but he asked for another chance. Any time one asks for another chance, I find myself saying, there is more than a chance.

The Systemic Failure and the Need for a More Active Stance

Looking back, the mistake I made with the adolescent who stopped responding after a few sessions was that I left the decision up to him and did not convey strongly enough to his parents the urgent need for their involvement in parent consultation or family therapy sessions. Clearly, the uncertainty I felt, as I had only seen him for a few sessions, my ambivalence about making the treatment an imposed experience for him, and the promise I felt in these early sessions and in what was emerging, made me feel hopeful in what was to come. Looking back, I regret that I did not reflect enough on the discontinuities that had marked his life and on his tendency to retreat and find safety and even a false sense of omnipotence in his denial of his need for the other. I regret not contemplating a different frame from the start, one that would involve consultations with his parents and the possibility of family sessions, as Scharff and Scharff (1987) advocated.

Novick and Novick (2013) made the case for a more active and collaborative stance when working with adolescents, one that would involve the parents' participation in joined or collateral sessions. It is a stance that most of us in the field are still struggling with as such an approach can intensify the paranoid and depressive anxieties the participants are likely to experience. As Fromm (2018) noted, working with highly resistant and avoidant clients often requires modifying the therapeutic frame. It is important, I feel, to be mindful of the systemic failures that exist in the families of the young Philoctetes, of the paralysis that has been created, and of the disillusionment and pain each family member feels. The young wrestler and the brilliant physicist resumed treatment after their parents insisted that they do so. But that was not the case with the self-conscious adolescent.

Writing about the difference between psychoanalytic technique and psychoanalytic creativity, Parsons (1990) made the point that the latter is not about the right way to do something but about "how to make something possible between two people" (p. 423). The same applies to the young Philoctetes who need our creativity so they can begin to take steps away from the remote existence they have sought refuge in. The young Philoctetes who prefer the safety of their isolation need to be claimed, otherwise they are at risk of living their lives as "isolates" (Winnicott, 1963, p. 190). They need to be sought out, just as Philoctetes was sought out when Neoptolemus and Odysseus sailed to Lemnos to persuade him to rejoin the expedition. This is not an easy task, as their negativity and rejection of others gives them, in the words of Green (1999b, p. 284), an "internal axis," a "genuinely invisible prosthesis" they are reluctant to let go of, and there are no demigods to rely on. But one needs to insist and persist despite their negativism and their claims not to need anything, so that they will not remain stuck in the desolate psychic spaces they have found themselves in. After all, Philoctetes' change of mind would not have been possible without Neoptolemus' persistence and his willingness to listen to Philoctetes' rage and to acknowledge how much he had been wronged by the Greeks.

References

Bion, W. R. (1962). *Learning from experience*. Basic Books.

Bion, W. R. (1967). Attacks on linking. In W. Bion (Ed.), *Second thoughts: Selected papers on psycho-analysis* (pp. 93–109). Jason Aronson. (Original work published 1957)

Britton, R. (1998). Libidinal and destructive narcissism. In R. Britton (Ed.), *Sex, death and the superego* (pp. 111–120). Routledge.

Durban, J. (2017). Home, homelessness and nowhere-ness in early infancy. *Journal of Child Psychotherapy, 43*(2), 175–191.

Ekstein, R. (1983). *Children of time and space, action and impulse*. Jason Aronson.

Fairbairn, W. R. D. (1941). A revised psychopathology of the psychoses and psycho-neuroses. *The International Journal of Psychoanalysis, 22*, 250–270.

Freud, S. (1918). From the history of an infantile neurosis. *Standard Edition, 17*, 3–122.

Fromm, G. M. (2018). *Taking the transference, reaching towards dreams; Clinical studies in the intermediate area*. Routledge.

Gottlieb, R. M. (2004). Refusing the cure: Sophocles's Philoctetes and the clinical problems of self-injurious spite, shame and forgiveness. *The International Journal of Psychoanalysis, 85*(3), 669–689.

Green, A. (1999a). An introduction to the negative in psychoanalysis. In A. Green (Ed.), *The work of the negative* (pp. 1–13). Free Association Books.

Green, A. (1999b). Primary anality. In A. Green (Ed.), *The work of the negative* (pp. 284–291). Free Association Books.

Green, A. (2005). The work of the negative. In A. Green (Ed.), *Key ideas for a contemporary psychoanalysis: Misrecognition and recognition of the unconscious* (pp. 212–226). Routledge.

Josephs, B. (1975). The patient who is difficult to reach. In M. Feldman & E. B. Spillius (Eds.), *Psychic equilibrium and psychic change* (pp. 75–87). Routledge.

Klein, M. (1957). *Envy and gratitude*. Karnac.

Kohut, H. (1972). Thoughts on narcissism and narcissistic rage. *The Psychoanalytic Study of the Child, 27*, 360–400. https://doi.org/10.1080/00797308.1972.11822721

Music, G. (2009). Neglecting neglect; some thoughts about children who have lacked good input and are "undrawn" and "unenjoyed". *Journal of Child Psychotherapy, 35*(2), 142–156.

Novick, K. K., & Novick, J. (2013). Concurrent work with parents of adolescent patients. *Psychoanalytic Study of the Child, 67*(1), 103–136.

Ogden, T. H. (2014). Fear of breakdown and the unlived life. *The International Journal of Psychoanalysis, 95*, 205–223.

Ornstein, P. H. (2015). Revisiting the negative therapeutic reaction: An example of comparative psychoanalysis. *International Journal of Psychoanalytic Self Psychology, 10*, 118–127.

Palombo, J. (1993). Neurocognitive deficits, developmental distortions, and incoherent narratives. *Psychoanalytic Inquiry, 13*, 85–102.

Parsons, M. (1990). Marion Milner's "answering activity" and the question of psychoanalytic creativity. *International Review of Psycho-Analysis, 17*, 413–424.

Rosenfeld, H. (1987). Narcissistic patients and negative therapeutic reactions. In H. Rosenfeld (Ed.), *Impasse and interpretation: Therapeutic and anti-therapeutic factors in the psychoanalytic treatment of psychotic, borderline and neurotic patients* (pp. 85–104). Routledge.

Salomonsson, B. (2011). Psychoanalytic conceptualizations of the internal object in an ADHD child. *Journal of Infant, Child and Adolescent Psychotherapy, 10*(1), 87–102. https://doi.org/10.1080/15289168.2011.575711

Scharff, D. E., & Scharff, J. S. (1987). *Object relations family therapy*. Jason Aronson.

Tustin, F. (1992). Psychotherapy with children who cannot play. In F. Tustin (Ed.), *The protective shell in children and adults* (pp. 97–101). Karnac.

Willock, B. (1986). The devalued (unlovable, repugnant) self. A second facet of narcissistic vulnerability in the aggressive, conduct-disordered child. *Psychoanalytic Psychology, 4*(3), 219–240. https://doi.org/10.1037/h0079137

Winnicott, D. W. (1963). Communicating and not communicating leading to a study of certain opposites. In D. W. Winnicott (Ed.), *The maturational processes and the facilitating environment* (pp. 179–192). International Universities Press.
Winnicott, D. W. (1971). The use of an object and relating through identifications. In D. W. Winnicott (Ed.), *Playing and reality* (pp. 86–94). Routledge.
Winnicott, D. W. (1989). Fear of breakdown. In C. Winnicott, R. Shepherd, & M. Davis. (Eds.), *D. W. Winnicott: Psycho-analytic explorations* (pp. 87–95). Harvard University Press. (Original work published 1974)
Wurmser, L., & Jarass, H. (2013). *Nothing good is allowed to stand: An integrative view of the negative therapeutic reaction*. Routledge.

7 I Rage, Therefore I Am[1]

Brent Willock

The Autistic-Contiguous Position

"The ego [the I] is first and foremost a bodily ego" (Freud, 1923, p. 26). In a footnote, Freud added: "The ego is ultimately derived from bodily sensations, chiefly from those springing from the surface of the body." Synthesizing two decades of research in the British Object Relations tradition, Thomas Ogden (1986, 1989) elaborated that the earliest sense of self derives from contact sensations that gradually give rise to a fundamental sense of a *bounded* sensory surface on which one's experience occurs – the beginning feeling of "the place where we live" (Winnicott, 1971, p. 104). Ogden posited an *autistic-contiguous position,* having primacy prior to, though always operating in dialectic tension with paranoid-schizoid and depressive positions. Each perspective generates characteristic forms of relationship and anxiety. In the autistic-contiguous position, the experience of impending or actual disintegration of one's sensory surface or 'rhythm of safety' (Tustin, 1986) results in feelings of leaking, dissolving, disappearing, or falling into endless, unbounded space.

Psychopathology reflects collapse of the generative dialectical interplay between modes of experience. Collapse toward the autistic-contiguous position obliterates 'potential space' (Winnicott, 1971) that requires interplay between the sensory and symbolic, between autistic-contiguous and depressive positions. When autistic-contiguous anxieties are activated, the depressive position, in which there is a subject who can contemplate situations, dissolves. Collapse in the paranoid-schizoid direction results in a sense of entrapment in a world of things-in-themselves. One does not experience oneself as the author and owner of one's thoughts and feelings. Cognition, affect, and sensation are experienced as objects or forces bombarding, entering into, or propelled from oneself.

Rage, Autistic-Contiguity, and Going-on-Being

For someone suffering autistic-contiguous anxiety, rage can prevent self-disintegration. Precursors of this idea can be found in Guntrip's (1966) description of schizoid personalities arising from early postnatal relational

DOI: 10.4324/9781003607120-10

difficulties. Aggression "arises out of the desperate struggle of a radically weakened ego to maintain itself in being" (p. 237). One of Guntrip's patients said: "I can only keep going at all by hating."

Bonime (1976) elaborated this developmental trajectory. Children raised in families that do not nurture a healthy sense of 'me' become hostile "as a way of life. Their sense of self develops in an internal milieu of anger" (p. 8) . . . the foundation for . . . [their] "sense of being" (p. 12). They battle to sustain anger because it is only in this modus operandi and the "simultaneous subjective sensations that the individual feels his identity" (p. 8). They fear "disintegration (p. 10) . . . losing their sense of 'me'" (p. 11), if they relinquish rage.

More recently, Sekoff (2009) discussed a patient whose hostility, violence, and despair "help form a shape, a felt experience of self" (p. 32) (cf. Tustin's, 1984, 'autistic shapes'). Sekoff's article is replete with terms embodying autistic-contiguous anxiety:

> confusion, helplessness . . . the tug of the whirlpool . . . threat of collapse . . . pull of the void. In her work on emotional vertigo, Mme. Quinodoz offers a lexicon of dizzying states: fusion-related vertigo . . . vertigo related to being dropped, suction-related vertigo . . . vertigo of imprisonment/escape . . . irresistible attraction to the void; anxiety about expanding into a world without limit . . . threat of dissolution . . . *living within* a state of dissolution . . . what had been torn asunder . . . black hole . . . toy figures swirling down a drain.
>
> (pp. 25–31)

Bonime and Sekoff did not link their work explicitly to Winnicott's (1956/1965, p. 303) going-on-being, Ogden's autistic-contiguity, or my hypothesis of rage defending against the most profound relational anxiety (Willock, 2015, 2018), but these connections pervade their writing.

Clinical Illustration

Briana typically arrived at our Ann Arbor clinic looking distressed and angry. She might be mad at me, or soon would be.

Growing up, her family said she was always miserable (angry, unhappy). No one understood why. They did not seem to care: "That's just how she is." In contrast, Briana felt I wanted to know what was troubling her, and she let me know, vehemently. People were always disappointing her. No one provided support and guidance. Her parents, and others, were so mediocre. Their heads were always "up their asses." She understood the *intensity* of her rage toward contemporaries was due to their triggering her ever present "wounded child."

We initially worked face to face. It enraged Briana that I sometimes jotted notes. She charged that these were for me whereas I should be fully attending to her (illustrating Kohut's [1971] concept, narcissistic rage). When Briana later chose to lay on my couch, her unbelievably acute hearing still detected my occasional notetaking. She would then suddenly stop, becoming silent, until simmering rage boiled over into a seething verbal assault on me for failing her.

Gradually this triggering by my notetaking became less frequent, less intense. It was replaced by a different, analogous phenomenon. Now her rage related to my silence. At these moments, although she had posed no question, she would claim I had not answered. I had abandoned her in her distress. She characterized this gap as chasmic. I was absent or preoccupied with my needs, oblivious to hers, content to observe her doing all the work. She derogated my 'method,' insisting it did not work for her. Contemptuously she declared I did not know what was going on, or how to help her. "You are useless, just like Father" or, more fundamentally, her emotionally absent mother. She often caricatured Father stroking his erection, or having someone suck it, in his chronic, self-preoccupied neediness that made him unavailable to her.

Briana had virtually no childhood memories of her mother. Since meals appeared, she knew Mother had to have been home, but she had no sense of that presence, except for two memorable, positive occasions – exceptions that proved the rule. In contrast, Father had been present. He chauffeured her to activities, beaming proudly as she excelled. Mother never attended those events – a chronic absence that troubled and puzzled adult Briana.

When Briana entered adolescence, her parents divorced. Paternal closeness diminished radically. He became preoccupied with his "chick of the month." When he picked Briana up for Saturday outings, a woman usually occupied the passenger seat. Briana fumed and pouted in the backseat. Father never inquired about her obvious upset.

Briana's repetitive traumatic states relate to Balint's (1968) 'basic fault' – the early realization that significant others are separate and can drop you from their minds. With this cumulative shock structured into her psyche, she constantly expected and confronted breaches in the continuity of being. She plugged those dreadful gaps with rage, restoring some sense of viability. She threatened to take heavy, framed pictures from my walls to hurl them about, smashing them to smithereens. In imagination, she repetitively stomped on her parents, strangled them, banged their heads against concrete, kicked them to death.

Briana's rage when feeling dropped from my attention reflected a fissure in autistic-contiguity. Having lost contact with her untrustworthy 'holding environment' (Winnicott, 1960), she suddenly found herself in a chasm of neglect. At these moments, she needed to rapidly generate an 'auto-sensuous object' (Tustin, 1983) that does not depend on anyone, to restore some sense of safety. Autistic children may do this via bodily motions that create sensations (hand flapping, tongue sucking, tip toeing, clenching a hard toy). Briana created sensations she needed to feel alive and connected (as opposed to dead, disconnected) via affect storms. She clenched her jaw and fists and launched word bullets (Bionic beta elements) – fire and brimstone – from her oral cavity. That intense autosensuous activity provided her some feeling of needed continuity.

When not exploding, Briana continued to be a volcano with a molten core. This necessary self sense served as the guardian of her core self. Briana could count on these sensations and their action potentials to protect and sustain her whenever fears of abandonment, loss, disconnection, and disintegration threatened her sense of going-on-being.

On relatively rare days when sessions began well, Briana would talk for several minutes, sometimes making interesting connections, generating insights, resolving problems, calming herself. I could relax and follow her process, or so I thought. Suddenly, she would switch into her silent, still pose, then attack me, charging that she was the only one working, etc. Countertransferentially, it was dangerous to relax. In this relational matrix, I was likely to be shocked if I did not maintain some guardedness, some readiness to defend myself from assault, perhaps with slightly tensed, ready to spring into (verbal) action, musculature. Always anticipating attack, it was difficult to fully greet Briana's arrival with calm, pleasurable, welcoming feelings, even though I did feel that way, too.

Briana's brief silences that preceded her vehement criticisms of me for being too silent (i.e., abandoning her) can be seen as a way of turning passive into active (A. Freud, 1937). When she experienced a dangerous quiet between us, she generated a terrible silence. That flow interruption always got my attention. I wondered if she was just pausing, reflecting (very rare), or preparing to attack (almost always).

If I mentioned that Briana's assault emerged right after she had achieved some significant realization that was satisfying and helpful, she would instantly reply: "Why didn't you provide that realization?! You're a useless, passive, no good therapist! If it were not for me, nothing would happen here. Thanks, Dad!"

Briana could not relax for long, enjoying talking and figuring things out, because her activity inevitably indicated my failure, my dropping her. I suggested she became scared when competently figuring matters out. Functioning autonomously implied some separation, thereby opening a gap, threatening going-on-being. That chasm had to be filled – fast – with rage. All the aforementioned created a challenging negative therapeutic reaction.

Knowing child Briana loved cartoons, I told her these attacks on me reminded me of Wile E. Coyote zooming off cliffs, running without any problem until, suddenly, realizing nothing supported him. At that instant, he plunged to his death – though always miraculously living to run another day. I wondered if it was like that for her when she talked, figured things out, made connections, then suddenly realized she was doing this 'on her own,' making her feel I was absent, not supporting her. She had lost contiguity with me, threatening her existence, then restored connection via vigorous assault. (Rather than feeling contentedly alone in the presence of the other – a developmental milestone Winnicott [1958] described – Briana was intolerably alone in the absence of the other, an unsustainable state that had to be obliterated via rage). These interpretations made sense to her.

Briana's anger not only papered over cracks in autistic-contiguity but also grounded her in a paranoid-schizoid perspective as she raged ruthlessly against her deceased parents in desperate, doer/done-to (Benjamin, 2004), orgies of violence. This sadism was reversed when she imagined her parents enjoying watching her struggle hopelessly with horrific feelings.

The depressive vertex of the neo-Kleinian trilectic was less apparent. On rare occasions, years into treatment, when Briana paused, I braced myself for brimstone but, instead, she would say, "I was scared when you did not respond." What a countertransference relief! We could now dialogue about her fear. There was space between stimulus and response. That gap could be tolerated, even valued. It facilitated curiosity, reflection, and communication. It did not have to be stuffed and sealed instantly with frantic rage.

Briana recalled attacking me for merely writing, or for not having something helpful to say after she had been talking, perhaps coming to her own productive realizations. At these rare, but increasingly frequent reflective moments, she saw that her rage served to protect her fragile self from archaic terrors. Soon, however, she would return to her default position: In rage we trust.

Briana usually works on current, personal problems, of which she finds no shortage. Free associations are rare as she struggles to comprehend and solve some quandary. If she/we are not actively struggling to figure something out, it is difficult for her to imagine any reason to be in the room. Just seeing what comes to mind ('passivity') is almost unthinkable. After many years of treatment, there were occasionally chances to do that. Sometimes departing from our grim modus operandi, we enjoyed a much-needed laugh. These moments of physiological discharge, relaxation, and relatedness were acceptable, even gratifying to Briana. Relaxing rage readiness continued, however, to be profoundly threatening and, therefore, was generally avoided.

Briana reported that although a recent session had been difficult, when she left, her (deceased) mother was out in the hall and hugged her lovingly. Briana cried. A gap had been transcended via wishful fantasy that generated an object very different from her previous 'autosensuous object' (i.e., her rageful bodily sensations).

Briana proceeded to discuss meeting up with her brother and his daughter for lunch. This niece was not doing well. Her brother encouraged his daughter to talk. Whereas such an invitation would have led to Briana freezing, her niece readily responded, saying life had no meaning. This niece could not see that conviction as changeable. "That's the chasm," Briana said, adding that if she could have talked like that to a receptive, loving parent, her own chasm would have been bridged.

Briana then reported a dream. "My feet were on the ground. I felt safe. A balloon descending." Floating away from planet earth (no gravitational bond) is a common expression of disrupted autistic-contiguity. Briana's imagery suggested restoration of necessary contiguity.

While that session had begun calmly, with Briana insisting she felt good and did not need to be here, she was soon fighting. She agreed this was a response to feeling separation from me derived from ancient maternal separation experiences. She proposed bringing Mother in to comfort her. The previous week I had said Briana was like an inconsolable preschooler left with a babysitter (me). That image resonated with her. I now suggested we should not immediately bring Mother into the room but, rather, deal with the reality that Mother was unavailable. Briana and the babysitter needed to make the best of this situation. We did not have to leap immediately from bad (absent) breast to good breast in a paranoid-schizoid manner. We might bridge the breach with depressive position linking words.

Briana instantly blasted me for not letting her bring Mother into the room. She demanded to know why I was being so untherapeutic. I suggested there were ways a child and babysitter might sort of bring Mother back. They could discuss how sad and scary it was to be left, how much they missed Mummy, and/or how marvelous it will be when she returns. They might draw beautiful and/or angry pictures of Mommy. They might engage in activities, knowing they could tell Mom about these interesting things they had done during her absence. Briana ragefully challenged me to explain what I was doing. She insisted my words were not working for her at all. I suggested maybe nothing a babysitter could say could bring quick relief. They had to endure and work through these difficult feelings, hopefully eventually finding creative ways of dealing with this distress.

At one point in this struggle, Briana pointed out that I swore. "Did I trigger you?" she asked. I responded that although I could not say for sure why I swore, I might have been trying to match and counter the intensity of her rageful denial of everything I said. Briana concluded that her anxiety and hostility had been because she initially felt I did not "get her." This feeling of misattunement created an intolerable gap.

I referred to a model scene (Lichtenberg, 2001) that we had not discussed in a long while. It involved a time when Briana's mother was about to leave to study in Los Angeles. Briana clung to her mother's legs, crying, begging her not to go. Having heard the story many times, I was pretty sure I had it right, but Briana corrected me, or clarified the situation, saying she had been in *grandmother's* hallway and, although she was crying, she had not been clinging *physically* to Mother. It seemed important for her to emphasize that she maintained some physical separation and that although she felt she was being abandoned by Mother, she did have a grandmother to, like me, babysit her.

Briana said she eventually told Mother going to LA was OK. This permission was a new element in this model scene. Previously, Mother simply did what she wanted, leaving Briana to cope with distress 'on her own.' Briana said she had probably told Mother she could go to LA out of guilt (concern for the object versus smashing it to pieces). That depressive position affect was now in the air. Mother seemed relieved to receive this permission and "probably felt guilty" about going. I believe these slight but significant revisions and elaborations of the model scene were made possible by work Briana and I had done on enduring separations, having the strength and support to do so, becoming capable of not hating babysitters (me, Grandma). Going-on-being was now conceivable, even when Mother was going away.

Progress continued very slowly. When Briana's boss is five minutes late for a meeting, she feels non-existent. She believes her sister reels her in to talk about something, then drops her.

> She's like Mother. She holds everything in and I spin. I try to mend the chasm with my sister while she only talks about the weather! . . . She drops off the face of the earth . . . I wander into space when you and me, or she and me disconnect.

Briana meets with a small group to work on a project that is important to her. Each time their collaboration ends for the day, she feels devastated.

> The chasm. The bridge under me is not solid. There's no connection to anything. I'm in this ether of loneliness. I'm pissed that the project gets interrupted! Working on the project was We, then it's gone. I want to work on it every day, all day.

During a bad weekend, Briana fought furiously with her friend. Furthermore, "My sister was so there recently, then so gone. That's the chasm. What did my mother do to me?!" She recalled, as a child, hating accompanying Mother on errands, but it was better to be included than "disintegrating and rotting to death at home" (autistic-contiguous anxieties).

In a dream at a friend's cottage, Briana missed Mother after having connected to her in our previous session. Here she manifested a new, or newly strengthened capacity to keep the absent 'breast' alive and in mind, even though absent, rather than it transmogrifying rapidly into the 'bad breast' against which she must rage. She cried to her friend about missing Momma. Her friend "comforted me, like a good mother . . . teaching me to wait versus, as you said, my being like an inconsolable child with a babysitter." To my surprise, Briana shared: "You've taught me lots about dialogue." This moment reflected significant progress along the developmental line that Klein (1975) delineated from paranoid-schizoid envy (of those who had or have supportive, loving parents, or partners) that had previously appeared so frequently, to depressive position gratitude for what she has (images, memories, and substitutes that are vividly, symbolically "like a good mother").

Conclusion

Briana is a poster child/adult for narcissistic rage. What is its function? Many answers have been given, including revenge, protest, turning passive feelings of helpless endangerment into active, omnipotent fury, maintaining a cohesive self, and so forth. Complementing these ideas, based on my experience with

Briana and others, I suggest a crucial function of these chronic rage reactions may be to obliterate breaches in autistic-contiguity to enable going-on-being.

Note

1 Thanks to René Descartes for his related, higher level, more intellectual aphorism: I think, therefore I am.

References

Balint, M. (1968). *The basic fault: Therapeutic aspects of regression*. Tavistock.
Benjamin, J. (2004). Beyond doer and done to: An intersubjective view of thirdness. *Psychoanalytic Quarterly, 73*, 5–46.
Bonime, W. (1976). Anger as a basis for a sense of self. *Journal of the American Academy of Psychoanalysis, 4*, 7–12.
Freud, A. (1937). *The ego and the mechanisms of defence*. Hogarth Press & The Institute of Psychoanalysis.
Freud, S. (1923). The ego and the id. *Standard Edition, 19*, 12–66.
Guntrip, H. (1966). The object-relations theory of W. R. D. Fairbairn. In S. Arieti (Ed.), *American handbook of psychiatry*. Basic Books.
Klein, M. (1975). *Envy and gratitude and other works, 1946–1963*. The Free Press.
Kohut, H. (1971). *The analysis of the self*. International Universities Press.
Lichtenberg, J. D. (2001). Motivational systems and model scenes with special references to bodily experience. *Psychoanalytic Inquiry, 21*, 430–447.
Ogden, T. H. (1986). *The matrix of the mind: Object relations and the psychoanalytic dialogue*. Jason Aronson.
Ogden, T. H. (1989). On the concept of an autistic-contiguous position. *International Journal of Psycho-Analysis, 70*, 127–140.
Sekoff, J. (2009). The touch beyond hate: Response to Danielle Quinodoz's "Aggression turned against the self also attacks others." *Fort Da, 15*, 24–34.
Tustin, F. (1983). Thoughts on autism with special reference to a paper by Melanie Klein. *Journal of Child Psychotherapy, 9*, 119–131.
Tustin, F. (1984). Autistic shapes. *International Review of Psychoanalysis, 11*, 279–290.
Tustin, F. (1986). *Autistic barriers in neurotic patients*. Yale University Press.
Willock, B. (2015). Psychoanalysis of prematurity. *Psychoanalytic Dialogues, 25*, 34–49.
Willock, B. (2018). The origins of relationality: The role of pre- and perinatal experience in the structure, psychopathology, and treatment of the relational self. In C. Bonovitz & A. Harlem (Eds.), *Developmental perspectives in child psychoanalysis and psychotherapy* (pp. 199–222). Routledge.
Winnicott, D. W. (1958). The capacity to be alone. *International Journal of Psychoanalysis, 39*, 416–420.
Winnicott, D. W. (1960). The theory of the parent-infant relationship. *International Journal of Psychoanalysis, 41*, 585–595.
Winnicott, D. W. (1965). Primary maternal preoccupation. In *The maturational processes and the facilitating environment* (pp. 300–305). International Universities Press. (Original work published 1956)
Winnicott, D. W. (1971). *Playing and reality*. Basic Books.

8 Accepting Death

The Role of Psychic Organizers in Death Awareness

Joy A. Dryer

Memento Mori

Dara shuffles into my office. Her slender frame sinks onto my couch. A shaft of morning sunlight etches out hollows in her cheeks. She looks paler than usual. She whispers, "My chest started to tighten as I drove here. Must be . . . the pear I was eating. . . . Damn . . .!" Dara's hand clutches her chest. She sucks in air.

I lean forward. "Can you breathe slowly?"

"I'm . . . trying . . ." She closes her eyes.

My own breath stops. My heart pounds. Call 911? My mind warns me. . . . Stay calm. Breathe. Please don't die.

Introduction

Until that day sitting with Dara in my office, I had not thought too deeply about how death awareness, let alone acceptance of my own death – might play a role in therapy. I wondered why nothing in my clinical psychology program, nor my psychoanalytic training, nor in any theory I had read, had prepared me for a patient literally dying on my couch. Why did I feel so ill prepared to come nose to nose with actual death and with a patient's terror of death? With my own terror? I never considered how such mortality awareness might help us all, therapists and those in therapy live authentically inside our fullest selves.

And, indeed, how does acknowledging, even accepting, our own mortality help us go-on-being?

Writing this chapter started a conversation with myself. We need to talk about death for three central reasons: a) to frame life by accepting death in order to live our lives more fully (Rodin, 2022; Shahar, 2022); b) to be able to participate in social change in our culture, and in our psychoanalytic community, and in order to deal more constructively with issues around aging and dying (Nicolo, 2021); and c) I have come to believe that it is our responsibility as analysts to expand our own awarenesses of death, and to help our patients expand their mortality literacy. After all, accepting that we die underlies all else we do as analysts and helps us to go-on-being.

DOI: 10.4324/9781003607120-11

Our western culture's phobic relationship to accepting death (Waraschin-ski, 2017), accepting our own mortality, is of course reflected in our psy-choanalytic literature and within our training institutes. Waraschinski (2017) noted that "contemporary Western civilization has a twisted relationship with death. Many scholars seem to agree on one point: we are living in a culture of death denial, death phobia and death illiteracy." Our profession in gen-eral tends to emphasize psychological conceptualizations of mortality – i.e. imputing symbolic meaning to illnesses, retirement, castration fear, narcis-sistic injury, disruptions in, or ending of, treatment . . . along with clinical approaches leaning toward neutrality, even abstinence, in death (Masur, 2020). Actual ending, real death, has received little full-throated discussion (Atwood et al., 2011; Solms, 2021).

In this chapter, I show why a binary of psychological perspective vs. bio-logic perspective is too simplistic. And I emphasize the need to talk about actual death. I have looked for language that helps frame a clinician's thinking when talking with a patient about their death thoughts and feelings, espe-cially regarding where on the continuum of accepting vs. denying death they may be.

Psychic Organizers

Thinking about death is hard. Writing about it is even harder. This chapter is my attempt to accept my own death. So I started, as many have done before me, to wrap my mind intellectually around the binary that death can be psychological and biological, or both. This dissonance is obvious. We as humans are caught between the mind's freedom and the body's somatic fate. The mind has unlim-ited energy to think beyond the physical. But the body cannot offer such a tran-scendence. At some point the heart and brain stop: the physical body dies. This dissonance may be akin to Kierkegaard's (1844) ultimate existential paradox of thought: "to want to discover something that thought itself cannot think," or to Bollas' "unthought known" (1987). The challenge is how to write about death that is thought about and observed, but not experienced? What symbols and metaphors are useful when "talking death"? How do we discuss the complexi-ties of both symbolic/psychological death, and actual death in reality? The goal I propose is to become "mortality literate," i.e. to be able to find the words to talk about death and dying along its range of complexities.

Thus, this chapter proposes Spitz's (1965) concept of "psychic organizer" as a useful frame to "talk death." He coined the term to refer to three aspects of how a baby's personality develops: their smile response, stranger anxi-ety, and the negativism that emerges during their first two years of life. This sequence of capacities helps the baby master the next developmental phases. Such psychic organizers function as a lens through which to interpret every-thing else. In reviewing the literature, and in the case study which follows, I will use this psychic organizer concept to unify the language and integrate the concepts.

In addition, I propose three psychic organizing dimensions of mortality literacy; 1) death as loss (different kinds of physical and emotional losses); 2) death as relational (how death makes meaning in an intersubjective context); and 3) death as reality (accepting actual physical death, not as fantasy or as symbolic).

Selected Literature

The scattered and sometimes confusing writings about death confirmed for me how much others have grappled with trying to describe with words an unknown unknowable physical experience, that of dying. The following three writers highlight the contradictory views expressed across the past century: Lippman (2011) proposed protecting our fantasies about death and an afterlife. He echoed Nietzsche's belief that human beings need their illusions to get by. Contrarily, Stolorow (2007) argued, "Human beings pay dearly for the evasive illusions of invincibility and invulnerability that shield them from reckonings with finitude." And Yalom (2008) concludes with the very question we ask ourselves and will eventually ask of our patients: How much truth can we stand?

Many writers hold Freud responsible for leaning heavily on death as symbolic and avoiding discussing death as real, actual dying (biologically). For example, Richards (2018) believes that Freud displaced his own fears of mortality onto concerns about sex and aggression (p. 150). However, I have concluded that Freud oscillated along the acknowledgement/acceptance . . . to avoidance/denial continuum just like most other humans, as in *Ego/Id, Inhibition*, and in *Thoughts . . . on War and Death* (1915), and in *On Transience* (1915, p. 305).

Sometimes Freud omitted specifying whether the "lost object" was psychological (abandonment/rejection) or actual. He languages the complexity of acknowledging actual death as an experience in real "life." In *Thoughts . . . on War and Death* (1915, pp. 289–300) Freud writes:

> everyone owes nature a death . . . that death was natural, undeniable and unavoidable . . . (but) in reality . . . show an unmistakable tendency . . . to eliminate it from life. . . . It is indeed impossible to imagine (believe in) our own death. . . . Hence . . . in the unconscious everyone of us is convinced of his own immortality.
>
> (p. 289)

Freud's (1920) much quoted sentence is: we "cannot wrap our minds around death because we've never experienced anything like it . . . it cannot be represented in the unconscious." Razinsky's explanation (2013, p. 289) is that "(Freud) evades the actual psychic impact of having to *die*. He converts death from an *external* event into something that is driven *internally*," through the death *instinct*.

Over time, it has become clear that the binary model of equally powerful life and death drives is too simplified. Other instincts operate simultaneously.

Solms (2021) contradicts Freud's (1920) comment that "the aim of all life is death" (p. 38). "Freud was conflating psychology with biology" (p. 1054). In fact, current biochemical research (Kirsch et al., 2022) lends evidence to how life instincts (i.e. "satisfactions") are experienced in the brain.

What makes most sense to me is Solms' statement regarding the falsity of a sharp binary in biological vs. psychological approaches. "We do not only have sex in order to fulfill our biological task of reproducing humankind. This is the evolutionary basis of our species. Psychologically, however, we have sex because of the exchange of lust and of attachment needs" (Solms, 2021, p. 1054).

I agree with Karbelnig's (2023) conclusion: "lay the death drive to rest (because) analytic writers fall along a continuum depending on the author's belief systems and clinical identity." Freud's writings are reflected in Handa's (2021) point that for most people death awareness oscillates along a continuum from denial to acceptance. Freud's thinking was complex and nuanced when it came to thinking about loss, grief and yes, death and runs along this continuum. However, this biological versus psychological binary, rather than the complexity, became the mistaken focus of generations of thinkers.

Moving from oversimplified false binaries, other writers use more complex psychic organizing lenses (Moss & Zeavin, 2022). The following seminal papers support my thesis that it is crucial, during any "death talk," to acknowledge actual dying. Highlighting such a talk's complexity, I frame it along the following three general psychic organizing dimensions:

1. **Death as loss**. As an early example from Freud's time, Rank's (1936) psychic organizer was how fear of death converted into loss of living a full life: "Neurotics scale back on their emotional investment in life in order to dilute the full sting of death." Loss experienced during midlife somatic changes such as weight gain, wrinkles, sagging skin, and hair loss can trigger an existential "crisis" with the fear of impending death: see Jacque's (1965) theory of "midlife crisis," and Vogelfanger (2020) body "variations" that "intrude" and announce time's passage and life's finitude.

2. **Death as relational.** Death is a communal equalizer in that we all die. While we each physically die alone, the meaning of our death is embedded in a context of friends and family. Shifting public discussion toward the patient's experience were: Kubler-Ross (1969) with her five stages of grief; Yalom's writings, first with existential theory then later clinically tracing many assorted physical and emotional problems back to their terror of death (2008); and Kohut (1977) who argued that death itself is not feared, but the loss of connection is (see Hagman, 2021). Marcuse (1955) and then Fromm (e.g. 1964) enlarged the relational context when they developed theories integrating philosophy, social theory, and cultural criticism. Becker (1973) specifically labeled the "denial of death" as having dire consequences within our culture, e.g. we avoid the biological reality of dying by erecting "worldviews, religious symbols, and beliefs . . . to feel less vulnerable" (Chambers, 2023). Terror Management Theory, or TMT,

builds its evidence based research on Becker's concepts that worldview and self-esteem are the two measures showing destructive human activity resulting from the unconscious fear of death. Character and culture are defenses to shield ourselves from the "devastating awareness of our underlying helplessness and the terror of our inevitable death" (Solomon et al., 2015, p. viii).

3. **Death as reality**. Many of the aforementioned articles accept the underlying and obvious reality of death as an actual event. Articles written during the Covid pandemic most poignantly spotlight the psychic organizer of death awareness coalesced around the body, that is, any of us could contract Covid and possibly die at any moment. Different psychic organizers languaged the awareness of the potential of death using various terms such as "intensified sense of loneliness, isolation" (Mimran, 2020) and "paradoxical separateness, seeking an optimal interpersonal distance" (Ingram & Best, 2020), Lombardi (2020); defenses such as "externalization, exporting, and shifting psychic suffering into the other" (Nicolo, 2021).

My conclusion from a range of Covid era papers is a broad acceptance that it is human nature either to deny death, and/or perpetually to oscillate between acceptance and denial of death (Mimran, 2020, Handa, 2021). And yet the those working in mental health need to support all attempts to develop a vocabulary for talking about death in both our personal and professional lives.

Death Talking With Patients

Emanuel (2022) raises a crucial question. What is different about people who have a capacity to be at peace with their mortality, accept their time limitations, and connect to things that really matter? She responds with her goal of *existential maturity*, the capacity to "internalize aspects of the deceased person whose memories function as self-objects." Also, gratitude reduces inside-outside dysfunction by keeping the lost object internally alive.

Frommer's paper (2016) illuminates his challenge in his analytic role in co-creating a safe space for him and his patient to talk death and reach for their most authentic selves. (Also see how Gerson, 2016, and Shabad, 2016, expand Frommer's clinical conversation about Death (as) Nothing at all: On contemplating Non-Existence). Frommer summarizes: "(we) must include mortality as central to the pain of being human. . . . Psychoanalysis must develop a more fully articulated ethos and existential framework to hold both analyst and patient in exploring how mortality shapes subjectivity."

Two additional researchers provide just such relational frameworks. They suggest how positive self-evaluations, and solid self-esteem, can function as a buffer against the anxiety engendered by death awareness (similar to TMT researchers). Both focus on shoring up ego strengths, building resilience, and softening a strict superego. Working with dying cancer patients, Straker (2020, 2021) integrates psychic organizers that connect reality-based issues with internal self-perceptions. He works to elevate a patient's self-esteem by affirming the patient's life contributions, establishing a legacy, healing relationships in mastering their longstanding psychological conflicts, and "forgiving oneself for past mistakes."

In a similar vein, Colarusso (2000) encourages developing a fully authentic self, with a capacity for gratitude (similar to Emanuel, 2022) and creativity. All these authors agree on the importance of helping the patient reduce ambivalence in respect to love by coming to recognize more "good" than bad.

In the case study I present, I use many of Colarusso's and Straker's concepts in my efforts to help my patient Dara acknowledge, then accept, the potentiality of her sudden death. First and foremost, we acknowledged this possibility in reality. Only then did we seek possible psychological and symbolic meanings.

Case Study

Start: Death as Reality

It took my patient Dara months to research her condition. She found an expert who helped her conclude that she had a rare disease that caused her to become allergic to various food types. The histamine reaction could happen suddenly, without warning. Like when eating the pear as she drove to my office. Her throat closed up. She could barely breathe. Her chest convulsed. She felt like she was going to die. This "felt like" experience is somatic or what the body feels. This is "death as reality," not death as symbolic. The terrible irony for Dara was that she was a chef who owned a well-known restaurant in the area. She loved designing recipes and tasting her creations. But now she was in danger and could no longer taste just *any* food. She began to think that she should give up her life's work. What she ate became an organizing function of *every day*. Food planning took up a huge space in her brain and a lot of time. Her food choices became the concrete representation for her death awareness. Food became a silent psychic organizer inside her head, as well as in her kitchen.

Add: Death as Loss

Dara's experience of allergic reactions to one food after another set off a series of mournings. She mourned not having a "normal life" and the pleasures lost. She had to reorder her career priorities. As she could eat fewer and fewer foods, she lost 35 pounds over six months. One day in session she was talking about these losses, one by one. I fully took in her much skinnier body. I was startled by my association. I imagined her disappearing like the Cheshire

Cat in *Alice in Wonderland*, gradually losing parts of herself until her voice, then her big round eyes, faded out of sight. With this metaphor, I realized that keeping her *physically* present in the room functioned as *my* own psychic organizer.

Before each session the Cheshire Cat image reminded me how her actual physical diminishment was the greatest danger in the transference. To keep us both authentic, I consciously looked for ways to keep her physically present in the room with me. We slowed down our words. We labeled and pursued each affect. We worked at keeping palpable the intersubjectivity between us, with no disappearing parts of sentences or veiled meanings. We both became experts at attending to how our bodies felt in the moment, and at staying open and vulnerable to painful feelings in the here-and-now. Such a "bottom up" approach – noticing and working somatically – added to our "top down," more frontal lobe intellectual and verbal, therapy work.

Integrate: Death as Relational

Dara's Inner and Outer Worlds. Resilience and Ego Strengths

As Dara more deeply understood how a severe histamine attack could cause her fairly quick death, we could trace changes in her defenses, her ego measures to adapt to her newest realities, her intrapsychic shifts in self-states, and her interpersonal shifts to gain support from her husband Evan and 15-year-old daughter Flora. She tolerated more and more the anxiety that these aware- nesses generated. Holding her own discomfort about uncertainty helped her speak of it to Evan. He, in turn, was relieved to admit his own terror. This allowed them together to develop assessment criteria to determine when a histamine attack was getting severe enough for Evan to rush her to the ER. Or whether in real time she could just lie down, deep breathe, get calmer, and wait for her throat to reopen. Also, she became adept at using her inhaler, another sign of growing competencies.

Getting feedback from her husband and daughter, Dara used their conversa- tions to role play what to do during histamine attacks. On one occasion in session Dara slapped the couch. "Why can't Evan just stay '*present*'? He can breathe. I'm the one who can't! If you were there, *you'd* stay with me. Why can't *he*?" I suggested: "Perhaps you want me to be the all knowing powerful mother who knows exactly what to do to keep you safe?" Dara laughed. "Well, aren't you?" Previously, we had identified her fantasy wish for my omnipresence and omnipotence to know and to tell her how to stay alive at one end and the actual reality at the other. In that intersubjective space, what does "*being present*" look like? "He could hold both my hands . . . breathe with me." She brought Evan's anxious voice into her consciousness, and into the room, his fear of losing her and how his own death fears might affect his ability to stay fully present. These fears were not derivatives of infantile conflicts. That is, this was not separation anxiety, or fear of loss. This was real death terror. Thus, anticipating and discussing behavioral options with Flora and Evan illustrates relational teamwork. This heightening awareness of her own mortality became a psychic organizing lens in all their lives.

Transference and Countertransference

Dara expected me to disappear on her, just as her father did, physically after her parents' divorce, and as her mother did by emotionally withdrawing. She was sure I would lose patience with her doubts and death fears, especially after her histamine attacks, when she would feel "exhausted and clingy." "I just wanna be taken care of." Dara increasingly could verbalize her longings for connection and support. The rhythm of her attachment longings seemed to oscillate between merger wishes, and then her recoil (Sirote, 2020) in shame when she became overwhelmed and frightened. She expected to be too weak and without agency to keep my interest.

To counter her hopelessness and helplessness, in my countertransference, I noticed my intense wish to control the situation, to race after the disappearing Cheshire Cat. I learned patiently to await her return. Our bond increased as we shared the uncertainty of the potential of death to her body and her grief in shedding, like a snake's skin, aspects of her changing body along with rearrangements of her identity. I worked hard not to sink into her despair as yet another food item became off limits. Gradually, I gained my own confidence in holding hope and letting go of my annoyance when she could become dangerously passive, once again.

My own important lesson is described movingly by Rodin (2022). He writes about (the) "letting go" process. He relates a fellow therapist's own torment with a patient while struggling to contain the hopelessness and despair. The therapist helped his patient find hope only after his "empathic immersion *in* his despair, rather than *resisting* it." In a parallel process, Dara learned, then accepted what she could control and what she could not. Akin to Ghent's (1990) framing of "surrender," Dara gradually accepted her condition rather than resisting its reality or becoming victim to it. Rather, we got there by sharing a common language and the physicality of dying as a psychic organizing lens. By therapy's end, she experienced less uncertainty and terror of dying with a bite of the wrong food, even a pear.

Discussion

Chambers (2023) noted that grief is a prerequisite for change. Moving through her grief and lessening her defenses (Sands, 2010; Nicolo, 2021), especially the dissociation of mind and body (Lombardi, 2020), Dara gained aspects of what existentialists call inner freedom from the "ashes" of a disappearing body. She forged a new identity as a cookbook writer which helped her transcend her fear of insignificance (Shahar, 2022).

We saw how Dara's early psychic organizers around her death awareness were focussed on loss of self (in reality) and loss of others. "Mortality salience," as described by Steele (2023), was an early psychic organizer around loss and separation anxiety: this linked her awareness of her possible sudden death to annihilation anxiety (Mikulincer et al., 1990). She increasingly earned security (Roisman et al., 2002) in her attachment (Main et al., 1985) with Evan as they bonded closer as a team. In the end, she learned to avoid potentially dangerous foods, as she greatly expanded her ability to take in the therapeutic process and feel symbolically sustained.

Conclusion

Thus, my omnipotent wish, embedded in writing this chapter, is to try to conquer death, at least intellectually. Accepting the impossibility of such a wish, this chapter proposes a clinical and narrower concept of "psychic organizers" to engage in "death talk." I have presented here a case study of how I used death awareness (i.e., being aware that we all die), then death acceptance, as psychic organizers in my therapy work with Dara. In spite of her medical condition, she gradually learned to fulfill her life's potential, an important existential mandate. Through therapy, she got better and better at confronting death's nothingness by learning to live obviously deathlessly.

Becker (1973) noted in *The Denial of Death* that Adam eats the fruit from the tree of knowledge and God tells him, "thou shalt surely die." Thus in his newly found dread, he learns the terror of his own mortality, what Becker calls the "final terror of self-consciousness" (p. 7). We have learned that the task of psychological therapy is expanded self-consciousness, or self-awareness. I propose this means that we as analysts invite our patients to taste of their tree of knowledge. Such self-awareness encompasses knowledge – and hopefully acceptance – of their inevitable death.

As a final entreaty, I urge expanding death literacy from our consultation couches to our cultural communities. While our western culture may be death phobic, death denying, and basically death illiterate, there is a tragic irony. Our current culture has fractured ideas of what is actual death, which is often depicted as violent and extreme.

Many in our country are confused about how real is real death. Death denial keeps alive a cultural delusion of a life without limits. Freud was correct when he noted, "in the unconscious everyone of us is convinced of his own immortality" (1915, p. 289). And thus, mental health professionals' availability to talk death with patients is one avenue to improve our culture's death literacy, one intersubjective conversation at a time. We all live in this always-Covid world: acknowledging and accepting the actuality of real death forever bonds us in the commonality as human beings who share the same final fate. An important contribution will be for us to help patients, and our culture at large, reach this final mortality literacy. As Handa (2021) so poetically expresses: we need to face death if we are to face life.

References

Atwood, G. E., Stolorow, R. D., & Orange, D. M. (2011). *The psychoanalytic review*. Guilford Press.

Becker, E. (1973). *The denial of death*. Free Press Paperbacks, NYC.

Bollas, C. (1987). *The shadow of the object: Psychoanalysis of the unthought known*. Columbia University Press.

Chambers, J. E. (2023). From mourning and melancholia to neurobiology in an era of global warming, pandemic disease, and social chasms: Grief as a requisite for change. *Psychodynamic Psychiatry*, *51*, 45–62.

Colarusso, C. A. (2000). Separation-individuation phenomena in adulthood: General concepts & the fifth individuation. *Journal of the American Psychoanalytic Association*, *48*, 1467–1489.

Emanuel, L. (2022). IPA Health Comm. Webinar 12/3/22.

Freud, S. (1915). Thoughts for the times on war and death. *Standard Edition*, *14*, 273–300. Hogarth Press.

Freud, S. (1916). On transience. *Standard Edition*, *14*, 73–102. Hogarth Press. (Original work published 1915)

Freud, S. (1920). Beyond the pleasure principle. *Standard Edition*, *18*, 3–64. Hogarth Press.

Fromm, E. (1964). *The heart of man: Its genius for good and evil*. Harper & Row.

Frommer, M. S. (2016). Death is nothing at all. *Psychoanalytic Dialogues*, *26*(4), 373–390.

Gerson, S. (2016). Psychoanalytic engagements with death: Discussion of Martin Frommer's "death is nothing at all: On contemplating non-existence". *Psychoanalytic Dialogues*, *26*(4), 400–403.

Ghent, E. (1990). Masochism, submission, surrender – masochism as a perversion of surrender. *Contemporary Psychoanalysis*, *26*, 108–136.

Hagman, G. (2021). Final reflections upon the psychoanalyzing the apocalypse panel. *Psychoanalytic Inquiry*, *41*, 76–77.

Handa, S. (2021). Mortality and finiteness. *British Journal of Psychotherapy*, *37*, 70–83.

Ingram, D. H., & Best, K. (2020). The psychodynamic psychiatrist and psychiatric care in the era of COVID–19. *Psychodynamic Psychiatry*, *48*, 234–258.

Jacques, E. (1965). Death and the mid-life crisis. *The International. Journal. of Psychoanalysis*, *46*(4), 502–514.

Karbelnig, A. (2023). Laying the death drive to rest. *International Forum of Psa*, *32*, 76–86.

Kierkegaard, S. (1844). *The concept of dread*. Univ. Press Edition, 1957 (W. Lowrie, Trans.).

Kirsch, M., Dimitrijevic, A., & Buchholtz, M. B. (2022). "Death drive" scientifically reconsidered: Not a drive but a collection of trauma-induced auto-addictive diseases. *Frontiers in Psychology*, *13*, 941328. https://doi.org/10.3389/fpsyg.2022.941328

Kohut, H. (1977). *Restoration of the self*. University of Chicago.

Kubler-Ross, E. (1969). *On death and dying*. The Macmillan Company, NYC.

Lippman, P. (2011). *"Disappearance." Presentation at Div39*. Published posthumously.

Lombardi, R. (2020). Corona virus, social distancing, and the body in psychoanalysis. *JAPA 68*, 455–462.

Main, M., Kaplan, N., & Cassidy, J. (1985). Security in infancy, childhood, and adulthood: A move to the level of representation. *Monographs of the Society for Research in Child Development, 50*(1–2), 66–104.

Masur, C. (Ed.). (2020). A psychoanalyst confronts mortality. In *Flirting with death: Psychoanalysts consider mortality*. Routledge.

Marcuse, H. (1955). *Eros and civilization: A philosophical inquiry into Freud*. Beacon Press.

Mikulincer, M., Florian, V., & Tolmacz, R. (1990). Attachment styles and fear of personal death: A case study of affect regulation. *Journal of Personality & Social Psychology, 58*, 2273–2280.

Mimran, M. (2020). Flirting with death: Psychoanalysts consider mortality. *Psychoanalytic Psychology, 37*, 259–261.

Moss, D., & Zeavin, L. (Eds.). (2022). *Reflections on Donald Moss and Lynne Zeavin's edited collection, hating, abhorring and wishing to destroy: Psychoanalytic essays on the contemporary moment*. Routledge.

Nicolo, A. M. (2021). The Covid-19 Pandemic and Individual and Collective Defences. *International Journal of Applied Psychoanalytic Studies, 18*, 208–213.

Rank, O. (1936). *Will therapy & truth& reality*. NYC Knopf.

Razinsky, L. (2013). *Freud, PsA, & death*. Cambridge University Press.

Richards, A. (2018). Dreams and the wish for immortality. *Canadian Journal of Psychoanalysis, 26*(1), 142–158.

Rodin, G. (2022). Hope and despair in the therapeutic relationship: The ParadoxPower of letting go. *Psychoanalytic Dialogues, 32*, 376–380.

Roisman, G. L., Padron, E., Sroufe, A., & Egeland, B. (2002). Earned-secure attachment status in retrospect and prospect. *Child Development, 73*(4), 1204–1219. https://doi.org/10.1111/1467-8624.00467

Sands, S. H. (2010). Body experience in the analysis of the older woman. *Psychoanalytic Inquiry, 40*:173–188.

Shabad, P. (2016). Will you miss me when I am gone: Death & our significance to others: A discussion of Frommer's 'Death is nothing at all'. *Psychoanalytic Dialogues, 26*(4), 391–399.

Shahar, G. (2022). Yalom, Strenger, and the psychodynamics of inner freedom: A contribution to existential psychoanalysis. *Psychoanalytic Psychology, 39*, 5–11.

Sirote, A. (2020). The Priest and the Rabbi meet in a bar: The dialectic between Merger and Recoil in psychoanalysis. *Psychoanalytic Dialogue, 30*, 336–351.

Solms, M. (2021). Revision of drive theory. *Journal of the American Psychoanalytic Association, 69*(6). https://doi.org/10.1177/00030651211057041

Solomon, S., Greenberg, J., & Pyszczynski, T. (2015). *The worm at the core: On the role of death in life*. Random House.

Spitz, R. (1965). *The first year of life*. International Universities Press.

Steele, H. (2023). An attachment perspective on the separation distress hypothesis account of depression. *Neuropsychoanalysis, 25*, 177–180.

Stolorow, R. D. (2007). *Trauma and human existence: Autobiographical psychoanalytic, and philosophical reflections*. Routledge.

Straker, N. (2020). The treatment of cancer patients who die. *Psychodynamic Psychiatry, 48*, 1–25.

Straker, N. (2021). Vicissitudes of death anxiety during the Covid-19 pandemic. *Psychodynamic Psychiatry, 49*, 384–387.

Vogelfanger, L. S. (2020). Midlife: When the body challenges time. *Revue Roumaine de Psychoanalyse, 13*, 153–176.

Waraschinski, T. T. (2017). *The necrophile self: Contemporary attitudes towards death and its new visibility.* https://hdl.handle.net/2440/113580

Yalom, I. (2008). *Staring at the sun: Overcoming the terror of death.* Jossey-Bass NYC.

Part III

Representation and Going-on-Being

9 Going-on-Being in Challenging Times

Greek Mythology and Mythic Approaches to Resilience

Renée Cherow-O'Leary

Introduction

The origin stories of psychoanalysis are replete with allusion to ancient myths. Whether we look at the term "psychology" from the tale of Psyche (which means soul or spirit in Greek) and her conflicted love affair with Eros (god of sensual love) as the prototype for Freud's theory of psychosexual development or Jung's theory that myths were expressions of the "collective unconscious" encoded in all humans through evolution or through universal spiritual processes, the rich complexity and deep emotion of the myths have emerged in story patterns around the world (Tyson & Tyson, 1990). We know these stories not only because we read them in school or heard snippets of these tales. We know them because they mirror universal stories that we experience in the contemporary world every day. They are, in a sense, "masterplots" (containing what Jung called "archetypes" or models of behavior) where the vagaries of human nature are on full display as well as visions of powerful forces that wish to control or destroy us (Mazzeno & Press, 2010).

Humans are storytelling animals. The myths can be seen as ancient psychological case studies of human emotions and their impact on spiritual and moral life. Joseph Campbell (1988), the author of *The Power of Myth*, says myths and dreams come from the same place and often serve the same purpose. They stem from deep, unconscious realizations that can only express themselves symbolically. Campbell (1988) calls the myth the public dream and the dream the private myth.

In his book, Campbell outlines what he calls "the four functions of myth." The first is *mystical*, opening the heart and imagination to the wonders of the universe and the mystery of existence. The second is *cosmological*, understanding that humans do not have all the answers and need explanations for the origins and development of the universe. The third function is *sociological*, supporting and validating or depicting certain social orders and natural phenomena like seasonal cycles with human characteristics. Finally, the fourth function of myth is *instructional*, teaching "how to live a human lifetime under any circumstances" (Moyers & Company, 2021).

DOI: 10.4324/9781003607120-13

Myths from the Greek canon have become, perhaps, the most well known of those of ancient cultures. How, amid the Chaos out of which the Greeks believe we humans emerged, did some mythic characters find paths to resilience, resourcefulness, and survival? How did they go-on-being to such a degree that we are still talking about them today? What lessons do they teach that we can apply in our own lives now? And how do these myths pertain to the art and craft of psychoanalysis?

Out of the many myths in the Greek pantheon, I have chosen three to discuss: The Oracle of Delphi, Pandora's Box, and Sisyphus to begin to answer these questions. I will also include a modern, Promethean invention with human capacities called Artificial Intelligence or AI. AI is new, only beginning to be explored, and mythic in its power and potentialities.

The Myths

I.   The Oracle of Delphi

Though the Oracle of Delphi is not technically a myth, its purpose was mythic – to tap into the mysteries of consciousness and contact ethereal wisdom beyond our human capacities to offer guidance to troubled seekers. Dating back to 1400 B.C., the Oracle of Delphi was the most important shrine in all of Greece and Delphi was considered to be the *omphalos* – the center, literally the navel – of the world.

People came from all over the ancient world to have their questions answered by the Pythia (the oracular being whose title came from the word for the Python snake). She was a priestess of Apollo, the god of light, music, knowledge, harmony, and prophecy, and her answers, usually cryptic, were said to come directly from Apollo through her. Arguments over the correct interpretation of an oracle were common. The path to the sanctuary was lined with gifts and statues given to the oracle in return for her prophecy. Having a statue on the Sacred Way was a sign of prestige for the owner who traversed there. There was a transactional as well as a spiritual dialogue ongoing at Delphi.

The lack of a strict religious dogma associated with the worship of the Greek gods also encouraged scholars to congregate at Delphi and it became a focal point for intellectual inquiry and an occasional meeting place where political rivals could negotiate.

The sanctuary was built around a sacred spring, and it was discovered, when investigating the temple ruins, that it sat on two faults in the earth's surface which meant it was prone to earthquakes. Sources say the friction along the lines of the fault would have released methane and ethylene gases. Mythically, the story was that the sacred site was protected by Mother Earth's daughter in the form of a Python. Apollo killed the Python, and it fell into a fissure in the earth and from this fissure emitted strong fumes as it decomposed.

During the nine days every year that the Pythia was to receive prophecies, she followed a ritual of fasting and bathing thought to purify her. From ancient sources, we know that the Pythia entered a sacred room where she sat on a bronze tripod seat close to a crack in the stone floor of the room that released noxious gases and would inhale the vapors escaping from the spring that ran beneath the temple. When the Pythia inhaled the vapors, she entered into a trance-like state. During this state, the god Apollo communicated with her. The priests interpreted the prophecies and delivered the message from Apollo to the supplicant.

The Oracle continued to make predictions until about 390 C.E. when the Roman Emperor Theodosius banned pagan religious practices. He also banned the Pan-Hellenic games which had been held at Delphi. Christian settlements took over the sacred site. It was not until the 19th century that Delphi was re-discovered (Miller, 2022).

There are many contemporary analogies to the Oracle of Delphi. First, America is a nation that gathers predictive data in all sorts of ways whether it be economic indicators, election polling, media ratings, health statistics, or through the constant proclamations of pundits on all the multiple channels of information. (Of course, other nations do these analyses as well.) Still, we cannot predict accurately what will happen despite our tools of analysis. There are stochastic processes at work in life – the random, the unexpected, the surprise, the totally mysterious factor that changes everything. Psychoanalysis studies the unconscious mind and relies on interpretation, intuition, and relational dynamics. It mines dreams, opens the opportunity to gain new insights, and offers a vision of new pathways and potentialities based on the premise that there is always an opportunity to change. Through interaction with another and a process of integration and awareness, it is possible to see our circumstances with new eyes. As in ancient times, being human means we seek guidance beyond our own understanding.

The Oracle of Delphi represents an elaborate attempt to delve into mysteries about the future. Historians say it was in use for almost two thousand years. The Oracle of Delphi allowed for "going-on-being" because it legitimized using intuitive tools of human understanding, going beneath superficial knowledge to a place of spiritual connection. The Oracle corroborated the wish to see manifestations of divine wisdom on earth. The Pythia offered a transcendental connection whether guiding plebians or kings.

In addition, what is fascinating and contemporary about the oracular process is its resonance with the latest directions in therapy – the taking of psychedelic drugs like ketamine, ayahuasca, and others formerly banned from use in treatment. Usually, a guide or a translator is required to process these deep, spiritual experiences. Evidence is accumulating for the power of these treatments in incidents of intractable post-traumatic stress disorder or to ease the passage of someone with a terminal diagnosis. Authors like Michael Pollan describe another way through substance-induced "trips" that are aligned with oracular experience. These drugs are now called "entheogens," which are "psychoactive substances that induce alterations in consciousness, cognition or behavior for the purpose of engendering spiritual development in sacred contexts." The term is derived from two words of ancient Greek – *entheos* which translates to English as "full of the god, inspired, possessed" (used as praise for poets and other artists) and *genesthai* which means "come into being." This seems to exactly describe the experience of the Oracle of Delphi (Pollan, 2018).

II.   *Pandora's Box*

The second myth, now a meme of our culture and a phrase we all understand, is the myth of Pandora's Box.

In the Book of Genesis in the Hebrew Bible, Adam was said to be the first man created by God. Woman was created out of Adam's rib. She was, thus, not so much a separate being but what we might call today "cloned" out of his flesh. Though this has many implications, in the classic story of the first book of the Hebrew Bible, Adam was lured by Eve, his wife, who had been cajoled by a serpent, to eat the forbidden fruit of the Tree of Knowledge. "She shared the fruit with him and he ate." They knew their nakedness and became wise. For this primal act of rebellion, God punished them – including pain in childbirth, the need to toil for a living, and the inevitability of death, "returning to the ground from which you were taken/for dust you are and to that you shall return" (*Tanakh: A New Translation of the Holy Scriptures According to the Traditional Hebrew Text*, 1985).

In a similar fashion, according to Greek mythology, Zeus, the king of the gods, was so angry when Prometheus stole holy fire from heaven that he created Pandora, the first woman, as a punishment to be visited upon humanity. Hermes taught Pandora lying and trickery. Aphrodite taught her grace and femininity. Athena gave her beautiful robes and taught her weaving. Zeus then gave Pandora a Box and asked the other gods to place in the Box so-called gifts for humans that were in reality deadly. Pandora was supposed to take care of the Box but never open it. Zeus knew very well that Pandora's curiosity would be too much for her to resist (sound familiar?). And, yes, Pandora opened the Box unleashing "all the afflictions that humanity could ever know." These included strife, disease, hatred, death, madness, violence, and jealousy. As all of these evils escaped the Box, Pandora rushed to close it. Inside the Box, only Hope remained (Sears, 2014).

Some say that the word "Hope" conjures perpetual unfulfilled expectations. But others would say Hope transforms us. By not letting it escape, Pandora was the one for whom possibilities were still open. The chance to change, even with evil unleashed, is the message we must have to go-on-being. Change is possible. So is "repair of the world." We can envision a better future through our Hope, and we can act to challenge the destruction around us. The 19th century poet Emily Dickinson called Hope "the thing with feathers," a suggestion of its delicacy, beauty, and elusiveness. The gift of Hope that Pandora gave us offers us an alternative to Despair. It enables us to go-on-being. We shall see where human Despair can lead in the next myth, that of Sisyphus.

III.   Sisyphus

Sisyphus was the first king of Ephyra now known as Corinth. He was a devious tyrant. Sisyphus killed visitors to his city to show his power and this violation of a sacred tradition of hospitality angered the gods. At the same time, Zeus, in the form of a massive eagle, carried Aegina, daughter of the river god Aesopus, and brought her to Ephyra where he encountered Sisyphus. Aesopus pursued them and Sisyphus revealed to the river god where Zeus had taken his daughter. When Zeus found out, he was so furious (again the issue was over a woman), that he ordered Thanatos, the god of Death, to chain Sisyphus in the underworld so he could not cause any more problems. However, Sisyphus was crafty. He asked Thanatos how the chains worked. Then, he quickly bound Death and escaped to the land of the living.

With Thanatos trapped, no one could die, and the world was thrown into disarray. Ares, the god of War, released Death since war was no longer "fun" without death and Thanatos was freed from his chains. Sisyphus knew his reckoning was at hand. Before dying, he asked his wife, Merope, to throw his body in the public square and it washed up on the banks of the River Styx. Now among the dead, he complained to Persephone, Queen of the Underworld, that his wife had disgraced him by not giving him a proper burial. Persephone granted him permission to return to the land of the living on the condition that he would return. Of course, he did not keep his promise. But Hermes, a son of Zeus and messenger of the gods, dragged Sisyphus back to Hades. His punishment was straightforward – roll a massive boulder up a hill and just as he approached the top, the boulder would roll down the hill forcing him to start over, and over, and over again (Cartwright & Saint-Pol, 2023).

Of all the myths of ancient Greece, Sisyphus holds a special place in contemporary life regarding the issue of going-on-being. Albert Camus, who wrote the essay, "Le Mythe de Sisyphe," in 1942, in the middle of World War II, used Sisyphus as the prototype of modern man dealing with the question of the "absurdity" of life (his term). What keeps any one of us from killing ourselves? Sisyphus' hubris was that he believed he could escape death. Nonetheless, he was reduced to performing a repetitive, meaningless task endlessly. It would seem this was the antithesis of freedom and nowhere near immortality.

The issue of the absurdity of life, particularly post-World War II, translated into artistic and philosophical movements of the mid-20th century. From the Theater of the Absurd (Beckett, Pinter, Ionesco, Genet) to Existentialism, the theory emphasizing that individuals are free and responsible agents determining their own development through acts of will (De Beauvoir, Sartre), the issues of absurdity and response to it were woven into the fabric of 20th century intellectual discourse (Bakewell, 2016).

Intentionality is at the heart of a human life, said Camus. In the terminology we have been discussing, conscious choice and intention are other ways to approach going-on-being. According to Camus, there is freedom at the core of human existence. It is up to us to create "the essence" of what we choose to become. Suicide, then, cannot be a generative response to the absurdity Sisyphus' life had become nor to our own struggles with meaning. "The only alternative is to rebel by rejoicing" in the act of rolling the boulder up the hill. Camus argues that with the joyful acceptance of the struggle, the individual gains an identity. He declares: "this is the price that must be paid for the passions of this earth" (Camus, 1942).

IV.   A Contemporary Mythic Colossus: Chat GPT

In the Fall of 2022, a company named Open AI introduced into the world an unprecedented creation. It was called a chatbot, a source of what is known as "artificial intelligence" (AI), created by humans, of course, but with the potential to supersede them (us). This invention was named Chat GPT. GPT stands for Generative Pre-trained Transformer, a large language model that is a framework for AI with the ability to create human-like text and content. Since it has been available for public use, (from 2022–2025) it has done nothing less than transform the world. Already, millions of people use it to answer questions called "prompts" instantaneously with the information "scraped' from innumerable postings on the Internet, another marvel that we now take totally for granted. Chat GPT can write books, essays, course materials, worker manuals, movie scripts, songs, and so much more. It can have policy implications and create false data called "hallucinations" (a psychological term that implies the bots can make errors that are often highly intelligent and plausible, though spurious). This technology can affect education, medicine, and creative invention of all kinds through its brilliant amalgamation of information. It can, through the stories it tells, confound the already complex issue of what is truth and what is falsehood (The White House, 2023). And yet, it is a science fiction fantasy that has now come true.

What is the mythic connection of Chat GPT/AI and its uses to psychoanalysis? What can it teach us about ourselves and how to go-on-being in challenging times when this invention itself is one of the largest challenges we have had to face technologically, besides, perhaps, the atomic bomb? As with the bomb, the technology poses an existential threat which has been mentioned by many scientists, even the inventors of the technology itself. They concede that if "bad actors" co-opt it, our civilization might be doomed. But others say Chat GPT can and will be a source of good – a vehicle for health breakthroughs, educational advancement, and planetary exploration that will enable us to have the capacity to become wiser than we ever thought possible.

Akin to the myth of Prometheus stealing fire from the gods which allowed the continued evolution of humanity, from cooking to forging tools to the capacity to control warmth and light, the circumstance of the appearance of Chat GPT has been called "Promethean" (Encyclopedia Britannica, 2024).

Interestingly, when the author Mary Shelley wrote her classic Gothic novel *Frankenstein* in 1818, she subtitled it "the modern Prometheus" (Shelley, 2021). Fire, like electricity eons later, is a key to technological advancement. When Prometheus stole fire, this angered Zeus and the god punished Prometheus severely, binding him to a rock and sending an eagle to feed on his liver. Then his liver would regenerate, and the Eagle would come again. But it was too late. Fire, lighting up the earth's darkness, was released and humanity used it (and, of course, has abused it, if we think of, for example, of a nuclear bomb as Fire). In the reputed words of Robert Oppenheimer, the lead inventor of the atomic bomb, citing the Hindu scripture, the Bhagavad Gita (Mitchell, 2002): "Now I am become Death, the Destroyer of Worlds" (Temperton, 2023). That realization is daunting and haunting.

We humans must go-on-being with a knowledge of the impact of our actions and a willingness to refrain from destructive consequences. Chat GPT has also awakened an urgent need to redefine the Collective. We are being forced as a species to find new ways to face challenging times through a recognition of the human and humane ways we must unify for the sake of ourselves and our planet.

The role of psychoanalysis is potentially profound in this new technological era. With this heretofore unexplored technological tool of AI comes great responsibility. What going-on-being will mean collectively is to develop a society with "technological maturity," the ability to harness these tools for the benefit of humankind (Cornish, 2004).

We must study the humanities to complement, balance, and support our scientific knowledge. In my view, going-on-being in challenging times with chatbots as companions will mean adding another dimension to the examples given in the three myths mentioned earlier by creating a new sense of the collective and our human destiny. Our technological challenges require new myths that teach us compassion, curiosity, cooperation, and community, new ways to integrate ourselves into nature for its salvation and making certain that our tools serve the common good. How psychoanalysis can assist in this provocative, and what will become persistent, presence of generative machine learning in our society is a question that has only begun to be considered. It may require new theory and new practice. Ancient myths can give us guidance in thinking imaginatively about human nature. The new myths may help us develop new evolutionary approaches to put human nature in relationship to technological change.

Conclusion

Could there be anything more akin to where we began – at the Oracle of Delphi? Chat GPT is another oracle of extraordinary capacities that is heralding a metamorphosis of society. The source of its wisdom is us, our technologies enabling repositories of huge caches of information. But some say these bots will not only learn to learn but become sentient, intelligent beings in ways we cannot yet define. Our human capacity for creating tools is undiminished, but this invention will require a recalibration of all that has gone before. As the "bioecological" theory of the developmental psychologist Urie Brofenbrenner states: "researchers should study not only the forces that have shaped human development in the past, but . . . those that may already be operating today to influence what human beings may become tomorrow" (Bronfenbrenner & Evans, 2000, p. 117).

Can we learn from the stories of our ancient ancestors, build new stories that speak deeply to our contemporary challenges, and establish channels for hope and resilience in our institutions and in ourselves that will fortify us and enable us to thrive? We are compelled now to ask the critical question: What does it mean to be human in an age of advanced and inexorable technological change (Wang et al., 2022)?

An imperative of going-on-being in this new context will require humans to be able to adapt, modify behavior, seek out innovative solutions, expand our consciousness, and open to the ancient wisdom of ethics, epistemology, and ontology from the Greeks and other human cultures. As we go-on-being, we will, we must, continue to invent and create, gathered together as a common humanity to decide collectively how to live guided by the wisdom of the past, gleaning the wisdom of the future, and recognizing that we are capable of insight and change (the basis, after all, of psychoanalysis). We must be committed to finding solutions for both individual fulfillment and the common good. The historical moment into which we are born also calls to us asking us to listen to what it requires. Our myths, ancient and modern stories of wisdom, can give us the guidance and the inspiration we need to go-on-being.

References

Bakewell, S. (2016). *At the existentialist café: Freedom, being, and Apricot Cocktails.* Random House.

Bronfenbrenner, U., & Evans, G. W. (2000). Developmental science in the 21st century: Emerging questions, theoretical models, research designs and empirical findings. *Social Development, 9*(1), 115–125. https://doi.org/10.1111/1467-9507.00114

Campbell, J. (1988). *The power of myth* (1st ed.). Doubleday.

Camus, A. (1942). *Le Mythe de Sisyphe: Essai Sur L'absurde.* Gallimard.

Cartwright, M., & Saint-Pol, B. (2023). Sisyphus. *World History Encyclopedia.* https://www.worldhistory.org/sisyphus/

Classical Mythology/Freudian psychology – Wikiversity. (n.d.). https://en.wikiversity.org/wiki/Classical_Mythology/Freudian_psychology

Classical Mythology/Jungian psychology – Wikiversity. (n.d.). https://en.wikiversity.org/wiki/Classical_Mythology/Jungian_psychology

Cornish, E. (2004). *Futuring: The exploration of the future.* World Future Society.

Dickinson, E. (1999). *Hope is the thing with feathers.* Poetry Foundation. https://www.poetryfoundation.org/poems/42889/hope-is-the-thing-with-feathers-314

Encyclopedia Britannica. (2024, June 18). Prometheus | god, description, meaning, & myth. *Encyclopedia Britannica.* https://www.britannica.com/topic/Prometheus-Greek-god

Mazzeno, L. W., & Press, S. (2010). *Masterplots.* Salem Press.

Miller, M. (2022, September 19). What is the Oracle of Delphi and how did she prophecize? *Historic Mysteries*. https://www.historicmysteries.com/history/oracle-of-delphi-pythia/14715/

Mitchell, S. (2002). *The Bhagavad Gita: A new translation*. https://openlibrary.org/books/OL7585657M/Bhagavad_Gita

Moyers & Company. (2021, March 28). Ep. 2: Joseph Campbell and the Power of Myth – "The Message of the Myth" | BillMoyers.com. *BillMoyers.com*. https://billmoyers.com/content/ep-2-joseph-campbell-and-the-power-of-myth-the-message-of-the-myth/

Pollan, M. (2018). *How to change your mind: What the new science of psychedelics teaches us about consciousness, dying, addiction, depression, and transcendence*. Penguin.

Sarah, V. a. P. B. (n.d.). *The origins of religious beliefs: Greek mythology vs Judaism*. https://web.archive.org/web/20230614185535/https://www.chicagojewishnews.com/which-came-first-greek-mythology-or-judaism/

Sears, K. (2014). *Mythology 101: From gods and goddesses to monsters and mortals, your guide to ancient mythology*. Adams Media.

Shakespeare, W. (1969). *The complete works*. Viking Edition.

Shelley, M. W. (2021). *Frankenstein: The 1818 text, contexts, criticism*. Norton Critical Editions.

Tanakh: A new translation of the Holy Scriptures according to the traditional Hebrew text. (1985). Jewish Publication Society.

Temperton, J. (2023, July 21). 'Now I am become death, the destroyer of worlds.' The story of Oppenheimer's infamous quote. *WIRED*. https://www.wired.com/story/manhattan-project-robert-oppenheimer/

The White House. (2023, November 22). Blueprint for an AI bill of rights | OSTP. *The White House*. https://www.whitehouse.gov/ostp/ai-bill-of-rights/

Tyson, P., & Tyson, R. L. (1990). *Psychoanalytic theories of development: An integration*. Yale University Press.

Wang, J., GPT-3, & Thomas, I. S. (2022). *What makes us human: An artificial intelligence answers life's biggest questions*. Sounds True.

10 Going-on-Being in the Body
From the Concrete Use of the Body to the Symbolic Use of the Mind

J. Gail White and Michelle Flax

The traumatic nature of the pandemic confronted us all with the fundamental existential question of "going-on-being". The Covid-19 virus brought in its wake the stark reality of a threat to our very existence. The existential threat of the pandemic flooded us all. In this chapter, we look at the question of what happens when we are emotionally overwhelmed whereby we cannot represent[1] our experience.

As recounted by Freud, "the ego is first and foremost a bodily ego" (1923) as it is derived from bodily sensations. Freud spoke of the enigmatic leap from psyche to soma, and from soma to the psyche (1914). When the process of mentalization fails, we can be left with concrete troubling somatic symptoms.

Psychoanalytic Approaches to Psychosomatic Functioning

The French Freudians, Pierre Marty (1968), Andre Green (1999) and Marilla Aisenstein (2006), address the psychosomatic question from a contemporary Freudian perspective. Their work has been helpful in comprehending how we structure and communicate our psychic pain and suffering through the body in symbolic symptom formation or through progressive disorganization.[2] Somatization is seen as the regressive alternative to mentalization. The question they pose is: how does the sick body triumph over the erotic body (Dejours & Fain, 1984).

As early as 1867, Maudsley attempted to "put a happy end to the inauspicious divorce between the physiology and pathology of mind" (p.v). In Maudsley's wise words: "the sorrow that has no vent in tears makes other organs weep". Historically, psychoanalytic treatment was attuned to psychosomatics only insofar as the symptoms were symbolically understandable. The organ affected was then seen to have symbolic meaning. Contemporary French Freudian theorists are more focused on somatic symptoms that present as inexplicable in a symbolic sense.

Marty et al. (1993) took a further step in noticing that the thinking of psychosomatic patients took on a particular pattern. It did not matter which organ was affected. Rather, their thinking style was operational.[3] There was

DOI: 10.4324/9781003607120-14

a paucity of dialogue with the analyst and poor expression with regards to internal and external objects. They asked the question: what happens when the pre-psychic[4] or primitive material of the psyche cannot become psychic or symbolizable? They posit that it can then disturb a somatic function.

Freud proposed that organs not only have a role in self-preservation, but they also strive to attain organ pleasure. Freud's framework was structured on neurotic illness and how conflict could result in somatic symptoms. However, in 1914, he wrote about how the narcissistic libido in regression returns to parts of the body. He saw this process as a regular feature in somatically ill subjects. Ferenczi (1926/1994), too, studied the psychoanalysis of organic illness. His theory of organ neurosis was built on Freud's early notion of the actual neurosis. Long standing repressed emotions, he thought, are conveyed along nerve pathways to the organs, which can lead to functional and organic disorders.

In 1920, Freud introduced the idea that the erotic and life-preserving drives were bound with the death drives and in opposition to them. Freud (1920) believed that there was a self-destructive force at the center of psychic functioning. We see great theoretical and clinical value in Freud's concept of the "drives" in understanding psychosomatic forces, as the body's endosomatic forces place a demand on the mind to work. Freud originally spoke of the libidinal life drive as related to sexual pleasure, but he extended this notion to other forms of pleasure necessary for survival, such as striving for knowledge, art, socialization and sublimation. The libidinal drive thus reaches out, is outwardly directed and is embedded in the drive toward symbolization (the process of thinking and making meaning and bringing creative forms into being). The destructive drive, on the other hand, is inward facing, static and concrete in the body where no symbolization or representation is possible. This state of rapidly reduced libido is characterized by its emptiness and its deadness. Here we see an unbinding of the drives where destructiveness prevails (Marty, 1966). The unrepresented tension is often bound by an organ and represents an attempt to survive in the face of what Marty (1966) labeled an "essential depression", or an existence depression where there is a rapid reduction of object seeking libido. For Aisenstein (2017) organ binding is a desperate attempt to prevent the mind from complete disintegration.

Contributions From the Biological Sciences

Recent developments in the biological sciences have lent support to these psychosomatic theories. For example, Ameisen (2007), a biologist and immunologist, similarly spoke of the destructive mechanisms at the very core of life that lead to programmed cell death. He noted that the organization of living systems is always in a process of disorganization followed by reorganization. The hypothesis is that during illness a dysfunction in the mechanism of cellular self-destruction creates pathological organ changes.

The recent biological concept of "interoception" helps us understand the mechanism through which the psyche and soma are in consistent communication. The term "interoception" refers to the "body to brain axis of signals originating from the internal body and visceral organs, such as gastrointestinal, respiratory, hormonal and circulatory systems" (Tsakiris & De Preester, 2019, p. v). Afferent signals from the inner body are in direct communication, particularly with the limbic system, the autonomic nervous system and the immune system. Signals are continuously unconsciously sensed and appraised in terms of the organism's contextual homeostasis (Barrett, 2017). Of course, the communication does not only proceed one way. The body and the mind are in constant and uninterrupted communication. Furthermore, since we are multicellular organisms, each cell in our body is in communication with each and every one of our 30 million cells. In the nucleus of every cell is a "bodymind", deeply adhesive and fully interconnected to every other cell.

How we experience ourselves in the phenomenological sense affects how we respond to the world. Both exteroceptive and interoceptive information shape cognitive and emotional processes, and vice versa (Berntson et al., 2019, p. 4). Interoception and exteroception are never just pure sensation but are shaped by interpretation. Having a language for this internal sensing is vital to our wellbeing. Our language about the interoceptive world remains impoverished (Leder, 2019, p. 309).

There is a link between psychological malfunctioning and the development of serious illness. Several recent papers have emphasized the role of dysfunctional interoception in somatic and psychiatric disorders (Bonaz et al., 2021; Khalsa et al., 2018). We now have scientific evidence that bodily immunity and psychic processes are deeply linked (Vasile, 2020). Psychoneuroimmunologists have long accepted that stress works to dysregulate our immune system functioning (e.g., Glaser & Kiecolt-Glaser, 2005; Bae et al., 2019). The idea that there is ongoing communication within the body, even at a cellular level, between biological and psychical processes is important and compelling. We have to understand what is being expressed somatically when we do not have the language to process the myriads of sensations, affects and appraised dangers that arise both from without and within.

Moving From the Concrete to the Symbolic

To explain psychosomatic disorders, two major approaches can be delineated: 1) a somatizing process through repression where the symptom is seen as a product of psychic conflict and is filled with symbolic meaning. We can think of this as occurring when the conflict is resolved through a somatic compromise formation. This approach refers to transitory reversible somatic symptoms; and 2) a somatizing process through drive unbinding,[5] where there is an incapacity to function symbolically and our sorrows are expressed through bodily concretization as in organ failure. Here, the psychic structure fails, resulting in the foreclosure of symbolic functioning. The inchoate, unrepresented aspects of the unconscious, those raw "beta elements" in Bionian terms, or Jouissance in Lacanian terms, are implicated in the illness. Essentially, the patient puts his soma in direct line of communication with external reality bypassing the mind altogether.

Levine (2022) comments that it is an open question as to whether any instance of somatic discharge can be assumed to have symbolic significance or whether it is "blind evacuation" (p. 135). He asks, "is somatic illness a manifestation of the 'speechless mind' or the 'communicating body'?" (p. 135). The Paris Psychosomatic school assumes that the somatic symptom holds no inherent symbolic value in the progressive disorganization process where the organ is used to bind, but it may secondarily acquire one, in the "apres coup" (cf. Green, 2010).

There is agreement among psychoanalytic psychosomatic theoreticians that the psychosomatic patient lacks or suspends the capacity to translate emotions and sensations into representational form, i.e., to reach the mind from a somatic form. Rather, there is an "evacuative discharge" (Bion, 1970) or bodily concretization in a physical malady. Green (1999) noticed in some patients that "affect could only be deduced from somatizations" (p. 133), that the affect never reached consciousness. As soon as it was mobilized, it could only be expressed in a somatic storm.

Rather than conceptualizing this as an either/or phenomenon, we contend that there is a range on the continuum of somatizing processes that can be identified. At the one end of the continuum, we see symptoms that are products of psychic conflict, full of semiotic meaning. These conflicted mental states are resolved through a somatic compromise formation.

At the other end of the continuum, we see a somatizing process through drive unbinding. As Aisenstein and Smadja (2010) understand it, potentially traumatic sensory traces have been invested with somatic excitation and have failed to be transformed into drives. Instead, they short circuit into the soma. In western society we have been influenced by the Descartian dualism of mind and body, and many would talk of these patients as being "organically" sick. Illness expression is of course multifactorial – genetic, environmental, cultural to name a few factors. It is our contention that among the bio-psycho-social determinants of illness is the factor that patients are more prone to becoming gravely ill under circumstances that call for great emotional resources that are presently unavailable to them.

Most patients we see seem to fall somewhere along the psychosomatic continuum. There may or may not be symbolic meaning to the symptoms *at the time*. And some patients lack capacity for symbolizing altogether. There are fluctuations in patients' states – sometimes the patient is able to represent and at other times the archaic, raw, unconscious bits are bound by somatic processes and here the concrete replaces representation. This is an attempt to arrest the progressive disorganization of the mind.

Clinical Illustrations

Following are clinical vignettes illustrating the range from the symbolic end of the continuum to the more concrete end of the continuum.

Claire, an opera singer, found herself unable to sing; her voice was reduced to a whisper. Upon medical investigation, no organic reason was found. Analytic work with Claire revealed that she was experiencing – what seemed to her – an unresolvable conflict between continuing to flourish in her career and her long-disavowed wish to have a family life. In analysis, over time, she found the words to conceptualize the conflict which resulted in her ability to find both her subjective and her actual voice. Through this process, Claire was able to live more comfortably with her conflict.

In the aftermath of my daughter's life-threatening illness, I (M. Flax) was struck with a partial vocal cord paralysis. I became aware over time that this somatic symptom was an expression of the surfeit of affect in me, a kind of wordless paralysis in response to my family's shared helpless despair, terror and rage. Coincident with my growing ability to articulate and process the enormity of the change for us all, my vocal paralysis thankfully largely resolved.

I (J. Gail White) am grateful to my analyst for her close bodily reading of my dream. During a session, I mentioned a vivid dream that I had that week. I dreamt that I was choosing the color of the satin lining of my coffin. The choice was between the color beige or pink. Knowing that I had not been feeling well, my analyst strongly suggested that I see my physician. Medical investigation revealed that I had Graves' disease. The sense that I was unwell was first symbolized for me in my dream.

Tom suffers chronic, persistent erectile dysfunction. While he can masturbate, he cannot get an erection during intimate encounters. Tom is the only son of a patriarchal European family. In the early 1980s, at the height of the AIDS crisis, he was diagnosed with prostatitis, following a case of untreated chlamydia. He never returned to the urologist who diagnosed him. For him, it was a lifetime sentence. It was revealed in our work that this diagnosis occurred around the same time that he told his father that he was gay. When he told his father that day, his father had a stroke, right there in front of him. In a defensive negation he came to believe that he could not have caused his father's stroke if he was not actively gay. And he could not contract AIDS (which to him revealed that he was gay) if he avoided having sex altogether. I (J. Gail White) came to understand Tom's dilemma in terms of Tom's tyrannical superego that demanded his masochistic surrender. Over the years, Tom has begun to language his shame, guilt and self-punishment exercises and we are more and more able to work with the symbolic meaning of his actions. While he has not fully been released from the belief that he was struck impotent by prostatitis, recently he has entertained the idea of contacting his urologist 17 years later for a follow-up appointment.

Further along on the continuum, we see Susan, who was plagued by dizziness since the start of the pandemic – spells that were interfering with her life. During reverie states with her, I (J. Gail White) would find myself think-ing of the "Stendhal Syndrome" (Bamforth, 2010), that medically recognized condition of dizziness felt after exposure to great art that evokes *immense* affect. It is a condition that is still regularly seen in emergency wards during tourist season in Italy (Bamforth, 2010). I found myself wondering if Susan's immense affect was overwhelming her mind and her ability to symbolize. It was during the pandemic that a previous childhood trauma (sexual abuse by her brother) surfaced from the distant corners of her psyche, initially in the form of dizziness with no narrative memory. Susan had bought a dog during the pandemic to stem her loneliness and to force herself to stay active. She had unwittingly bought an identical dog to the one she had had in childhood who had been witness to her sexual abuse. Memories of the childhood abuse surfaced first in daily dizzy spells, then months later in dreams. The current pandemic trauma echoed and resonated with her previous trauma, as indeed has happened for so many during the pandemic. As we worked through the childhood sexual abuse, tears came to replace the dizzy spells and a sea of sadness – such a valuable feeling – emerged. Her manifest dreams always involved water in various states – foggy rooms, scenes of drowning, missing the cresting wave. Then she dreamt of two big waves that came over her. And she wasn't afraid anymore. In our work together the tears started to flow unin-terrupted, no longer requiring the body's dizziness to communicate. There have been no dizzy spells since. In the place of feelings, Susan had only physical sensations, the residue of a stifled unformulated affect that failed to achieve symbolization. As the symbolizing function did its work, the physical symptom of dizziness no longer served its purpose.

Even further along the continuum we find Jessica. Jessica cannot stay still on the couch; she writhes in constant action, twirling her fidget spinner to display the agitation she feels. The capacity to symbolize regularly collapses and she communicates primarily through the body. Kullman (2018) posits that those with eating disorders think with their bodies rather than their minds. Jessica balks at being asked to tell me how she feels in her body[6] while at the same time she displays to me her battered, gaunt body. Jessica's body is a foreign country, mysterious to her, and at the same time colonized with a violent disregard.

Jessica feels desperate to feel held. She describes a fantasy of being weight-lessly carried in the arms of a desperately loved protective woman. When I (M. Flax) met her some years ago, she had been in and out of in-patient units to help her survive her extremely disordered eating – she alternated between restricted anorexic eating and bulimic expulsion of food from her body. She made suicide attempts and was regularly self-harming. Her body was crisscrossed with scars from burns and cuts. The word FAT was carved into her thigh. The first couple of years of treatment were extremely harrow-ing, as she communicated only with her body. In rapidly oscillating moods, she displayed the terror of abandonment at the end of our sessions and would contact me after to say that she was standing at the edge of the subway and no longer wished to live. Her fantasy was that I would save her, weightlessly carrying her off the platform. For her, going-on-being on her own without a call for help to the powerful other was unthinkable; her body was put to work to express all her dread, rage and ungovernable affect storms. She was constantly talking of death, and demonstrating to me her bleeding cuts, her skin and bones, her easily broken bones. She longed for my constant care but also resisted any attempts to be helped. In my countertransference, I felt rendered professionally incompetent by her bodily attempts to engage me and at the same time, I was desperately afraid for her.

Jessica's somatization seems to be a screaming cry for help to manage her overwhelming and terrifying affect. She both pulls away from her intrusive parental imago, and at the same time seeks and defends herself against her fusion with the other. She hates those upon whom she depends (at times including me) and constantly attacks her internal objects in a physical form by being inconsistent in taking her medications, not eating for days, binging, purging repetitively and carving words into her body.

At times of late, she has been able to better describe her internal states, but she is still prone to storms. Recently, after a particularly intrusive interaction with her mother, she cut herself with a razor quite deeply and only realized what she was doing when she saw the blood. At the same time as cutting, she inadvertently urinated, in both a regression to infancy and a release of control. In our next session, we were able to talk about her rage with her mother, her turning that onto herself, her fear that the rage would damage the loved object, and her regression to a child state to stay fused and connected. We work to bring words to the painful, repetitive acting in through her body, to find the memory traces and dream fragments that can be spoken, symbolized and wrested away from an immediate concretization through the body, to find a more comfortable place between fusing with me and losing me.

Clinical Approach

While we may be limited in how much we can help when a destructive process has taken hold, we attempt to accompany our patients in their ongoing struggle. We have found certain approaches to be helpful, with both those who can symbolize some or all the time and with those who concretize some or all of the time. It is possible to oscillate from one end of the continuum to the other.

Clinically, we have found it important to embody an image of the early mother who seduces and captivates the baby into the life forces through her own desire, thereby structuring the child's psyche (Levine, 2020). The concept of "reverie" (Bion, 1962) is useful here, as most often the countertransference can precede or be simultaneous with the transference. As we create the story together using shared metaphors and mutual play, we begin to generate a workable representational space. It is here in the three-dimensional space where mentalization work can germinate. In most cases, the forming of images takes place in the mind of the analyst first, and the patient can be ushered into the symbolic through the analyst's interest, curiosity and enthusiasm in the work of representation. Repetition in the transference allows for the opportunity for early traces to be transformed into representations and thereby assigned meaning.

Conclusion

We have attempted to show in this chapter how psychoanalysts can understand and work with somatic symptoms. One could say that the overwhelmed psyche speaks the anguish through the body that the mind cannot utter in words. Patients present on a fluctuating continuum from the concrete level to the symbolic level in terms of whether they are presently capable of mentalization and symbolization. We are all more prone to becoming gravely ill under circumstances that call for great emotional resources that are presently unavailable to us, even if we have some capacity for symbolization. The very art of aiding representation and meaning making can help our suffering patients in that hardest of struggles, that of going-on-being.

Notes

1 Representation is to make present. To represent is to associate, which creates binding. Representation is the presentation of bodily experience and primitive drive iterations to the psyche so that the organism may use such experiences in the process of thought. Representations may be in the form of images or words. In the absence of representation, presentation of experience and drive may be primarily somatic and motoric.
2 Progressive disorganization is a retrograde movement expressed concretely in the body itself through organ binding (Marty, 1968).
3 Operational thinking is characterized by a deficiency in mentalization and a hyper cathexis of the concrete, seen in severe psychosomatic illness.
4 The pre-psychic is a sphere that either can or cannot become psychic (Green, 2010).
5 According to the French Psychosomatic theoreticians, drive unbinding is when the life and death forces lose their state of equilibrium, and the unbinding allows the destructive forces to reign.
6 Alexithymia is a common aspect of eating disorders (Westwood, Kerr-Gaffney, Stahl, Tchanturia, 2017).

References

Aisenstein, M. (2006). The indissociable unity of psyche and soma: A view from the Paris Psychosomatic School. *International Journal of Psychoanalysis*, 87, 667–680.
Aisenstein, M. (2017). *From the art of archery to the art of psychoanalysis*. Karnac Books.
Aisenstein, M., & Smadja, C. (2010). Conceptual framework from the Paris Psychosomatic School: A clinical psychoanalytic approach to oncology (S. Jaron, Trans.). *The International Journal of Psychoanalysis*, *91*(3), 621–640. https://doi.org/10.1111/j.1745–8315.2010.00256.x

Ameisen, J. C. (2007). La mort au cœur du vivant [Death at the heart of the living]. *Revue Française de Psychosomatique* ('Illness and self-destruction'), *32*, 11–43.

Bae, Y. S., Shin, E.-S., Bae, Y.-S., & van Eden, W. (2019). Editorial: Stress and immunity. *Frontiers in Immunology, 14*, 10. https://doi.org/10.3389/fimmu.2019.00245

Bamforth, I. (2010). Stendhal's syndrome. *British Journal of General Practice, 60*(581), 945–946. https://doi.org/10.3399/bjgp10X544780

Barrett, L. F. (2017). *How emotions are made.* Houghton, Mifflin, Harcourt.

Berntson, G. G., Gianaros, P. J., & Tsakiris, M. (2019). Interoception and the autonomic nervous system: Bottom up meets top down. In M. Tsakiris & H. de Preester (Eds.). *The interoceptive mind: From homeostasis to awareness.* Oxford University Press.

Bion, W. R. (1962). The psycho-analytic study of thinking. *International Journal of Psychoanalysis, 43*, 306–310.

Bion, W. R. (1970). *Attention and interpretation.* Tavistock.

Bonaz, B., Lane, R. D., Oshinsky, M. L., Kenny, P. J., Sinha, R., Mayer, E. A., & Critchley, H. D. (2021). Diseases, disorders, and comorbidities of interoception. *Trends in Neurosciences, 44*(1), 39–51.

Dejours, L., & Fain, M. (1984). *Corps malade, corps erotique (sick body, erotic body).* Masson.

Ferenczi, S. (1994). Organ neuroses and their treatment. In S. Ferenczi (Ed.), *Final contributions to the theory and technique of psycho-analysis* (pp. 22–28, J. Rickman, Comp. & J. I. Suttie, Trans.). Karnac. (Original work published 1926)

Freud, S. (1914). On narcissism. *The Standard Edition of the Complete Psychological Works of Sigmund Freud, 14*, 67–102.

Freud, S. (1920). Beyond the pleasure principle. *The Standard Edition of the Complete Psychological Works of Sigmund Freud, 18*, 1–64.

Freud, S. (1923). The ego and the Id. *The Standard Edition of the Complete Psychological Works of Sigmund Freud, 19*, 26.

Glaser, R., & Kiecolt-Glaser, J. (2005, April). How stress damages immune systems and health. *Discovery Medicine Journal, 5*(26), 165–169.

Green, A. (1999). *The fabric of affect in the psychoanalytic discourse.* Routledge.

Green, A. (2010). Thoughts on the Paris School of Psychosomatics. In M. Aisenstein & E. Rappoport de Aisemberg. *Psychosomatics Today: A Psychoanalytic Perspective.* Karnac Books.

Khalsa, S. S., Adolphs, R., Cameron, O. G., Critchley, H. D., Davenport, P. W., Feinstein, J. S., Feusner, J. D., Garfinkel, S. N., Lane, R. D., Mehling, W. E., Meuret, A. E., Nemeroff, C. B., Oppenheimer, S., Petzschner, F. H., Pollatos, O., Rhudy, J. L., Schramm, L. P., Simmons, W. K., Stein, M. B., Stephan, K. E., Van den Bergh, O., Van Diest, I., von Leupoldt, A., & Paulus, M. P. (2018, June). Interoception and mental health: A roadmap. *Biological Psychiatry: Cognitive Neuroscience and Neuroimaging.* https://doi.org/10.1016/j.bpsc.2017.12.004

Kullman, A. (2018). *Hunger for connection: Finding meaning in eating disorders.* Routledge.

Leder, D. (2019). Inside Insights: A phenomenology of interoception. In M. Tsakiris & H. de Preester (Eds.), *The interoceptive mind: From homeostasis to awareness.* Oxford University Press.

Levine, H. (2020). Reflections on therapeutic action and the origins of psychic life. *Journal of the American Psychoanalytic Association, 68*, 9–25.

Levine, H. (2022). *Affect, representation and language: Between the silence and the cry.* Routledge.

Marty, P. (1966). La dépression essentielle. *Revue Française C de Psychanalyse, 30*, 595–598.

Marty, P. (1968). A major process of somatization: The progressive disorganization. *International Journal of Psychoanalysis, 49*, 246–249.

Marty, P., de M'Uzan, M., & David, C. (1993). *L'investigation psychosomatique: Sept observations cliniques [Psychosomatic Investigation: Seven Clinical Observations]*. Presses Universitaires de France.

Maudsley, H. (1867). *The physiology and pathology of mind*. Appleton and Company.

Tsakiris, M., & De Preester, H. (2019). *The interoceptive mind: From homeostasis to awareness*. Oxford University Press.

Vasile, C. (2020). Mental health and immunity (review). *Experimental and Therapeutic Medicine, 20*(6), 211. https://doi.org/10.3892/etm.2020.9341

Westwood, H., Kerr-Gaffney, J., Stahl, D., & Tchanturia, K. (2017). Alexithymia in eating disorders: Systematic review and meta-analyses of studies using the Toronto Alexithymia scale. *Journal of Psychosomatic Research, 99*, 66–81.

11 So Close and Yet So Far Away

Psychoanalytic Treatment and Recovery From Psychosis-Inducing Trauma[1]

Burton Norman Seitler

In 1953, Wittgenstein wrote: "Whereof one cannot speak, thereof one must remain silent." And so, it is the task of the analyst to act as the patient's interlocutor. This presentation is about a youth whose trauma was so profound that he initially could not speak of it.

After experiencing his mother's agonizingly protracted illness and eventual death, Carl manifested symptoms of a psychotic episode; initially characterized by severe regression, extreme withdrawal, diminished verbal communication, and, subsequently, by the development of an elaborate delusional system. At first, Carl was unable to verbalize his inner state. Ultimately, the medium by which contact was established occurred through Carl's pencil and paper drawings. While all art forms, such as music, poetry, comedy, sculpture, writing, etc. utilize imagistic symbolic processing (Paivio, 2007, 1971; Bucci, 1995; Fosshage, 2005, 1997, 1983), this presentation will deal exclusively with drawing, and how Carl used his drawings:

> to communicate and begin to relate to his therapist; to safely express his private feelings; to protect himself from certain inner fears or forbidden wishes coming into conscious awareness, except in pictorial form, and to maintain sufficient space so as to form or maintain human interrelationships at a safe distance.

Through his drawings in general, Carl was able to symbolically illustrate his struggle to separate from and simultaneously preserve the image of his lost mother. One specific drawing starkly depicted this conflict. Carl referred to it as: "the earth as seen from the surface of the moon." Through this particular drawing, Carl was able to make contact with me at a safe distance and learn whether I was cold, barren, and distant or not. His drawings created the possibility of creating a relationship with me. I believe that our co-created relationship is what ultimately contributed to Carl's resilience in the face of trauma. His progress occurred in non-linear stops and starts – which can be traced from his initial episode to psychotic symptom, to artistic expression, to symbol formation, and finally (but not easily) to complete remission.

DOI: 10.4324/9781003607120-15

Freud (1905, 1916–17, p. 370) defined traumatic events as ones in which the ego is bombarded and overwhelmed by excessive amounts of stimuli, either intrapsychic or interpsychic. He asserted that the sources of the stimuli are due to sexual and/or aggressive drives.

This chapter is about Carl, an adolescent traumatized by the death of his mother and his painful struggle over her loss. When Carl's father and stepmother brought him in for psychotherapy, he appeared to be a skinny, freckle-faced, slightly disheveled 16-year-old, who looked bedraggled and unkempt. His bright red hair was uncombed, his shirt was half out of his pants, his pants were slightly stained, and even his shoelaces were untied.

He was referred because of an incident in his high school Biology class. During a dissection of a bullfrog, Carl started to wreath and wretch. This was followed by rhythmic rocking movements, crawling on the floor, curling up into a fetal-like position, becoming motionless and unresponsive to anyone for several minutes. The school psychologist was consulted. She concluded that Carl may have been in the throes of a psychotic episode. To be sure, she recommended a complete physical examination, including a neurological evaluation. Results indicated no tumor, lesion, cerebral insult, or any disease.

Family Constellation

Carl's father, a research scientist, was described in the intake report, as "cold, rigid, domineering, critical, suspicious, and intent on denying that there was anything wrong with his son." He said, "my boy's problem is he's lazy. He doesn't work hard in school, and he avoids things. That's all!" Regard for Carl's feelings were either denied, minimized, or delegitimized. All that mattered was that Carl achieve in school.

Carl's mother died tragically of stomach cancer two years (almost to the day) prior to the above Bio lab episode. It was slow, insidious, and prolonged, lasting five years from the time of diagnosis. Carl was unusually close to his mother and witnessed the final moments of her life, an event that he tape-recorded. One year after her death, Carl's father, Dr. T, remarried. Carl's stepmother had previously been married.

To briefly recap, Carl was only 9 years old when his mother's illness was discovered, 14 when she died, and a helpless observer of her agony during the intervening years of her suffering, with radiation, surgical, and chemotherapy treatments.

Preverbal Phase of Treatment

During our early sessions, Carl was taciturn. Despite numerous attempts on my part to initiate conversation, Carl curled up in his chair in a fetal position, head down, arms around his legs, and knees drawn in to his face. He had withdrawn from interacting with the world and appeared more receptive to internal stimuli. Fromm-Reichmann (1954) commented on this:

> I believe it is of interest to state that many clinicians have been accustomed to describe stuporous states as a result of the schizophrenic's withdrawal of interest from outward reality. Hence, the oversimplification of interpreting them only as a response to catatonic fear of rejection becomes quite understandable. . . . As we know, from our reports about the experience while in stupor, which these patients furnish after their emergence, they are, more frequently than not, keen observers of what is going on in their environment. Withdrawal of the ability for interpersonal communication is what characterizes the condition of the patient in stupor, not withdrawal of interest in the environment per se.
>
> (p. 410)

Assuming Carl was not "out of reach," I continued to attempt to find some way to communicate with him. Initially, my attempts were mostly verbal. I spoke to Carl; tried to ask him "neutral" questions. When he did not respond, I then accepted his (need for) silence. His silence, and all that it signified, were to be accepted and understood as important to Carl – for as yet unknown reasons. So, I sat quietly with him; waited and observed, while at the same time, delighting myself in my own reverie.

At about our fourth session, Carl furtively peeked out from his curled-up posture, as if playing "peek-a-boo" with me. And, with a fleeting glance, appeared to catch sight of me smiling at him. During our fifth session, Carl spontaneously spoke up in a hurried, mumbled, staccato-like stammer. He said, "I can draw, you know, you know, you know. I draw a lot. I can draw all kinds of things, and I'm good at it too. My favorite things, I'll show you." I quickly furnished him with paper and pencils, and he began to draw. He described his first drawing as an "ice cube." For the next few sessions, Carl's drawings were exclusively of inanimate objects, such as ice cubes, rocks, buildings (with windows), and so forth. His drawings opened the therapeutic possibility of serving as a medium for communication between the two of us.

Several crucial aspects of Carl's perception, defensive network, and delusional system are illustrated by his drawings. Most of his drawings reflected the preponderance of a particular motif. Accordingly, I selected one specific drawing as a representative sample of the imagery he employed and the recurrent theme that ran through most of his drawings, namely, relating to objects at a distance.

Carl described that drawing as "the earth as seen from the surface of the Moon." Upon inquiry, he explained that the shaded portion indicated that the Northeastern section of North America was in darkness . . . because it was nighttime. Attempting to bring things closer by degree, I asked Carl if he could see where he lived. He responded that the distance was too great and that his home could not be seen – although he emphatically added, "It's there, you know, you know. It's not gone, no no no no!" Carl added that the earth was observed from the dark (unknown) side of the moon.

Although his drawings were a step or two removed from him, his feelings, and his reality, the drawings provided an inkling (albeit vague, veiled, and indistinct) of what he was going through. Also, his very being, or for that matter, non-being was expressive of his felt experience.

If we conceptualize therapy as a "recapitulation of developmental phases," then a sense of trust, the initial stage of development, described by Erikson (1950), must first be established. The question then is how can one trust someone that one has never met before? How was Carl to trust me, whom he did not know, or from whom he did not know what to expect, much less what was expected of him? How was he to find out how I would greet him? The drawings became the means by which Carl could develop a transitional space in which he and I could safely make contact.

Carl's drawings may have been attempts at "feeling out" the environment to see whether it was cold, hard, or unfeeling (like an ice cube, or a rock – or perhaps something resembling his father) or to see if the opposite was true.

Via graphic imagery, he simultaneously expressed his feelings about the environment and himself. He depicted his feelings about self and other as dualistically bound or fused together. His drawings not only served as communication and as a device for eliciting reactions from the environment, but also as a gift to the therapist. Greenacre (1957, 1958, 1963) describes this as "the artist's love affair with the world" in which his artistic productions are not to be kept or hoarded, so much as they are to be presented as gifts to a loved one, a potential love object, or someone "standing in the place of" a love object. She sees this as a displacement of libidinal strivings and the provenance of a love gift to the viewer.

In this drawing, Carl has not lost total interest in the environment. After all, he has depicted an environment for us. Admittedly, the nature of the environment is rather peculiar in that it is far removed and devoid of people, save for whomever is doing the observing of the earth (whom Carl did not identify). He provided a distance perspective, as well as a relationship between two celestial bodies – the earth and its satellite, the moon. Nor has he tampered, through symbolic tricks or pseudo-logic, with any principle of astronomy or physics. Instead, he represented himself symbolically, through an already existing system in which objects revolve around each other in accordance with cosmic influences (i.e., gravity and centrifugal force). He had a vast amount of knowledge and understanding of astronomy and various "laws" of physics said to govern the universe, and scrupulously abided by them in his pictorially represented mini-delusional system. Thus, his thought process bore a quasi-realistic aspect to reality, and at least paralleled realistic thinking. The difficulty arose when he tried to apply his "system" to his interpersonal relationships via the use of highly personalized, magical symbolic equivalences, as though his view of the solar system held sway for the interpersonal universe as well.

Many Meanings Comprise the Meaning

The interpretation of the possible meanings of Carl's drawings is intended here merely to provide a glimpse into his complex, highly personalized imagery and symbolic thinking in its most relative sense. My intention is to simply make a few inferences in the hope of generating some hypotheses.

Interpretive Inferences

Because the moon is a satellite of the earth, it thus may be said to occupy a subordinate position to the larger earth. A reciprocal relationship also exists. The moon orbits around the earth, partly because of the earth's larger mass and gravity which attract the moon. Simultaneously, the distance from the moon to the earth (its relative position to the earth) determines the ebb and flow of the earth's tides. Also, the earth is colloquially referred to as "Mother Earth." In this respect, a child can have an effect on his mother's "tides" or moods and vice versa. For that matter, a child's magical, omnipotent thinking might conceive of himself as responsible for his mother's illness (or even worse, her death). As one would expect, her loss is tough enough for someone entering young manhood, without the additional burden of guilt being superimposed upon that tragic and traumatic event.

Carl's drawing suggests a dualism consisting of a graphically depicted separation/distance from the mother (i.e., mother earth), which Mahler refers to as an attempt to achieve separation and initiate individuation (1967). Paradoxically, this represents an attempt to maintain an umbilical-like or possibly symbiotic relationship with the mother. The latter constitutes Carl's possible denial or non-acceptance of the reality – and finality – of her death. For Carl, out of sight did not mean out of mind.

The loss of his mother, with whom he was heavily identified, meant a loss of self. In his words, "to lose is to be lost." Carl's lack of acceptance of his mother's death is evidenced by the tape recordings of her voice as she was dying, which he played over and over each day. An over-identification with the lost object may have resulted in feelings of being lost, or even feelings of being dead. Ironically, the reasoning behind his denial of her death may also be – "She and I are one (via the process of identification with the lost object). She is dead. Therefore, I am (or I feel) dead. Yet, I somehow know that I am alive, so she must also be alive." Identification with the lost object is also a way of expressing anger at the departed person "for having left me in my time of need," as well as a way of expressing one's feelings of guilt (possibly for feeling this way and for not being with the departed one in death). This can also represent a wish for self-punishment for being the survivor.

The complete nature of the existence of his guilt feelings is not fully known. Perhaps Carl was angry with his mother for not being able to meet his needs and may have "wished her to be gone," a thought that many children have at various times. Perhaps too, her progressive pain was more than he could bear, and he wished death would spare her further agony, only to subsequently regret that wish.

The existence of guilt feelings may be understood as based on thoughts or behaviors for which Carl may have felt that he might be punished and for which he anticipated retaliation. This hypothesized fear of retaliation adds yet another rationale for dissociating from others, as well as from his own feelings and for cutting off close interpersonal interactions. It also makes understandable Carl's maintenance of distance between himself and others, as well as maintaining distance between aspects of his own self-states.

Defenses

I believe that there was a splitting of Carl's ego, and that this represented a last-ditch effort at psychological survival. We see Carl attempting to institute defenses against the onslaught of anxiety emanating from the ego's excruciating trauma of his mother's loss, and a possibly archaic superego's invocation of guilt and the ensuing fear of punishment. Understandably, his defenses would seek to vitiate or deaden the anxiety via distancing, loss of contact with external reality, depersonalization, and isolation of affect, as well as regression and a reduction in secondary process thinking.

Carl's preoccupation with distance provided a defense against hurtful thoughts from within, as well as the threat (or reality) of harm experienced from without. Despite resultant distortions of interpersonal reality, Carl's obsession with "outer space" provided him with a modicum of relief. Since his defenses paralleled realistic thinking to some extent, he maintained them. This provided a sense of continuity so Carl could exist and function. Curiously, although Carl was failing practically every subject in school, he was a master of the most arcane facts. His extensive in-depth knowledge was related to areas involving distance. He knew the mean distance of every planet from the earth, every planet's satellite to the "mother" planet [his wording], the mean diameter of every planet, and each one's satellite.

Progress in Therapy

Carl's drawings were of great value to the treatment in that they facilitated our communication by helping me better understand where he was emotionally, while at the same time helping me appreciate what he was going through. Of even greater importance, his drawings helped focus my empathic attunement to his feelings.

As treatment progressed, Carl increasingly engaged in conversation. However, still needing to maintain control over aspects of our sessions, he began to choose specific games in the playroom which allowed for this.

In particular, he preferred the game Monopoly. Here we begin to see progress in the direction of remission. Through the *game*, Carl was able to reinstitute some compulsive defenses that could eventually serve to structure and/or control the obsessive ideation that was besieging him earlier. One particular Monopoly game lasted for four months. Carl was winning throughout and could have dispensed with me at any time. He did not do so, not out of a sadistic desire to slowly beat me "by inches," but rather out of genuine compassion, perhaps to "preserve" me somehow. Each time that he had the opportunity to win, Carl manipulated aspects of the game to "keep me going." Obviously, this game had great personal and literal significance for Carl. My sense is that it was a relational re-enactment of his feelings about his mother, and the enormous impact that losing her constituted.

When I asked him why he so kindly let me continue to play, he insightfully explained "when the game is done, it's all over. That's it, the end." Once again, he invoked his mythic formula, "to lose is to be lost." Carl identified with me as the "good mother," thus, defeating me would cause me to lose, and if I lost, *I would be lost to him*, and gone. If I lost, Carl would feel lost himself.

Since I would, in reality, neither be gone physically, nor less emotionally available for Carl, the factor of loss could now be dealt with more readily via *the game* than it would have been when Carl first came for therapy when any sort of loss, no matter how seemingly inconsequential, would have been experienced as monumental. However, his presumed guilt feelings (possibly for having "caused" the loss) and anticipatory fears of punishment or retaliation would have to be dealt with.

Eventually, Carl understood his need to perceive the *game* as his tie to my life and death. Ultimately, he relinquished this literal life/death meaning, substituting in its place one that was predicated on how I would feel about him if he were to "win" or I were to "lose." He slowly recognized that I would feel about him as before and that it was fine with me if I lost the game. On one specific occasion, he showed great surprise when we were talking about winning and losing. He said, "you mean you aren't mad. I mean, you won't be angry?" Two sessions later, apparently believing me, or at least exhibiting a willingness to test out what had been said to him, he won the game. He was thus able to see that I still was alive, and what is more, that he was too. I was not annihilated, nor was he. Of equally important significance, our relationship did not die. Commenting on what recovery requires, Ferenczi (1928) compassionately observed:

> The process of recovery consists to a great extent of the patient putting the analyst (this new father) in place of the real father who occupies such a predominant place in his super-ego, and his then going on living with the analytic super-ego thus formed. . . . Only a complete dissolution of the super-ego can bring about a radical cure.
>
> (p. 98)

As time went on, Carl's advances continued, along with the expected regressions. After two and one half years of psychotherapy, three to four times a week, Carl could now interact with new people and make friends, something that was previously avoided. He took better care of his appearance. His grades skyrocketed. Although he did not put away his tape-recorder, he no longer replayed his mother's voice. It was sufficient for Carl that he had her with him as his transitional object.

Through the years, I have received an occasional letter or holiday card from Carl. He got married, had a son, whom he adores, and has achieved his dreamed-of career.

Finally, as Shakespeare wrote:

Give sorrow words: the grief that
Does not speak, whispers o'er
Fraught heart, and bids it break.

(Macbeth, IV, iii, p. 218)

Note

1   This chapter is a revised version of La tierra vista desde la superficie de la luna (The Earth as seen from the surface of the Moon), which was first published in Sandor Ferenczi y El Psicoanalisis del Siglio XXI [Ed. Pedro Boschan] Buenos Aires: Argentina, Letra Viva Publisher, 2011, p. 439–450.

References

Bucci, W. (1995). Dual coding: A cognitive model for psychoanalytic research. *Journal of American Psychoanalytic Association, 33*, 571–607.

Erikson, E. H. (1950). *Childhood and society*. W.W. Norton & Company.

Ferenczi, S. (1928). The elasticity of psycho-analytic technique. In *Final contributions to the problems and methods of psycho-analysis*. (Maresfield Reprints, 1980)

Fosshage, J. (1983). The psychological function of dreams. *Contemporary Psychoanalysis, 33*(3), 429–458.

Fosshage, J. (1997). The organizing function of dreams. *Contemporary Psychoanalysis, 33*(3), 429–458.

Fosshage, J. (2005). The explicit and implicit domains in psychoanalytic change. *Psychoanalytic Inquiry, 25*, 516–539.

Freud, S. (1916–17). Mourning and melancholia. *Standard Edition, XIV*, 237–260. Hogarth Press.

Freud, S. (1905). Three essays on the theory of sexuality. *Standard Edition, VII*, 123–246.

Fromm-Reichmann, F. (1954). Psychotherapy of schizophrenia. *American Journal of Psychiatry*, 204–219.

Greenacre, P. (1957). The childhood of the artist. *The Psychoanalytic Study of the Child, 12*, 47–72.

Greenacre, P. (1958). The family romance of the artist. *The Psychoanalytic Study of the Child, 13*, 9–43.

Greenacre, P. (1963). *The quest for the father*. International Universities Press.

Mahler, M. (1967). On human symbiosis and the vicissitudes of individuation. *JAPA, 15*, 740–763.

Paivio, A. (1971). *Imagery and verbal processes*. Rinehart & Winston Publishers. (Shakespeare, W. *Macbeth*, IV, iii, p. 218)

Paivio, A. (2007). *Mind and its evolution: A dual coding theoretic approach*. Lawrence Erlbaum Associates.

Wittgenstein. (1953). *Tractatus logico-philosophicus*. Humanities Press.

Part IV

Going-on-Being Through Social-Political Upheaval

12 Dehumanization and Going-on-Being After Catastrophic Trauma

John A. Sloane

Ever since Donald Trump began his irrational rise to power, I have been flooded with psychotic anxieties about what was happening to the world and to me. His utter disregard for truth and humanity in his quest for power, profit and privileged "greatness" was chillingly like the rise of the Third Reich, the most dehumanizing event of the last century, one that was in the air and on the ground as I was growing up.

Like many, I have been haunted by a "praecox feeling" emerging from Pandora's box outside and inside myself. The disintegration of world order (illusory as that may be) gives rise to rage in search of an "object". In the absence of effective agency to get rid of the offender or get through to a *person* who cares, we're left in a state of despair and dehumanization – or itching for a fight.

Those feelings are compounded by an invisible virus that makes infants of us all; vulnerable, ignorant and powerless, but nonetheless deadly "doers and done-to's" (Benjamin, 2018) whether we know it or not, whether we accept or reject responsibility by denying and projecting that inconvenient truth in the form of blame. We have been locked up with – and away from – what we love in ways that feel unbearable, arousing hate and all-out infantile destructiveness (Winnicott, 1969) toward whatever impinges on us, limits our freedom or controls our behaviour. We all feel endangered, imprisoned, isolated and robbed of our birthright to be, enjoy and bring joy to the world. Instead, we dehumanize others at times, not only those "below" us, but those "above" us to whom we attribute all-knowing, all-powerful, super-human importance. When we elevate (idealize) someone or something beyond question or objection – or degrade them beyond caring, listening and learning from them, we set the stage for abuse of power.

There is no such thing as a self without others to lovingly hold and oppose us, bearing with us but holding us responsible for the effects of what we do with our infantile omniscience/omnipotence.

The climate crisis is making its presence felt in equal measure to its very denial in high places (Weintrobe, 2021). Putin has launched an inhuman assault on Russia's neighbour, Ukraine. His "special military operation" is boundlessly destructive to innocent civilians both Ukrainian and Russian, and to their societies, not to mention to truth, life and democracy all over the

DOI: 10.4324/9781003607120-17

world. His military assault invades our living rooms and relational unconscious, day by day. Even the word "war" normalizes mass murder and crimes
against humanity in the service of reclaiming or avenging lost or stolen power
and glory. This state of mind we know is developmentally prior to the capacity
to recognize and care for the humanity of the Other.

Although "the catastrophe we fear has already happened," we all know
it can be repeated in enactments, unconsciously co-created between and
around two or more – up close and personal or on the world stage, split
to its nuclear core. This is more than metaphor. We have been splitting the
Adam forever and are now reaching a critical mass. Nuclear weapons are a
finger-tip away from those at the top of our endangered species, faced with
the existential question that Einstein asked Freud back in 1932, "Is there any
way of delivering mankind from the menace of war?" (Einstein et al., 1939). Is
there any way of transforming our all-out infantile destructiveness into viable
limit-setting and capacities for truly human relatedness?

Winnicott thought so – as long as the (m)Other had the capacity to survive,
stand her ground and say "No" without retaliating, withdrawing or collapsing
(Winnicott, 1969), the prototype for constructive use of "hate in the countertransference" (Winnicott, 1947). Then, the discovery and "use" of otherness
(reality) could take place, and our initially necessary infantile omniscience
and omnipotence could be gradually limited, mourned and responsibly harnessed in the service of critical thinking, confident action, humble acceptance and co-creative dialogue with others. Doing that with someone who
knows they need help is difficult enough. Doing it on the world stage without taking what psychoanalysis is learning into account is hard to imagine.
We need a process whereby our species can draw on whatever capacities for (m)other-infant mutuality are there, defended against by one-sided
all-knowingness and power-over others. Theoretical formulations and explanations, however, are not useful, socio-politically.

Ignorant as I am of the vast complexities of socio-political, economic,
technical and historical processes to which developmental needs and
defenses against vulnerability and interdependency contribute, this chapter
will draw on personal and clinical experience (Bromberg, 2006a) to imagine what that process might look like in an expanded frame. It is vital to
bring psychoanalytic ways of being, knowing and relating to bear on what
goes on beyond individuals, dyads, triangles and groups that call upon us
to facilitate reconciliation of splits that spawn primary passions and relational dysfunction.

A scholarly review of the psychoanalytic literature on the topic is beyond
my scope and the purpose of this chapter, so I will begin with self-disclosure
of developmental experience. It has been reactivated "in the transference"
(Bird, 1972) to what I'm up against in the world, a sick and dangerous Other
we all wish we could understand and affect.

When I was first learning to express myself in words, I used the word
"hate" – a fitting word for what I was feeling. My mother responded, gently

but with absolute authority, "Oh, no you don't dear". Although she no longer considered herself a Methodist, she could not bear to hear that the apple of her eye was rotten.

It is only gradually that I have realized the full gas-lighting (Dorpat, 1996) impact of that denial/negation (Stern, 2019) of a vital aspect of my own humanity. She hated my hate more than she knew. She was a very loving, creative person, a "good-enough mother" in many ways, but those well-intentioned words were swords that cut deeply into my sense of self, my grasp of reality and my capacity for critical thought. Both love and hate can smother the Other. Both love and hate are essential to the healing, humanizing process so beautifully described in the last chapter of Mitchell's book, *Relationality* (Mitchell, 2000).

My trans-generationally "troubled" Irish father was another matter. He was someone I looked up to with a mixture of affection, fear and god-like idealization until he became irrationally angry, judgemental and punitive from a place of absolute authority that I've gradually come to realize, defended his own troubled vulnerability. Finally, he aroused an equal and opposite, rageful authority in me. At that point, as a boy of 10, I erupted with all-knowing, all-out infantile destructiveness from a safe place at the top of our basement stairs – with him at the bottom. To my everlasting guilt and need to make reparations (Klein, 1937) through pathological accommodation to the needs of others (Brandchaft, 2007), that explosion had the visible effect of extinguishing the light in his eyes and rendering him weak and useless in mine. Shortly after that, he died of the brain cancer that had gone undiagnosed too long – leaving me with recurrent nightmares of nuclear holocaust. The arms race in the '80s, the attack on the Twin Towers and now the rise of Trump and Putin, are stirring that cauldron again. The Doomsday Clock is 90 seconds to midnight as I write.

As many like me do from such a compelling preverbal place, I went into medicine, psychiatry and finally psychoanalysis to find out what goes so wrong and to rectify it if I could, one patient at a time. It took time to learn that I couldn't be Superman and to harness my hate in the service of containing regression (Winnicott, 1947). Not-knowing (Bion, 1967; Eigen, 2011), and self-revelation of shameful states (Bromberg, 2006) are useful, too.

Out there in the world, though, the word "hate" still refers to something unequivocally "bad", something to be stamped out or denied and projected in ways that are crazy-making and destructive to society. It's not me, it's you. Not us, but them who are bad – or weak. But as Aichhorn wrote about antisocial youth, and Brent Willock observed in his work with hyperaggressive children, delinquent behaviour also embodies hope if it can be held, owned and harnessed for effective communication (Aichhorn, 1951; White, 1963; Willock, 1986, 1987).

Dickens wrote, "I love these little people and it is not a slight thing when they who are so fresh from God love us" (Dickens, 1841). The corollary is that "it is not insignificant when they hate the way we use our authority over them rather than respecting and working with them to find words that work" – as we learn to do in analysis.

Robbie Burns wrote; "O, would some Pow'r the giftie gie us/to see ourselves as others see us" (Burns, 1786) – a "prayer" that Relational analysts have been responding to. "Whose bad objects are we anyway?" (Davies, 2004) And where would we be without them (Mendelsohn, 2002)? Whose good objects are we trying to be? Are not "good-enough" (m)others those who can hear and bear it when they are not good enough? Are we not learning to learn from the ways our patients sometimes drive us crazy in the service of healing, enabling us to facilitate their healing (Searles, 1959, 1979)? Are we regressing in the service of a new beginning or is what we are going through malignant (Balint, 1968)?

As world events re-create the madness of mutually assured destruction, many of us regress to borderline if not psychotic, psychopathic and manic modes of functioning in the service of the Ego with a capital "E". Self-supremacy and theocracy are rampant, amplified by lies and conspiracy theories, spread as though they were "Gospel" – and by derogatory, dehumanizing rhetoric. All children lie to themselves and others when they fear being found out by an all-powerful, punitive Other. Words can be used as weapons of mass deception. We all wish we could get rid of what ails us and threatens to overwhelm, humiliate or annihilate us – even by selling our souls (Brandchaft, 2007) as a shocking number of otherwise respectable politicians are doing. I've heard the most loving, level-headed people I know confide how much they wish they could kill both Trump and Putin – or their own neighbours. Some even feel that way toward the medical profession and the democratically elected powers that be in governments that mandate injections of substances against the will of some people – arousing defiance of authority. Whose body is this, anyway? Whose choice? Whose birthright to say, "No"?

What is it, then, that allows some traumatized folk to become wounded healers (Farber, 2016; Sloane, 2016) while others become dehumanized killers, destroying "the Other" with intimidating, derogatory language that becomes inflammatory and contagiously violent? And greedy, of course. Ravenous, rapacious hunger of mercenaries, selling souls and bodies for money or becoming suicide-bombers in search of glory in the next world. Anti-democratic autocrats misusing the name of a "Grand Old Party" in the service of conserving Self to the exclusion of the Other, a perverse form of original unity (Loewald, 1950). Nuclear powers locked-in to MAD-ness in the absence of a living, loving Third (Gerson, 2009).

When Alyona Chukanova issued an invitation to IARPP to join her Ukrainian colleagues wrestling with questions of ethics and the maintenance of human integrity at ground zero of Putin's attacks, I felt like a moth drawn to the flame in order to bear witness and find out in real time how some manage to remain human in the face of inhumanity, while others become one with a heartless aggressor.

It was very moving to witness what happens to all of us more than we remember from the timeless mists of early catastrophe – or in the fog of "adult" wars that leave many traumatized by what they have done as well as by what was done to them and their companions (Benjamin, 2018; McNamara, 2005). It can be impossible to remember, let alone formulate who's doing what to whom (Benjamin, 2018) in the present. It is not just what's done to us that is traumatically dehumanizing, but what we do to essential others with what erupts from within. Post-traumatic stress can be boundless, timeless and impossible to locate, exactly.

One of the questions raised in those monthly Zoom meetings was whether to continue talking with Russian colleagues who supported what Putin's forces were doing. Like New York analysts after 9/11, Ukrainian analysts were as traumatized as those they were trying to help, but in an ongoing way where boundaries are blurred between victim and villain. How can one be true to oneself if one cooperates with "the enemy"? How can one hold others in mind (Spezzano, 2007) when one's own mind is driven to madness by what one Ukrainian analyst called "information warfare"?

Those were the questions so agonizingly asked by our Ukrainian colleagues. Can one say "No! I hate what you are doing to me" – and get it through to a "hearing heart" (1 Kings, 3: 1–9) (Eshel, 2019) and get the destruction to stop?

As William Blake wrote,

O for a voice like thunder, and a tongue
To drown the throat of war! When the senses
Are shaken, and the soul is driven to madness,
Who can stand?[1]

Can a Republican stand against his own? Can a Democrat be receptive to the emotional truth of those who see something seriously wrong with a "system" that has broken its promises and robbed them of human dignity and equal opportunity? Can an honest politician pretend it's "politics as usual" when he or she is destroying what has taken millennia to build? What do we do with a patient before us who buys into paranoid-schizoid lies that threaten our own existence (Sloane, 2019)? How can one participate in a process of inquiry into the truth of relational experience when one is the target of all-out destruction, awash with misinformation (Dorpat, 1996)?

I had one patient who identified with the terrorists on 9/11 – and treated me as though I were as privileged as those in the Twin Towers (Sloane, 2012). She relentlessly tore me down and rejected all my efforts at respectful, empathic recognition of her impoverished, degraded, dehumanized childhood experience. To her, "empathy" was pity from someone who had no idea what it was like. I was the despicable, "useless" enemy; someone to be destroyed. I finally reached a point of putting my thoughts on paper that I read aloud in one of our sessions. I was no longer willing to pretend that the process was one of truth-seeking, let alone healing. It had become one of satisfying her compensatory need for destructive power and punishment – and mine for self-sacrifice. Vengeance was hers until I told her we would have to stop after another three months, during which time we might come to terms with what-ever that meant to her. For reasons I'm not sure of, I was no longer in the grip of paranoid/depressive anxiety that she would commit suicide or homicide in response. But she was shocked to realize I "had a choice" (as she put it) and was flooded by memories of a pivotal betrayal of trust by her passive but relatively benign father obeying her mother's command that he brutally beat her for disobeying the matriarch.

Recalling that opened a door to how hurt she had been, how much she hated her father for obeying her mother, and how much she was punishing me in his stead. As Freud wrote, "For when all is said and done, it is impossi-ble to destroy anyone in absentia or in effigie" (Freud, 1912, p. 108). It is only possible "in the transference" where that person comes alive and survives our all-out destructiveness. By the end of three months, we had found ways of communicating and reflecting in ways that felt productive to both of us. It was as though her basic mistrust made room for a measure of basic trust – with mutual respect and affection that grew over several more years with sanity and satisfaction in the end for both of us.

I am at a loss to recall the details of conversations that followed my unilat-eral decision to terminate – which then made it possible to change my mind at the end of three months. Somehow, my carefully considered, non-retaliatory decision to stop what we were doing worked. I had stood up for a part of her as well as myself by saying "Enough is enough," giving voice to a part of her with which I was introjectively identifying more than I knew.

In the correspondence we have continued since she left analysis to find work in another city, I found a letter from me in response to a question she asked.

Dear . . .

It's good to hear from you – and that your work is going well. Sorry, though, that your brother was so ill. So many reminders of our own vulnerability, these days, and how lucky we are to be alive!

You also raise a good question, "How did I cope with your rage for so long?" I've wondered the same thing. It would take much longer than this to explain, but it occurs to me, now, that part of it has to do with a part of me that felt I deserved it. Another part of me identified with it and wanted to understand where it was coming from. Another part of me did not want to destroy you as I had my dad – as another part of me wishes I could do to the powers-that-be in the world, right now. All that has taken me back, as you did, to the psychotic core and multiple self-states of the child I was – and still am in some ways.

Michael Eigen's writing has helped me with that, especially his book "Rage" that I needed the help of others, reading and discussing it with me, to under-stand. One quote from it rings especially true for me; "I don't know anything

in human history that has done more harm than the sense of being right."
(Eigen, 2002)[2] p. 172

Thanks in part to you, I reached a point of being able to say, "No" – and to feel I had that basic "right" – on behalf of both of us, as it turned out.

All that's more than you were expecting, I'm sure. But a good question from a colleague who has found a different way of working with "Flames from the Unconscious" (another of Eigen's books) (Eigen, 2009) deserves a thoughtful answer. Those of us who are crazy enough to go into this field are drawn like moths to the flame – the mysterious scene of an original crime against our humanity and that of those we love.

Thank you for prompting me to formulate that much.

Warmly,

John

Another patient identified with Trump's suspicion and hatred of Muslim immigrants, and disdain for the mainstream media and left-wing politicians in power in Canada. Our therapeutic alliance foundered, regrettably, on my impulsive, unprocessed countertransference hate of his dangerous public protests and scapegoating of Muslims for a terrorist attack by a misanthropic INCEL member on the street where my office was located (Sloane, 2019). He felt categorized (dehumanized) by me as "an Islamophobe", and said, "No" in a way that accurately pointed out my failure to recognize and use my countertransference in the service of his analysis.

My point in relation to the Ukrainian experience is that despite my bias toward the essential function of dialogue, an assumption based on experience, memory and desire (Bion, 1967), I was able to see and understand the necessity of saying "No" to talk at times – even though it can be heart-wrenchingly difficult to know what else to do. Kill or be killed? Stand by and do "nothing"? Dissociate in ways that are necessary to one's mental health but feel irresponsible if not delusional in their non-recognition of reality? One can err in many ways.

One Ukrainian therapist who dared to speak openly in that surprisingly intimate forum received a call from the trenches in the Donbas from a tormented man who needed to talk. He was fighting for the Russians and had no way of paying, except to promise to shoot into the air instead of at Ukrainians.

Stop for a moment and think about what that might feel like, and what you would do. . . .

We did not hear the end of that story. Even writing about it in a public summary on the IARPP listserv, afterwards, conjured up dread and guilt, for me. Was I breaking an unspoken, implicit confidentiality and putting her – or her would-be patient – at risk of being identified by an all-seeing "Lord High Executioner"?

I take heart from the capacity of those we spoke with in those deeply moving moments of meeting (Gotthold & Sorter, 2006) to maintain their love of Life and Truth and their determination to find a Way.

Visceral truths, such as mistrust, disgust and hate, undigested by compassionate recognition and respectful reasoning give rise to lies, contempt and derogatory rhetoric that perpetuates reciprocal emotional abuse and leads to scapegoating of despised, dehumanized Others – unless it finds a "home in the mind" of an Other (Spezzano, 2007). In a marital relationship, hate can sometimes be held by marital therapists in ways that trace triggers and origins of old wounds, yielding unexpectedly valuable reconciliation (Edwards, 2016). In toxic work environments, it can sometimes be neutralized and transformed into mutual respect and cooperation among those who otherwise founder on the rocks of dominance-submission hierarchies. In the socio-political arena, however, it not only causes discontent over real injustices, but polarization and breakdown of civilization itself. The Destroyer is trying to destroy himself – taking creative goodness with it unless we can find ways to take what Freud wrote to heart.

> *If the propensity for war be due to the destructive instinct, we always have its counter-agent, Eros, to our hand. All that produces ties of sentiment between man and man must serve as war's antidote. . . . The psychoanalyst need feel no compunction in mentioning "love" in this connection; religion uses the same language, "love thy neighbour as thyself". A pious injunction, easy to enounce, but hard to carry out! The other bond of sentiment is by way of identification. All that brings out the significant resemblances between men calls into play this feeling of community, identification, whereon is founded, in large measure, the whole edifice of human society.*
>
> *(Einstein et al., 1939)*

Respectful empathic enquiry into what is not yet known or understood, in conjunction with judicious acknowledgement of vulnerability and fault, together with truthful confrontation, can promote mutual recognition and identification. We need time and space to stand (Bromberg, 1996) and hear the hurt behind hate – and the shame behind rage and contempt. Not-knowing or being-able to do anything can be excruciating but can also be borne with the help of an Other who has been there and takes some responsibility for causing or allowing it.

In the absence of a loving Other, capable of regressing in the service of empathic identification and authentic relatedness, we are lost. That's what good-enough mothers have always done instinctively, and men are learning to do over time.

Notes

1 From "Prologue intended for a dramatic piece of Edward the Fourth" in *Blake's Poetry and Designs: William Blake 1757–1827*. W.W. Norton & Co. 1979, p. 9.
2 Citations not included in my letter.

References

Aichhorn, A. (1951). *Wayward youth*. Imago.

Balint, M. (1968). *The basic fault*. Tavistock.

Benjamin, J. (2018). *Beyond doer and done to: Recognition theory, intersubjectivity and the third*. Routledge.

Bion, W. R. (1967). Notes on memory and desire. *The Psychoanalytic Forum, 2*(3), 271–280.

Bird, B. (1972). Notes on transference: Universal phenomenon and hardest part of analysis. *Journal of the American Psychoanalytic Association, 20*, 267–301.

Brandchaft, B. (2007). Systems of pathological accommodation and change in analysis. *Psychoanalytic Psychology, 24*, 667–687.

Bromberg, P. M. (1996). Standing in the spaces: The multiplicity of self and the psychoanalytic relationship. *Contemporary Psychoanalysis, 32*, 509–535.

Bromberg, P. M. (2006a). The analyst's "sel-revelation": Not just permissable but necessary. In *Awakening the dreamer: Clinical journeys* (pp. 128–150). The Analytic Press.

Bromberg, P. M. (2006). *Awakening the dreamer*. The Analytic Press.

Burns, R. (1786). *To a Louse*. Kilmarnock Edition.

Davies, J. M. (2004). Whose bad objects are we anyway?: Repetition and our elusive love affair with evil. *Psychoanalytic Dialogues, 14*, 711–732.

Dickens, C. (1841). *The old curiosity shop*. Chapman & Hall.

Dorpat, T. L. (1996). *Gaslighting, the double whammy, interrogation, and other methods of covert control in psychtherapy and analysis*. J. Aronson.

Edwards, J. K. (2016). *Why are you driving me crazy?: How the dramas of marriage can change you for good*. Langdon Street Press.

Eigen, M. (2002). *Rage*. Wesleyan University Press.

Eigen, M. (2009). *Flames from the unconscious*. Routledge.

Eigen, M. (2011). *Faith and transformation*. Karnac.

Einstein, A., Freud, S., & Gilbert, S. (1939). *Why war? A correspondence bewteen Albert Einstein and Sigmund Freud*. Peace Pledge Union.

Eshel, O. (2019). *The emergence of analytic oneness: Into the heart of psychoanalysis* (Vol. 50). Routledge.

Farber, S. K. (2016). *Celebrate the wounded healer psychotherapist*. Taylor & Francis.

Freud, S. (1912). The dynamics of transference. *Standard Eedition, XII*.

Gerson, S. (2009). When the third is dead: Memory, mourning and witnessing in the aftermath of the Holocaust. *International Journal of Psychoanalysis, 90*, 1341–1357.

Gotthold, J. J., & Sorter, D. (2006). Moments of meeting: An exploration of the implicit dimensioms of empathic immersion in adult and child treatment. *International Journal of Psychoanalytic Self Psychology, 1*(1).

Klein, M. (1937). Love, guilt and reparation. In *Love, guilt and reparation & other works 1921–1945* (pp. 306–343). Delacort Press/Seymour Lawrence.

Loewald, H. W. (1950). Ego and reality. In *Papers on psychoanalysis* (pp. 3–32). Yale University Press.

McNamara, R. S. (2005). *The fog of war. Lessons from the life of Robert S. McNamara*. Rowman & Littlefield.

Mendelsohn, E. (2002). The analyst's bad-enough participation *Psychoanalytic Dialogues, 12*(3), 331–358.

Mitchell, S. A. (2000). *Relationality: From attachment to intersubjectivity*. The Analytic Press.

Searles, H. F. (1959). The effort to drive the other person crazy – an element in the aetiology and psychotherapy of Schizophrenia. *British Journal of Medical Psychology, 32*, 1–18.

Searles, H. F. (1979). The patient as therapist to his analyst (1975). In *Countertransference and related subjects: Selected papers*. International Universities Press.

Sloane, J. A. (2012). The loneliness of the analyst and its alleviation through faith in "O". In B. Willock, L. C. Bohm, & R. C. Curtis (Eds.), *Loneliness and longing: Conscious and unconscious aspects* (pp. 197–209). Routledge.

Sloane, J. A. (2016). Wounded healer – Healing wounder: A personal story. In S. K. Farber (Ed.), *Celebrating the wounded healer psychotherapist: Pain, post-traumatic growth and self-disclosure*. Routledge.

Sloane, J. A. (2019). *A tale of two terrors: Early parental loss and the search for safety*. Paper presented at the IARPP Annual Conference, Tel Aviv.

Spezzano, C. (2007). A home for the mind. *The Psychoanalytic Quarterly, 76*, 1563–1583.

Stern, S. (2019). Airless worlds: The traumatic sequella of identification with parental negation. *Psychoanalytic Dialogues, 29*, 435–450.

Weintrobe, S. (2021). *Psychological roots of the climate crisis: Neoliberal exceptionalism and the culture of uncare*. Bloomsbury Academic.

White, R. W. (1963). *Ego and reality in psychoanalytic theory* (Vol. 3, Issue 3). International Universities Press.

Willock, B. (1986). Narcissistic vulnerability in the hyperaggressive child: The disregarded (unloved, uncared-for) self. *Psychoanalytic Psychology, 3*(1), 59–80.

Willock, B. (1987). The devalued (unloved, repugnant) self – a second facet of narcissistic vulnerability in the aggressive, conduct-disordered child. *Psychoanalytic Psychology, 4*(3), 219–240.

Winnicott, D. W. (1947). Hate in the countertransference. In *Through paediatrics to psychoanalysis*. Hogarth Press.

Winnicott, D. W. (1969). The use of an object. *International Journal of Psycho-Analysis, 50*, 711–716.

13 Striving to Create a Safe Space in an Unsafe World

Responding to Students' Needs in the Days After October 7[1]

Ionas Sapountzis and Amira Simha-Alpern

Introduction

We would like to begin this chapter by expressing our appreciation to the editors, Michelle Flax and J. Gail White, for pointing out that a book with the title *Going-on-Being in Challenging Times* should also attempt to grapple with the horror that unfolded on October 7 in Southern Israel and the untold pain this has caused to millions of Israelis and Palestinians. It is a tragedy that will continue to affect the lives of millions of people for many years to come, people who will have to find a way to go-on-being despite the losses they have experienced and despite everything that has happened to them and everything they have witnessed.

This chapter does not dwell on what happened in Israel that day or on what has followed since then in Gaza, nor does it offer an account of how people in Israel and Gaza are trying to go on despite what has happened. Instead, it offers an account of the effort that was undertaken at the Derner School of Psychology of a small nonprofit private university in the U.S. to respond to the level of anxiety and confusion many students, administrators, and faculty members were experiencing at the time.

With tensions rising on many campuses across the country and with an increasing number of students complaining about the University's response and stating that the letters of support that the University posted failed to sufficiently acknowledge how wounded many students felt, the director of the postgraduate programs at the Derner School of Psychology proposed offering, as a trial, four group processing sessions over a period of two weeks to any interested participant on campus. If participation and interest were deemed to be strong, the administration and the faculty were open to extending the group sessions for several weeks more. Joining her as co-leaders were a faculty member and a postgraduate candidate with considerable experience in leading groups of individuals who have experienced trauma.

Going into the meetings, there were no set agendas and no roadmaps. The co-leaders could not rely on previous practices because, as will become clear later in this chapter, the circumstances were unique. Moreover, they could not anticipate who would attend the meetings as they were designed

DOI: 10.4324/9781003607120-18

as "drop in" group meetings open to the entire University community. The insights shared in this chapter developed over the course of the meetings and mostly in retrospect.

Planning the Meetings

The meetings were announced via listserv to students and faculty across campus. With little time to prepare and without a clear sense of who the participants would be, the group leaders found themselves wondering what these group meetings could offer to the students and what they could do to ensure that the experience would not feel injurious to any participant. Such anxieties are likely to be experienced by all facilitators before the start of group processing meetings in the aftermath of traumatic events. But the brutality of what had happened and the intergenerational traumata that were stirred gave these meetings a sense of the unexpected as well as a sense of risk. Adding to these anxieties were the reports of demonstrations and counter-demonstrations on the campuses of several prestigious universities across the U.S.

After 9/11, the nation was more or less united and the delineation between friend and foe was clearer. By contrast, the events of October 7 were more unsettling. The binary categories that typically serve to contain and process traumatic experiences – good-bad, right-wrong, friend-enemy, ally-suspect – had broken down, melting into an unformulated mush that contributed to a profound sense of confusion and threat. Facilitating a group in which members felt that they could not trust and share their minds with others made these groups intrinsically unsafe. Thus, the possibility that the meetings could escalate to loud confrontations and leave students feeling hurt and unprotected felt very real to the group co-leaders. Nevertheless, that possibility made the need to provide students and faculty members with a space to express themselves and to find support more urgent. As Coates (2003) pointed out in the aftermath of 9/11, being with others, sharing experiences of a traumatic event with others who have also experienced it, mitigates the traumatizing effect of that event. Therefore, creating a space for students to come and share their experiences with each other would serve to offer a holding experience to students who needed that kind of a response from the University.

Prior to the first meeting the co-leaders found themselves discussing the uncertain position they found themselves in, that of wanting to offer something meaningful to the participants, most of whom were likely to be the age of their own children or even younger, and also knowing that there was not much that they could do to help the students. They were also fully aware of the counter-transferential pressures the group meetings were bound to evoke, such as the need to *do something* to allay the pain and to lessen the fears of the participants, as well as to lessen their own depressive anxiety that what they were striving to offer was not likely to be enough. As is often reported in the literature, therapists who work with severely traumatized patients or are thrust into deeply traumatizing situations often experience guilt at not being able to offer something more tangible to these individuals. Although the group leaders were aware of the importance of offering a space for reflection and support to group participants, they were also mindful of the fact that the deep emotional scars the event had caused might have rendered that goal unattainable. They were aware of how hard it would be to create and maintain a reflective space when the pressure to do, to offer something tangible, was likely to be acutely felt.

The Group Meetings

The initiative to offer the groups was generated by experienced clinicians who were not identified with the administration and were not expected to represent the University's line, even though they were faculty employed in the Department of Psychology. They encountered challenges immediately after the invitation to participate in these groups was distributed campus-wide. The original subject line read: "Process Groups for Those Impacted by the War in Israel." The University's administration, however, asked the facilitators to change the subject line to "Process Groups for Those affected by the ongoing Israel-Hamas conflict." This was not a small editorial semantic change. It reflected the administration's understandable hypersensitivity to political correctness and the fear of appearing non-inclusive and insensitive to affected groups. However, the word "ongoing" deflected the focus from the acute events of October 7, nesting it within a historical context. This by itself intensified the already existing concerns of the co-leaders, as it bore the danger of placing the groups in a socio-political arena, which they were carefully trying to avoid. The title was eventually changed to "Process Groups for Those affected by recent events in Israel & Gaza."

The first group meeting was offered at a dormitory so that many undergraduate students could attend. Going into the meeting, the leaders were expecting a large attendance, so there was a sense of disappointment when only one student showed up. There was also a sense of relief at not having to face the prospect of students of different religious and ethnic groups accusing each other, which would have added to the sense of hurt and insecurity that many students were experiencing in those days.

There were several possible reasons for the very low turnout: Lack of enough publicity was one reason, and another was the fact that the meeting took place at a time and day when many students were not on campus. But according to the student who attended the meeting, the main reason was that, for many students, the meeting did not feel safe and as a result, they opted not to come even though they had expressed an interest in attending it. This emotion resonated with the co-leaders as well, who were very mindful themselves of the real risk that the space they were hoping to create would become an "anti-space" (Fromm, 2018) for the group participants, one that would add to their sense of persecution. The feeling of unsafety, though, went beyond the immediate group. As the participant pointed out and as confirmed in conversation with other students in the days after the first meeting, Jewish students felt that the campus was an unsafe place, an experience that mirrored how they felt in the community. They also felt that they could become the targets of hateful projections at any time.

After the first meeting, it occurred to the co-leaders that creating a *safe space* in an unsafe world was an ambitious task. However, doing nothing at the institution with responsibilities for its students' wellbeing was not appropriate either. The group facilitators gathered that perhaps, at best, they could serve as "unobtrusive companions" (Grossmark, 2016) and just tolerate the sense of unsafety all the participants felt, navigating it as best as they could.

The second meeting took place in a classroom. As had happened with the first meeting, several students had expressed their intention to attend, but in the end only four students attended in person and two via Zoom, one of whom had to leave midway through the meeting. The students who attended in person had been in the same cohort the previous year and were quite familiar with each other. They had encouraged each other to attend the meeting and felt supported in sharing their emotions and the sense of injustice they had experienced. They all expressed their appreciation that such a meeting was offered and also that faculty members were willing to make arrangements for them so that they could attend it even though the time conflicted with the time of their evening classes. They also expressed their appreciation for the University's and the School's efforts to recognize how traumatizing the experience had been for them. They compared their experience with that of their peers at other universities and felt deeply appreciative of the effort that was made to reach them and to listen to them.

The third meeting was offered three days later. The composition of this group was very different from that of the first two meetings. It was attended by graduates and members of the postgraduate community who were only loosely actively involved in the University's day-to-day operation. The concerns attendees shared were related to living in their respective communities in the political atmosphere that permeated at that time.

The fourth meeting was again attended by a small number of students. It was the first meeting in which a Muslim student attended, and therefore, it was the first meeting when the leaders had to face the prospect of contrasting views. But even though the students identified strongly with their respective groups and felt victimized by the aggression of the other, the participants were able to listen to each other's experiences and perspectives and were able to understand how wounded the other felt.

Reflecting on These Meetings

These groups were offered early, amid the traumatic events. The much lower than expected student turnout was a disappointment to the leaders. Clearly, the issue of safety was a significant reason for the low level of participation as was the fact that most participants had, directly or indirectly, sought and found support elsewhere in their communities, families, and circle of friends. Over the course of the two weeks of group meetings, more and more details about what transpired on October 7 were uncovered and further acts of aggression were committed that intensified the horror the students felt, rendering these experiences unbearable. The main challenge in running a group at times like this is that the verbal and symbolic sharing that therapists are trained to do can be compromised or close to impossible. With such overwhelming emotions, there was the fear that any attempt to link experiences between members would come under attack (Bion, 1959), preventing the group from becoming a containing experience and from developing a sense of cohesive meaning.

Yet, although it was hard to put experiences into words and to place them in context, and also to find a cohesive narrative or logical explanations, the group meetings did not disintegrate into heated exchanges. As it became apparent from the beginning, by joining these meetings the students were not seeking to develop a better understanding about themselves and how they had been affected. Even though they repeatedly expressed how distraught they felt and wondered how an incident like this could have happened, what they primarily needed from these meetings was not insight so much as the symbolic gesture of the University's being with them and being there for them. They needed the comfort of knowing that others shared their experiences and that the University took the initiative to offer these meetings and recognized the need for faculty members to be accommodating to students who had been affected by the events. Mostly, they needed to know that a place existed for them to turn to if they needed it, a place where they would be listened to without an agenda and without judgment.

According to Eshel (2013), an Israeli analyst herself, the therapist's availability to take in a patient's subjective reality and to be there for them is both an act of being there with them and also of being present for them. She has called such acts "withnessing" and "presencing" (p. 925). Although the co-leaders were not thinking of Eshel's terms at the time, their desire to make themselves present for the students and to take in their reality helped to make the students feel, as several of them reported when contacted after three months to inquire about their experience of these meetings, "very comforted in the face of global attacks." It was important for them to know that the University was mindful of their needs and was offering such meetings, especially as they learned from their peers at other institutions that such initiatives were not available. As one participant said, it was very important for students to "have a safe space to explore feelings about the event with others who are experiencing the global trauma similarly." This sentiment was echoed by another participant who emphasized how "extremely important" it was that these meetings were offered "immediately after the events of October 7th." What mattered therefore – more than the number of students attending the meetings – was the fact that these meeting were offered. In much the same way, what was important was not what happened during these meetings and what kind of insight was generated as much as the fact that these meetings happened at all.

It is important to note that the participants in these groups were all in the U.S., while the events took place in the Middle East. They experienced the events vicariously through the media or reports of family members in Israel, Gaza, or the West Bank. A very important contributor to the intense reactions to the events was an activation of intergenerational collective trauma that was, more often than not, unconsciously transmitted. Many mentioned the experiences of their ancestors during the Holocaust and even the pogroms in East Europe and Russia in the late nineteenth and early twentieth centuries, which they vaguely knew about and rarely directly talked about.

Even though the initial fear that these meetings would lead to intense confrontation and hateful encounters was not realized, and even though the last meeting gave a glimpse of the coexistence that is possible, there was feedback from a student suggesting that the facilitators should have limited participation to those meetings exclusively to Jewish students, and only invite students from different religious and ethnic groups at a later stage. As the student stated,

> In my current state, it is not practical to demand while I am in shock, anger, and mourning to feel compassion for the people who were behind the massacre of my tribe. While I was in the group space, I attempted to do so, and it served a purpose, but it did not meet what was needed at that time. . . . It turned into a debate a bit.

In retrospect, although not intended, the fact that these group meetings were open to students of different ethnic and religious backgrounds, specifically Jewish and Muslim students, did seem to undermine the experience the leaders were seeking to create for the participants as it did impose expectations of acceptance and integration. The students who participated at the last group meeting did an admirable job at trying to do that. This, however, may have been more a reflection of their strong alliance with some of the group leaders and the high regard they had for them than an indication of openness on their part to listen to other perspectives and experiences. Although this was not the intention, the expectation that the students would display a level of integration and acceptance while still grappling with intense emotions of anger and betrayal might have been premature and might have felt as if it were being imposed on them. The specter of having to be accommodating to statements and respectful of views from participants of different faiths and political beliefs could be experienced as disrespectful to the profound emotional wounds of most participants.

Looking back at these meetings, it is clear that they did not help the students to better cope with what happened and what they experienced at the time in and of themselves. But to the 12 participants who attended them, the meetings were an acknowledgment of the faculty's desire to make themselves available to them and for them. Although not realized at the time, it was also important for the faculty members to be able to offer these meetings to the students and in doing that to care for them. It was important for the faculty to convey their concern to the students and to know that their presence and availability had been a source of comfort.

Further Thoughts and Associations

James Foley was an American freelance videographer who was decapitated by the Islamic State (IS) in 2014. His brutal murder was videotaped and posted on the internet. Several years after this event, his mother took the very unusual step of agreeing to meet with her son's executioner against her family's protests. She was not clear as to why she wanted to do so other than feeling the urge to better understand why what happened did happen. She wanted to understand but also to be with her son, an act of symbolic but much needed "withnessing" (Eshel, 2013), as she was certain that he would have approved and, in fact, would have done so himself. To her surprise, when she was brought face-to-face with her son's executioner she found a gentle, soft-spoken young man who in doing what he did had lost everything: Himself, his children, his wife, his hold on life. "We all lost," she said and added, "That's what hate does" (Foley, 2024).

In the very act of seeking to maintain a compassionate stance, the group leaders ran the risk of colluding with hateful statements and attitudes, which could inadvertently stoke further hate. There was the fear that in an effort to be compassionate and accommodating that the group leaders may have ended up encouraging students to become lost in their hate and adding to divisive stereotypes. Such a breakdown in linking would not only make symbolic expressions difficult to entertain but, even worse, would annihilate the object of hate, rendering any attempt to ask for empathy for the "other" to feel like an impossible task. But although there were moments when the students became emotional and found themselves being carried away by their anger, they never became lost. They needed, first and foremost, not a place to vent and to direct their rage and hurt, but a place to be with and to feel listened to by others. They needed to be in a space that they knew others had sought to create for them.

In her foreword to Teju Cole's (2018) evocative book, *Blind Spot*, Siri Humstvedt writes that inside every human eye is a spot where the retina meets the optic nerve that is insensitive to light and thus receives no visual information. And yet, Humstvedt notes, humans do not experience a blind spot in their actual vision because the eye adapts to the blind spot and makes up for it. The eye does not just passively see, in other words, but also creates some of what is seen. In the photos he put together and in the text that accompanied them, Cole focused not on the ophthalmological blind spot Humstvedt was referring to, but on the blind spot that is always present in everything we see. He was focusing on the perceptual and, one might add, the psychological blind spot that is always present – in fact is always created – when one focuses one's gaze on a single aspect. It is the blind spot that is created when one becomes absorbed by what one sees and ends up missing what else is there and what else can be found.

Bion (1963) made a similar point about the psychotherapeutic encounter. The very act of focusing on a particular piece of information to the exclusion of something else, the "selected fact" (p. 39) as he called it, prevents the possibility of focusing on or attending to another fact. Stern (2004) made a similar point as well. The "I," he wrote, cannot see itself. In other words, one cannot see what one does not see while engaged in the act of seeing. These unavoidable experiences of not seeing, which are all part of the human condition, become even more pronounced and blinding when emotions and cultural norms are involved. And, one might add, when there is a history of trauma. When that is the case, when one's reality and sense of being are overshadowed by what has happened to them, not seeing and not reflecting are not as much blind spots as acts of self-preservation, of protecting oneself from what has been experienced. Being lost may be a way to cope with all that has been lost. It is not clear how one comes back when one has experienced a profound loss or trauma. The body keeps the score, writes van der Kolk (2015), but so does the mind. The issue, therefore, is not the impossibility of coming back to what was and what has been, but how one goes on in spite of what happened and what was experienced.

Sometimes – many times – the force of what happened makes the effort to integrate and understand feel unreachable or irrelevant. When thinking links are broken, unshakable absoluteness and overgeneralization reign. There is no differentiation, distinctions are erased, and nuances are flattened. This was how Hamas-Palestinian-evil became an undifferentiated entity on one hand and Israel-occupier-evil on the other. Facilitators' attempts to facilitate differentiation, to usher "mind-deadness" into "mindedness" (Amir, 2023) can be futile. Nevertheless, one must keep doing that, especially when what happened feels so overwhelming and annihilating. One must keep striving, knowing that often, what one can hope for is, to paraphrase Bion (1979), to make the best out of a bad situation.

What the group meetings sought to achieve in the aftermath of October 7 was to make the best out of an impossible, indeed horrifying, situation. The participants were not the disturbed individuals Bion was referring to in his paper. They were young adults at a small university who, like the group leaders themselves, were trying to cope with a very disturbing reality. Striving to create a space for them and to listen to them was the best the group leaders could do at the time for these young individuals and for themselves.

Note

1   The authors wish to thank Ms. Rakefet Einav-Grunberg, LMSW, for her contribution to this endeavor.

References

Amir, D. (2023, December 20). *If a tree falls alone in the forest, it should make a sound. We deserve to hear.* https://www.betipulnet.co.il/particles/If_a_tree_falls_alone

Bion, W. R. (1959). Attacks on linking. *International Journal of Psychoanalysis, 40,* 308–315.

Bion, W. R. (1963). *Elements of psychoanalysis.* Heinemann. (Reprinted Jason Aronson, 1979)

Bion, W. R. (1979). Making the best of a bad job. In *Clinical seminars and four papers* (1987, pp. 247–257). Fleetwood Press.

Coates, S. (2003). Introduction: Trauma and human bonds. In S. Coates, J. Rosenthal, & D. Schecter (Eds.), *September 11: Trauma and human bonds* (pp. 1–14). Analytic Press.

Cole, T. (2018). *Blind spot.* Random House.

Eshel, O. (2013). Patient-analyst "witness": On analytic "presencing," passion and compassion in states of breakdown, despair and deadness. *Psychoanalytic Quarterly, LXXXII*(4), 925–963.

Foley, D. (2024, February 10). 'We all lost. That's where hatred leads': 10 years after her son was beheaded, Diane Foley on why she met one of his killers. *The Guardian.* https://www.theguardian.com/global/2024/feb/10/diane-foley-mother-james-foley-beheaded-islamic-state-interview

Fromm, G. M. (2018). *Taking the transference, reaching towards dreams; Clinical studies in the intermediate area.* Routledge.

Grossmark, R. (2016). Psychoanalytic companioning. *Psychoanalytic Dialogues, 26*(6), 98–712.

Humstvedt, S. (2018). Foreword. In T. Cole (Ed.), *Blind spot* (pp. ix–xvi). Random House.

Stern, D. B. (2004). The eye sees itself: Dissociation, enactment and the achievement of conflict. *Contemporary Psychoanalysis, 40,* 197–237.

Van der Kolk, B. (2015). *The body keeps the score: Brain, mind and body in the healing of trauma.* Penguin Books.

14 Going-on-Being in Two Cultures

Nepantla – In-Between the First and Second Generation of Latinx Immigrant, Higher Education, Scholarship Students

Helen Quiñones

If one were to visualize the initial journey of an immigrant one can imagine seeing a familiar port or city receding as you embark by land or sea to a destination that will bring safety, solace, hope and opportunity. As the distance between that which is familiar and that which is yet to be, widens an undefinable space is created. Upon arrival this space can represent an in-between state of being – one that holds the world view of the home country and that of the new land. The Aztec Indians of the 16th century called this state of being in between as Nepantla. Duran (1984) as cited in Perez and Castany (2011) told the following story that illustrates the state of being in between two cultures.

> A Jesuit priest was angry when the natives whom he had converted to Christianity celebrated a wedding using rituals to honor their deities rather than the Christian God. A native confidante consoled him by pointing out that this was just a moment of Nepantla where the old demon gods were honored along with the Christian deity.

During this in-between state the clashing religious views were placed side by side. The story of Nepantla applies well to a more contemporary immigrant experience. An immigrant does live in between two cultures. Like the Aztec Indians they initially maintain their dual identity in recognizable ways that remind them of their home country. For example, in my childhood neighborhood composed predominantly of working class, Latinx, first generation immigrants, the local bodega not only carried Caribbean produce, but also became a place to share the neighborhood news. Credit was extended based on an unspoken honor system. These ethnic neighborhoods provided a cultural transitional space. In this space the mother country is held in mind through the familiarity with certain objects, traditions, routines of daily living. Akhtar (1999) describes the importance of this transitional space and objects in the following:

> the distance between two lands (two mothers – "the mother of symbiosis" and the "mother of separation") is also bridged by ethnic ties in

DOI: 10.4324/9781003607120-19

the new country, international phone calls, and listening to one's native music. These serve as "transitional objects" (Winnicott, 1953) and help bring what has become externally "too far" a bit nearer.

This dual identity becomes more difficult to sustain as the developmental cycle of the family proceeds. Families who foster educational ambition or have marketable skills leave the neighborhood. As they walk into the mainstream of America, sustaining their biculturalism becomes more difficult. They are faced with the challenge of acculturating to the adopted country while sustaining their connection to the native country. Continuing with the metaphor of Nepantla one can visualize an immigrant traveler entering an in-between space which is ambiguous, complex yet moving and vibrant. It is in this in-between space that the immigrant faces the challenge of developing an identity that accepts the new culture while retaining their cultural roots.

Given certain conditions the psychoanalyst can create an 'in-between' space where this duality of self-representation can be sustained. A self-representation that doesn't negate aspects of their identity that temporarily 'live' in different cultural contexts. Akhtar (1999) recommends that a psychoanalyst who works cross culturally needs to: maintain cultural neutrality, that is, remain equidistant from the native and adopted culture; recognize one's own cultural stereotypes; and adopt a developmental stance that focuses on the fulfillment of innate capacities. These guidelines are an adaptation of key psychoanalytic praxis-neutrality, analysis of countertransference, and self-actualization.

There is yet another principle underlying contemporary psychoanalytic praxis. It is related to extracting knowledge from the intimacy that is created between patient and analyst. It is the vibrant here and now experiences that can capture the complex facets of a cross-cultural encounter. An encounter that contains both subjectivities that are caught in the relational matrix of analyst and patients. The value of this ontological perspective is reflected in the following statement by Rosemarie Perez (Perez et al., 1996, p. 18):

Aside from our common and fundamental belief in the unconscious . . . we all have at our disposal the manifold experience of the ongoing co-participant connection with our patients. Whether we choose at any given moment to address this interaction at a conscious, pre-conscious or unconscious level, the evidence now shows that these human co-experiences are capable within themselves, of generating a self-sufficient empirical field of systemic inquiry.

In my work I have shifted to working in the analytic space that is defined by the intersubjective therapeutic experiences. As you will see in the subsequent clinical material, entering the cultural and psychic space of intersubjectivity can facilitate the recognition of culturally significant objects that decrease stranger anxiety. It can also bring to subconscious awareness the affect missing in empathic failures.

It is by working with both subjectivities that a dual narrative emerged in the clinical work with Latinx, youths attending a prestigious higher education university. In the following clinical vignettes, the narrative of this clinician – also Latinx – is contained in the reveries that occurred spontaneously during key moments in the treatment. The narrative of the student is revealed in the material that follows the analysis of the reverie.

In the first two vignettes, the reveries occurred during the initial phase of engaging the student in treatment; the third and final reverie emerged as both I and patient worked through the issue of familial ties. Each vignette consists of the student's presenting complaint, cultural history pertinent to the symptoms, and the clinician's reveries. Each will be followed by a discussion section that includes the self-analysis of the reveries.

Clinical Material

Prior to the vignettes, I would like to start with a brief personal history that helps elucidate my perspective as a bicultural analyst. My personal search for a bicultural identity began with a course assignment by a psychology professor in my second year of a master's program. The students were asked to address the question – Who Am I? I was puzzled by the question and wanted to fully represent myself as a Puerto Rican and an American. I found myself researching the history of Puerto Rico, its folklore, and customs, trying to affirm my heritage. Over the course of childhood, my parent maintained our connection to Puerto Rico via summer visits to my grandparents' home and my aunt's farm. However, as I went through a long educational journey in New York City – master's in social work, doctorate in psychology, and psychoanalysis – this bicultural identity was sometimes lost, rediscovered, and lost again. In fact, there was a period in my life when I hid my Puerto Rican background and feigned being a White American. I remember the emptiness of disassociating a significant part of myself. I learnt then, what continues to be my credo – only by claiming all aspects of an identity can you truly go-on-being fully yourself.

The three students included in this presentation – Miguel, Socorro, and Maria – are Latinx and come from families who were economically stable in their country of origin and region of the Mexico, Columbia, S.A. and Los Angeles, California. They were awarded full scholarships based on merit. Their immigration was not based on economic or political survival. Instead, they were motivated by intellectual curiosity and the dream of becoming who they want to be relationally and professionally. Two of the three students were also motivated to give back to their communities at home.

Vignette 1: Miguel

Miguel was a young adult Mexican man, who had married before migrating to N.Y. He presented with symptoms of anxiety that were increasingly interfering with his sleep and academic performance. The anxiety was initially ascribed to his repeated failures in his scientific experiments which consisted of regenerating brain cells in simple organisms. He feared that his repeated failures could lead to his expulsion from the program. I initially reassured him by stating that other students with the same scientific zeal had also experienced repeated experimental failures but were not expelled. I added that failed experiments were not equated with failure in scientific competence. I offered this reassurance and suggested that perhaps he obtain comparative feedback from the other students who may also be experiencing similar rates of failure. As Miguel and I spoke of repeated failures I remembered:

> *Reverie* – My own failure at not passing a licensing examination. I initially felt intense shame and defeat that made it difficult to recover my self-confidence. Therefore, I decided to join a study group of doctoral students who had taken diverse preparatory courses. As we went over the sample tests, I recognized that each of us had a different way to analyze the sample tests. I wasn't just memorizing the answers, I was also learning how to analyze them differently. I was drawn to how another person not only thought but also developed different strategies. I regained the confidence to take the test again, this time, successfully.

After this reverie I suggested to Miguel that he form a study group with his peers. He rejected this idea as he felt it could label him as a student who needs academic remedial support. I recognized that I had made a mistake offering a solution that was acceptable in my social context but not that which was appropriate for Miguel.

To explore an alternative way of supporting Miguel, I asked him to compare his learning experiences in his hometown in Mexico to those in the current department. He remembered the weekly meetings held at the main campus where his peers would share their research along with a beer. He became increasingly nostalgic as he recognized that there was little opportunity to collaborate with his current peers who were also spending long hours alone in the laboratory. The nostalgia led him to recognize that he was lonely in a way that "he had never been before". He also felt lonely in his marriage. As we continued exploring the loneliness, it became apparent that he was ashamed about needing support from his spouse as well as his academic colleagues. This vulnerability threatened his image of a man who could stand alone, that is, supporting others without needing support. As he continued working in treatment, he came to view independence differently. I was once told by an analyst that you can only be as independent as you are dependent. Utilizing this analytic wisdom, I asked him to look at independence as interdependence. As an example from his own life, I added that he contributed to his wife's ambition of working with a dance troupe by his move to N.Y. and she in turn was supplementing his student salary. They both were supporting each other's dreams by depending on each other in different ways. By the end of our work the shame that had diminished his sense of manhood abated along with his symptoms of anxiety.

My initial reaction was a quick solution to alleviate his sense of shame elicited by his failed experiments. However, I failed to place this idea into his social context which was that of a first-year student in a scientific department in a prestigious school. In this highly competitive environment, a peer study group can be perceived as a form of remediation rather than expanding your analytic ability. I was culturally mis-attuned. However, I was attuned to the cultural expectations of a recently married, Latino man. It was with these expectations in mind that I reframed independence as a mutually collaborative process. In essence depending on another, be it spouse or colleague, didn't mean that he was failing as a man.

Given the significance of loneliness, I researched different types of loneliness. I found that loneliness is felt when surrounded by ingenuine companions (Fromm-Reichman, 1990). It is also experienced when an individual fears depending on another (Searles, 1965). It is these two sources of loneliness that Miguel was experiencing within the context of the immigrant experience.

The transition from present situation to his cultural past occurred when I failed to provide an effective source of academic support. This inquiry into his academic past in his country of origin brought back what he was missing in the current situation – the comradeship that compensated for the solitary times of research. Their fraternity-like meet-up was also a playful way of ending each academic week. What was captured by the nostalgia was his astutely recognizing his loneliness. As we followed the thread of loneliness we shifted to a more significant aspect of his identity – the balance between independence and dependence. It was reframing the relationship between independence and dependence and how it related to his sense of manhood that helped him recapture his confidence and competence.

Towards the end of treatment Miguel did have successful scientific trials and started a department-wide soccer team. On the playing field you not only need to collaborate, but all are equal in achieving the same goal.

Vignette 2: Socorro

Socorro was a 23-year-old, single woman from East L.A. who was earning her master's in comparative literature. Her parents owned a multifamily home in which several families pooled their income to afford the property. Socorro and her family had lived in the poor neighborhoods of Los Angeles, and she could still "remember the helicopters" that would monitor the streets. As she spoke of her family, she highlighted the pride the family felt when they were able to move to a better neighborhood.

At the time she sought treatment she felt inhibited during classroom discussions. She remained silent, not expressing her ideas for fear that others wouldn't be able to "understand her point of view". I explored the inhibition by asking if she had had other academic experiences in which she was able to participate. She described two such experiences. The first was when she was selected for a leadership program by a teacher who mirrored her innate capacities and valued what she said. The support from this leadership program helped her succeed in both middle school and high school. The second experience that had been helpful to her was a college-based religious group. As she described the group, I realized that it was based on pastoral counseling. The sessions consisted of reflections of biblical excerpts which were applied to problems of everyday living, such as alcoholism and relational impasses. As she spoke, I knew that I could not replicate this model of healing, having only a high school level knowledge of the Bible. I asked her directly if she was hoping to find a pastoral counselor. This was so. Wishing to engage her I offered a psychological facsimile of pastoral counseling – she could bring to her session biblical statements that were selected by her, and we could discuss their meaning for her. She didn't accept the idea so I then suggested that she return to the University services to explore if they could provide her with a referral to a pastoral counselor before deciding to continue treatment with me. Later that night I found myself reviewing the session and felt guilty for the abruptness of my actions. As I attempted to process the session I had the following reverie.

Reverie – My now deceased aunt guided her life by daily reflections of Bible readings. She was a fervent believer and for a while hoped that I would convert to the religious sect she attended. She brought this up frequently until I stated that if our relationship depended on my conversion, I wouldn't be able to continue it. However, neither one of us wanted a rift in our relationship. Given our wish to sustain our connection we negotiated a way to be together. I listened to her interpretations which were inspirational, but I also added my way of understanding the life issues being addressed. Once this impasse was resolved we continued teaching and learning from each other. We had found a way of coping with life's challenges – religiously and psychologically. In this way we were able to share such complex discussions as gender identity.

This reverie gave me a new perspective on the enactment. The motivation behind the referral back to the counseling center was not based on an unrecognized intolerance but on the fear that the patient's religious fervor wouldn't allow me to connect with her as a psychologist. It was a similar relational impasse I had reached with my aunt.

Socorro did return to my practice, giving me a second chance to engage her. This time I decided to launch the therapeutic endeavor with a simple query: your relationship with God is. It was a basic question that could be answered by both of us. The treatment did begin with her journaling biblical excerpts and her reflections. Once she found a community church which sponsored a youth group, she transitioned in the sessions to speaking directly about herself. Over the two years that we worked together I discovered that religion: prevented her from overusing alcohol in college; helped her forgive her parents for the tragic, early childhood accident that had left her partially disabled; and fueled her belief in herself. In treatment we worked through a main issue: the anger at her parents for failing to supervise her around dangerous machinery. In retrospect I recognized that she needed to know that she could forgive her parents before fully confronting the anger intrinsic to the trauma that had left her permanently, albeit, partially disabled.

As with Miguel there was a transition to the educational experiences in her neighborhood home of Los Angeles. This time her memory helped her recapture the belief in her shown by a teacher. This belief in herself became more constant as she worked through her trauma while simultaneously becoming a teacher's assistant with a professor who trusted her academic and administrative skills. The recognition of her academic capacities, along with her working through the trauma resulted in her sustaining a good feeling about herself. A feeling that when necessary was refueled by her belief in a God who "always believed in her".

By the end of her treatment and the master's program, Socorro was presenting her ideas in the classroom and professional conferences. She had found her voice.

Vignette 3: Maria

Maria was a young adult South American woman who entered therapy because of depressive symptoms and feelings of academic inadequacy despite having successfully completed her first year of a doctoral program. She was in a long-distance relationship with her boyfriend who had migrated with her but was living in a different county. Shortly after beginning treatment the pandemic hit New York City, at which time she migrated north to join her boyfriend before the borders closed. She felt relieved of the loneliness she had been experiencing but was ambivalent about her decision to stay in the USA. As treatment proceeded, she shared what had prompted the initial decision to immigrate. She began the educational history by recalling her experiences as a medical student in an impoverished area of her country.

As a medical student, she had found it overwhelming to treat patients in a hospital system that didn't have the necessary equipment or staff to meet the needs of the patient. She felt frustrated and helpless at her failed attempts to persuade the overburdened resident-in-charge to respond to her patient's medical needs. During one of her rotations, she was monitoring a newborn who began having breathing difficulties. She repeatedly asked the resident to minister the necessary medications. Unfortunately, the newborn died while she waited.

This theme of being responsible for another's life reverberated in her family as well. At home she oversaw the medical and mental health needs of her sister and her father. The mother was described as withdrawn. Maria posited that the mother's withdrawal had been triggered by the burden of having complete financial responsibility while the father recuperated from a life-threatening cardiac crisis. The brother was also described as distant from the family as he pursued a demanding career in another part of the country. Neither her family nor her medical patients had enough support to adequately address their needs. Feeling alone and overwhelmed both at home and in the hospital, she became increasingly depressed and considered dropping out of medical school. She was dissuaded by the program director who considered her one of his best students. It was at this juncture that she began her first course of psychotherapy. Upon completion of her medical studies the clinician recommended that she pursue her education abroad.

By migrating she did escape temporarily the family's overdependence on her. This lasted until the Covid wave hit her hometown in South America. It was at this point that survival guilt converged with her wish to separate. She knew first-hand the lack of medical services which were further curtailed by Covid clinic closures. She also knew her family's limited capacity to support each other. She was at yet another crossroad – does she go home without knowing when she would be able to return to her studies and boyfriend or does she remain? In the analysis I felt as though I was holding the hand of someone (Maria) who in turn was holding the hand of someone else (her family) hanging over a precipice. I couldn't rescue Maria, nor could she do so for her family. It was at this point that I had the following reverie.

Reverie – At 22, I was standing on the railroad platform waiting for the train that would take my family to Florida. I stood steadfast in my decision to remain in New York where I had been awarded a full scholarship to attend an Ivy League school. In the excitement of this opportunity, I underestimated the pain of this separation, until I found myself waving goodbye to my mother, brother, sister, and dog as they entered the railroad car. They took off to find a new life in Florida and I took off to follow an ineffable dream.

It was this reverie that brought back to me the pain of separation felt when you leave your family to follow a dream that is uniquely your own. I had also felt envious of Maria's closeness with her family. It contrasted with the distancing that had occurred between myself and my family. However, the reverie helped restore the empathy needed to recognize the intensity of her guilt and the pain experienced by her family (and mine). I remained at this relational impasse until I asked myself – does Maria need to sacrifice her strong connection to her family to fulfill her ambitions?

I recognized then that the only way to alleviate Maria's survival guilt was to increase the emotional (not physical) presence in her family. I hoped that she could continue going-on-being with her boyfriend and her studies if she could sustain the family to the best of her ability. Fortunately, her boyfriend shared his wish to continue his studies while being supportive of each other and their prospective families.

Subsequently, Maria and her boyfriend (independent of the treatment) promised each other that they wouldn't leave unless there was a dire family emergency. It was a promise they were able to keep for the remainder of the pandemic. Additionally, I helped Maria develop strategies that would increase her emotional presence across two countries. This included sending N95 masks, keeping the family informed about CDC recommendations, mobilizing her medical colleagues to monitor her father's cardiac condition, and finding a psychiatrist that would provide her sister with the necessary medications. I don't believe that either Maria or I had recognized the extent of her influence in the medical community of her hometown. The survival guilt was alleviated as she took care of her family in the same way she would have if she were home. As she mobilized resources to care for her family, she also developed study strategies for her oral examinations which she passed with distinction. She had taken care of her family without abandoning herself.

Maria ended treatment as the pandemic dissipated. During the final session, she shared with me the lesson she had learnt from our work. She recognized that she had hidden her needs behind those of her family. In essence she could not face her own fears, or her relational ambivalences, in the fog created by the needs of the family. In this fog she not only lost sight of her own needs but also the recognition of her capacity to mobilize the network she had established in a self-made consulting group. In essence she could not feel her needs or her capacities. The pandemic, in this case, provided physical boundaries (border closures) that prevented her from escaping the guilt of self-fulfillment.

The treatment had also awakened in me the wish to involve myself further with my family. We both had learnt a lesson – one can establish an emotional presence that securely holds our connection to the family while fulfilling our ambitions. To this date Maria and her husband live in New York City while she continues her doctoral studies.

Conclusion

The cross-cultural work that led to recognizing the patients' past experiences in their country of origin did help identify what was missing in the immediate social environment of the adoptive country (Bhabha, 1994). By contrasting his peer group in Mexico with those in his science lab, Miguel felt the nostalgia and loneliness inherent to losing supportive, collegial companions. Hearing about Socorro's past experiences in the leadership programs of East Los Angeles led to my recognizing the importance of the teachers' belief in her when she couldn't believe in herself. Maria's personal history revealed the familial and systemic burden of rescuing another when there are insufficient resources. It is by eliciting their past experiences in their country of origin within the context of their adoptive country that their symptoms became part of a greater narrative. A narrative of loneliness, belief in oneself, and hiding behind a family. These narratives opened the door to the clinical work described in the vignettes.

My clinical work with these students also taught me lessons that emanated from each of their narratives. These were the importance of recognizing the intense empowerment (both religious and psychological) that is needed to heal the wounds of early childhood physical trauma, that belonging depends on equality, and that the optimal distance for the family (Akhtar, 1999, p. 85) is one that maintains the familial connection without losing oneself.

In conclusion, by entering the transitional space of Nepantla where temporality is condensed one can travel many years into the past while in the present and the future. By reflecting on one's own earlier self-experiences, one can pass onto the next generation the hope and perhaps the next step needed to continue actualizing their own dreams.

References

Akhtar, S. (1999). *Immigration identity-turmoil, treatment and transformation*. Rowman & Littlefield Publishers Inc.

BhaBha (1994) as cited in Beltsou, J. (2016). *Immigration & psychoanalysis*. Routledge.

Duran, D. (1984). As cited in Perez, T. R., & Castany, B. (Eds.). (2011). Tierras Prometidas. De La Colonia De la Independencia. *Nepantla, Una Aproximacion al Termino* Barcelona, Centro para la Edicion De Los Classicos Espanoles. UAB, p. 375.

Fromm-Reichman, F. (1990). Loneliness. *Contemporary Psychoanalysis, 26*, 305–329.

Perez Foster, R., Moskowitz, M., Javier, R. A., & Pérez-Foster, R. (Eds.). (1996). *Reaching Across boundaries of culture and class-widening the scope of psychotherapy*. Jason Aranson Inc.

Searles, H. (1965). *Collected papers on schizophrenia and related subjects*. Hogarth Press.

Winnicott, D. W. (1953). transitional objects and transitional phenomena – a study of the first not-me possession. *International Journal of Psychoanalysis, 34*, 89–97.

15 Beyond Neutrality

The Role of Political Beliefs in the Therapeutic Relationship

John O'Leary

Introduction

Political polarization has been with us for years. In the therapeutic space, political polarization is the uninvited guest who refuses to leave, turning each session into a tightrope walk between therapeutic alliance and personal bias, and pressing psychoanalysis to redefine its boundaries. Political polarization is exacerbated by our media, and has wrought some terrible consequences, such as half the country hating the other half. How can we go-on-being both individually and collectively when we are divided, angry, and convinced (no matter which side you are on) that we are right? Some have predicted the outbreak of a civil war. In the least, the recent elections have stirred up feelings of fear, pessimism, and what is seen as political revenge.

That we are in an historic period in need of resilience, endurance, and going on is not debatable. This country's divisiveness has taken its toll on *psychoanalysis by disenfranchising millions of our own citizens from the full benefits of psychoanalytic healing in part because most of us analysts are attached to liberalism and its attendant beliefs* (Duarte et al., 2014; Silander et al. 2020; Tublin, 2017). This adherence makes it difficult to resonate to opposing beliefs and leaves a great many ordinary folks feeling misunderstood and alienated. Animosity becomes the default position.

Ideological opinion within the profession is significantly more left-oriented compared to the broader populace, highlighting a potential incongruence between psychotherapists and their clientele (Saad, 2021). A substantial ideological difference between client and therapist could be a precursor to negative therapeutic outcomes (Berzins, 1977; Beutler, 1972). Disparities in clinician-client attributes – encompassing ethnicity, socio-economic status (SES), and religious/spiritual beliefs – have been extensively scrutinized, yielding mixed results on therapeutic alliances and clinical outcomes (Silander et al., 2020). Contemporary demographic analyses indicate a sustained conservative inclination among the U.S. population, though liberal viewpoints have seen recent augmentations (Saad, 2021; Whitesides, 2017).

Unfortunately, our profession has given the topic scant attention (Duarte et al., 2014 are notable exceptions to this general silence). These

DOI: 10.4324/9781003607120-20

authors have made a strong case that our universities, and especially our psychology faculties, are overwhelmingly liberal with the consequence that nearly everyone loses. Faculties lose because their teaching, research, and curriculum are slanted towards a liberal ideology. The mission should be about striving for truth: a balanced truth. Students lose because when they are not exposed to other views they fail to develop an open posture towards the wisdom of a major constituency. Worst of all, they come out of their extended training experience even more convinced of their moral righteousness.

Political Talk

Political talk is fraught because it taps into some of our most deeply held values and stirs very strong feelings. Tublin (Aibel, 2017) argues that meaningful political dialogue is near impossible. Because of its intensity, political speech in our sessions requires greater scrutiny and reflection. This chapter emphasizes the importance of building trust through inclusiveness, and through a commitment to a fuller range of diversity. It suggests that there is a new trend for many in the profession to talk about politics freely in their sessions. Karen Starr (2018) is a case in point. Her patient, Theresa (24), is secretly dating a young Muslim man whom her parents regard as a terrorist, a man who could only be imagined to be a coercive and controlling partner – despite never having met him. Theresa, herself comes from a very authoritarian family where all the men bully the women. From the get-go, the analyst struggles with the following questions:

> [is] it our responsibility to bracket our subjective experience and political beliefs in order to allow our patients' voices to emerge, or is it in fact our responsibility to speak up to give voice to that which is not being said? Given our position of influence, what do we have to teach our patients about the value of political engagement, and, if we allow ourselves to be influenced, what might we learn from them?
>
> (Starr, 2018, p. 392)

In the course of this treatment the therapist is of the mind that the patient is partly in collusion in allowing this "secret" to stand. According to Starr, "Theresa's lack of political consciousness seems almost deliberate; I suspect it's her way of protecting herself from venturing too far from her family." An unexpected visit from the patient's mother to the therapist's office has the mother screaming, "radical Muslim extremists are a threat to our safety to our country. . . . I don't want you to be in an oppressive relationship. Does he let you talk?" The daughter answers, "he lets me talk. He is the only man who lets me talk." This is the only time the mother has heard anything directly from this daughter about the boyfriend. The author does not share the finale of the story, but we learn much about how an important dialogue begins.

Origins of Modern-Day Polarization

The American sociopolitical landscape is gripped by an intense state of polarization which has led to animosity between millions of people holding differing political ideologies. This division has become so pronounced that an increasing number of individuals would even sever family ties over opposing beliefs (Whitesides, 2017). The disturbing events of the assault on the nation's capital offer a stark illustration of the political violence resulting from this polarization.

The history of modern-day polarization in North America can be traced back to the Civil Rights Act of 1964, with the southern Dixiecrats' departure from the Democratic Party. This initiated a process of homogenization along party lines that endures today (Klein, 2021). Central to the development of polarization is the role of race, along with other contributing factors such as conservative religious influences, the decline of union power, the emergence of heavily partisan news networks, shifting demographics (e.g., urbanized Democrats and rural Republican), and the influence and the ubiquity of social media (Klein, 2021; Pinsker, 2022).

These political transformations have led to stagnation and impasse, as political parties become increasingly dogmatic and reluctant to compromise. Party identity has evolved into a crucial concern, prompting many individuals to vote for their party even when it conflicts with their personal interests, in part, driven by the dynamics of the "culture wars" (Jouet, 2017; Klein, 2021). The "culture wars" was a counter movement launched by the right after the "licentious" 1960s to bring us back to a period in which male, Christian, heterosexual, middle-class family values could be embraced again. The contemporary branches of this development have led (on the far-right) to the notion of replacement theory: "the assertion that demographic changes are causing long-established cultural, racial, and ethnic groups to be downgraded to the status of displaced minorities in their own homeland" (Walle, 2023).

In this environment, empathy atrophies and othering proliferates. The repercussions of these political shifts are significant, with party membership transforming from a marginal concern to a defining aspect of one's identity. Consequently, political identity has become a paramount facet of many people's lives (Iyengar & Krupenkin, 2018; Klein, 2021).

One immediate and potentially catastrophic factor is the role of war. The Gaza-Israeli war is a case in point. Because of the provocations of several proxy states, and the insistence of Israel on wiping out Hamas, the war has the potential to explode into a regional, large-scale war.

The support for then-President Biden's pro-Israel stance diminished within the Democratic Party, as shown by a Times/Sienna poll taken in December 2023 (Weisman et al., 2023). This decline in support is largely due to the influence of younger voters, left-leaning individuals, and many independents who usually back the Democratic candidate. In contrast, Republican support for Israel remains high, nearly 70%, with almost unanimous backing from Evangelicals. Only recently has there been a diminishment in Republican support. At any rate, this new situation has led to internal conflicts within the Democratic Party, including increased acts of antisemitism. It has become a case of liberals clashing with other liberals, which blurs traditional distinctions. New party configurations could encourage bipartisan cooperation. Such intra-party discussions could potentially reduce overall political polarization.

Two Conservative Patients

Within my practice, I am currently working with five patients who identify as Republicans. I shall present vignettes of patients Katelyn and Anya, illustrating the ways in which political affiliation permeates the therapeutic relationship.

Katelyn, a long-term patient, ultimately terminated treatment due to her unwavering pro-life stance. A former nun, she harbored vehement anti-abortion sentiments that only intensified upon discovering my support for Biden, whom she denounced as a "murderer." I brought up Biden without conscious intent, when the political parties were still having primaries. I carelessly thought she already knew my party affiliation and could have easily guessed my political choices. Katelyn had met me first as a professor when I was teaching a very politically oriented class. Katelyn's recent affiliation with an ultra-conservative group, fervently opposed to abortion, further exacerbated this tension. When my support for Biden was inadvertently revealed, Katelyn perceived me as complicit in the act of taking unborn lives.

Reflecting on our therapeutic process, I recognize that an enactment or impasse emerged, as Katelyn's political beliefs veered further to the right. *Unbeknownst to me, my detachment from her and her politics echoed her early childhood experience of painful dismissal by her mother, who perceived her, in Katlyn's words, as a drama queen. Personally, I was so lost in trying to rescue our relationship – during that most difficult session – that I failed to see my role in this enactment.* I remain stung by my trauma surrounding this patient. I take most of the responsibility for that failing. Going forward, I cannot imagine taking on this subject of political difference without the patient's permission.

Anya, a 55-year-old Catholic divorcee, sought therapy to help mend her relationship with her daughter, who held vastly different political beliefs. A staunch Trump supporter, Anya grappled with her daughter's Goth-like demeanor, replete with tattoos, a nose ring, and purple hair. The daughter lived with her boyfriend 60 miles outside New York and had severed all communication with her mother. She couldn't bear sharing the same space. Though anguished, Anya persisted in her political and religious messaging until recent shifts in the therapeutic process softened her approach, eliciting a reciprocal response from her daughter. The principal strategy I started employing with her was a posture of active listening. I summarized in my own words what I heard her saying and conveyed the major feeling she was having about the topic in question. I did not challenge her premises, or her political content even though I often wanted to. I sometimes used an approach articulated by Feldman (Aibel, 2017) where I invited Anya to collaborate with me as to "How should we talk about this?" We decided together how to proceed. *Anya attributed this transformation in her relationship to her daughter to therapy and began expressing curiosity about my political beliefs, mirroring my own interest in hers.* Concurrently, she displayed a renewed interest in dating and reconnecting with old friends, as well as being able to share her anxieties about aging and loneliness – topics with which I could readily empathize.

In presenting Katelyn's and Anya's brief narratives, I aim to underscore their inherent humanity and complexity, cautioning against the perils of stereotyping. Furthermore, I remain cognizant of the fragile nature of our therapeutic alliance with politically different patients, many of whom are likely to perceive the majority of psychologists and analysts as aligned with the opposition (Silander et al., 2020; Tublin, 2017).

The Psychotherapy Community

The political uniformity of the psychotherapy community is a problem! As Tublin argues:

> It reinforces the tendency to pathologize right-leaning ideology and the inclination to merely tolerate right-wing positions rather than to work to contextualize and respect them. . . .
>
> Can the analyst dig in and truly appreciate, truly recognize the web of attachments and the organizing principles of a "conservative" subjectivity and honoring, the person's love of country, of tradition, and religious devotion?
>
> (508)

Tublin (2017) continues:

> Right-leaning patients are justified in feeling the disapproval and distaste of their left-leaning analyst. . . . At a minimum the right leaning patient cannot expect the comfort of left-leaning twinship that the more common urban left-leaning patient is free to anticipate.
>
> (506–507)

The Shift Towards Political Disclosure

The noticeable shift in clinical practice towards more openly discussing political beliefs with patients is a marked departure from previous approaches within analytic psychotherapy. Therapists of most stripes emphasized neutrality and avoided political topics, as they were seen as potentially damaging to the therapeutic alliance (Farber, 2018). However, a recent study by Nili Solomonov and colleagues (involving 604 self-described Democrats and Republicans from 50 states) found that most therapists and patients disclosed their political stances to each other (Solomonov & Barber, 2018). Patients who perceived political similarity with their therapists reported stronger therapeutic alliances, more political disclosure, and found the political discussion to be useful. The editor, Barry Farber of the *Journal of Clinical Psychology*, has reported:

> Based on my own practice and from speaking to many other practitioners, politics (broadly defined) have seeped into many psychotherapeutic sessions, perhaps in an unprecedented fashion – or perhaps in a way reminiscent only of the unrest and divisions that defined much of the 1960s.
>
> (Farber, 2018, p. 717)

When Our Ideologies Get in the Way

Therapists who adopt a relational approach may find it especially challenging to establish a strong therapeutic alliance with conservative Republican patients – as political differences can create a barrier to the development of trust and mutual understanding. Relationists, while seeing themselves as hyper-alert to their own biases and avoiding any pretense of neutrality, often advocate for social justice causes, such as supporting immigrants (Akhtar, 2010; Tummala-Narra et al., 2018); the Black Lives Matter movement (Gaztambide, 2021); as well as promoting accessibility to healthcare for marginalized groups (Altman, 2010). They have also sought to challenge traditional binary distinctions, such as queer-straight as well as male-female gender identities (Aron, 2014). In general, they lean into a post-modern sensibility. All these issues have a distinct political loading.

Yet, from a relational perspective, political differences are seen as an integral part of the therapeutic relationship, and therapists are encouraged to acknowledge and explore these differences as they arise. This can help to promote greater understanding and empathy between therapist and patient and can also contribute to the development of a more robust therapeutic alliance. Aibel (2017) makes the argument, citing Samuels (2004), that there may be an intensification of affect, a low volume exchange that gets turned up. Ultimately, the aim is to create a safe and supportive space where patients can explore their thoughts and feelings about politics, without fear of judgement or condemnation. From a relational view, these differences and tensions are alive and well. The "elephant" and the "donkey" are already in the room and they cannot *not* be addressed. From this angle, political sensitivities are never too far from the surface and the patient usually has a plausible idea of what your politics are anyway (Hoffman, 1983).

This chapter would hardly be complete if it failed to deal with the topic of why there are some analysts who tend to skip over political differences in their scrutiny of transference-countertransference. First, some analysts may still be allied with an earlier posture which put politics outside the reach of discussion. These analysts may be super careful of preserving the neutrality between analyst and patient. Crastnopol (2015) warns against "the analyst's expression of unbridled indignation." A second reason might be that ethnicity, race, gender, sexuality, and socio-economic status often take center stage because these aspects are frequently associated with systemic disparities, and discrimination which can be big psychological stressors. These groups may have historically been marginalized, oppressed, and underrepresented. Also, political beliefs are often perceived as more of a choice compared to those more intrinsic aspects of personhood. Finally, there might be worries about the ethical implications of engaging one's political beliefs, especially as it concerns imposing the therapist's values on the patient.

The Troubled Road of Political Engagement

We are prone to numerous biases because of belonging to a particular in-group like liberal democrats. In-group vs. out-group biases have been well documented in the standard psychological literature (Gershon & Fridman, 2022; Sherif, 1956). Experiments have shown that people will endure physical pain as well as significant losses of money just to witness a loss to an out-group member (Jouet, 2017). Third, our usual sense of empathy and collaborative inquiry becomes significantly disturbed when it comes to political affiliations. *In other words, while embracing diversity in all its forms, we seem to have special difficulty with political differences (this may be a function of good faith efforts to center historically marginalized communities without considering right-leaning working class constituents as being one of them).* Yet, the dangers of political engagement are considerable! What is the knowledge base that allows us to be the arbitrator of what is fair to the Republican patient, or for claiming issues have been worked through, or for labeling something an enactment when we have no set of postulates to bring to the table? There is no training in our analytic programs for dealing with political content. There is a paucity of articles about strategies for dealing with Republican patients. This knowledge gap is even further amplified when it comes to strong pro-Palestinian or pro-Israeli patients. Who of us can claim a plentitude of experience?

Reliance on Cognitive Styles

There is another facet of this argument that needs to be addressed: the growing literature attesting that there are fundamental personality differences between liberals and conservatives. This body of work implies that we liberals and conservatives are wired very differently, both emotionally and cognitively. These differences easily lead to disjunctions and misconstruals when a liberal therapist treats a conservative patient or vice versa.

One prominent study (Jost et al., 2003), a meta-analysis based on 22,888 cases, found that certain psychological traits predict conservatism. These include death anxiety; system instability, needs for order, structure, and closure; the fear of loss; being less open to experience; and being less tolerant of ambiguity. Put together, conservatives tend to see the world as dangerous, whereas liberals see the world as a place of safety and cooperation. My concern here is that almost all the traits ascribed to the conservatives are negative, even pejorative. This hardly represents an impartial assessment. How many therapists does it hold sway over?

Another study employs the NEO, better known as the Big Five (Gerber et al., 2009, 2010). The NEO is the most widely used and reliable test of personality traits in the psychological community. Gerber et al. (2009, 2010) are known for having done extensive studies on the linkages between ideology and the Big Five traits. The most consistent finding from their work is that liberals score high in *Openness to Experience* which defines itself as greater appreciation for diversity, novelty, and unconventional ideas. Whereas conservatives score high in *Conscientiousness* which is defined by showing greater appreciation for orderliness, diligence, and reliability.

While interesting, this literature has problems. These traits don't apply uniformly to everyone within a political ideology. Political beliefs are influenced by a myriad of factors beyond personality, such as cultural, environmental, and situational factors. Also, responses in such studies might be influenced by what participants perceive as socially or politically desirable, rather than their actual beliefs or traits.

This Can't Happen to Me

At this juncture, the reader might ask, what is the main concern in this chapter? Aren't analysts, regardless of politics, typically accustomed to dealing with diverse and idiosyncratic content from their patients? What prevents us from approaching political content with the same sensitivity and empathy as other analytical subjects?

There are some key differences! First, we have all been exposed to an overwhelming amount of propaganda through our news media, through our associations with like-minded people, and from our families. We often perceive conservatives as ignorant, racist, conspiracy-prone, and violent, while they view us as socialists, anti-American, elitist, and soft on crime. I plead guilty to many of these prejudices. Albeit we try to be our best selves.

It should come as no surprise that when political beliefs become a source of tension in therapy, there is a serious risk of unconscious enactments (as witness my case with Katelyn) and countertransference. This can lead to even deeper negative attitudes or judgments towards our patient's character, like pathologizing what should be labeled as a political belief – resulting in resistance or defensiveness on the part of the patient. Experienced clinicians may be skilled at maintaining distance in fraught moments, but political beliefs can be especially potent in driving passionate evaluations. As Tublin (2017) notes, "The psychoanalytic community is almost uniformly left leaning. That homogeneity fosters a sense of moral community and belongingness but limits the theoretical and clinical grasp of issues with powerful emotional valence among right leaning patients" (505).

Had I to do it over again with my pro-life patient, Katelyn, I would have paid more attention to my irritability when our talk turned political; I would have inquired earlier into her joining a right-wing group within her community; I might have delved into our process with greater scrutiny when there was the first hint of political difference. Not only would I have scrutinized my own countertransference but also the transference that emanated from her relationship with her dismissive and devaluing mother.

Political talk is different from all other talk. It is more intense, more emotional. The stakes are higher because our very identity is on the line with our political affiliation. Political beliefs are very similar to deeply held moral beliefs. There are ways to make this talk more respectful, and certainly, more easily tolerated. For example, could understanding a patient's political views wind up calcifying that patient's ability to hold uncertainties? Or does this stance help revitalize someone whose identity revolves around political activism? I would also monitor how correlated their personal issues are with their political views. If the correlation is strong, I would be more willing to engage politically. On the other hand, following Bromberg (1996) I can imagine politics as an alternative persona. The best way of determining this is how playful and flexible the person can be around political issues of the day. How well do they "stand between the spaces."

I offer the following suggestions where the climate seems right:

1. When political topics arise, focus on the emotional underpinnings and psychological significance for the patient rather than the content of the beliefs.
2. Emphasize shared human experiences and emotions rather than political differences. This helps to build rapport and trust.
3. If the therapist finds their own reactions are interfering with their ability to remain neutral, seeking supervision or consultation can provide a space to process these reactions without involving the patient.
4. Be vigilant and reflective about transference and countertransference dynamics. The therapist's own reactions can be informative, even incisive, but should not dictate the entire therapeutic process.
5. Continue to educate oneself about different political perspectives and the cultural contexts from which they arise to better understand where the patient is coming from.

It is so easy for things to go asunder when the talk turns political. I think we analysts need to be on guard not just because of our privileged access to vulnerable patients but also because many of us lean leftward politically. It is my firmest hope that we begin tackling this overlooked intersubjectivity and give it the attention it cries out for.

References

Aibel, M. (2017). The personal is political is psychoanalytic: Politics in the consulting room. *Psychoanalytic Perspectives, 15*(1), 64–101.

Akhtar, S. (2010). *Immigration and acculturation: Mourning, adaptation, and the next generation.* Jason Aronson.

Altman, N. (2010). *The analyst in the inner city: Race, class, and culture through a psychoanalytic lens* (2nd ed.). Routledge.

Aron, L. (2014). "With you I'm born again": Themes and fantasies of birth and the family circumstances surrounding birth as these are mutually evoked in patient and analyst. *Psychoanalytic Dialogues, 24*(3), 341–357. https://doi.org/10.1080/10481885. 2014.911601

Berzins, J. I. (1977). Therapist-patient matching. In A. S. Gurman & A. M. Razin (Eds.), *Effective psychotherapy: A handbook of research* (pp. 222–251). Pergamon Press.

Beutler, L. E. (1972). Value and attitude change in psychotherapy: A case for dyadic assessment. *Psychotherapy, 9*(4), 362–367. https://doi.org/10.1037/h0086789

Bromberg, P. M. (1996). Standing in the spaces: The multiplicity of self and the psychoanalytic relationship. *Contemporary Psychoanalysis, 32*(4), 509–535. https://doi.org/10.1080/00107530.1996.10746334

Crastnopol, M. (2015). *Micro-trauma: A psychoanalytic understanding of cumulative psychic injury.* Routledge.

Duarte, J. A., Crawford, J. T., Stern, C., Haidt, J., Jussim, L., & Tetlock, P. E. (2014). Political diversity will improve social psychological science. *Behavioral and Brain Sciences, 38.* https://doi.org/10.1017/s0140525x14000430

Farber, B. A. (2018). "Clowns to the left of me, jokers to the right": Politics and psychotherapy, 2018. *Journal of Clinical Psychology, 74*(5), 714–721. https://doi.org/10.1002/jclp.22600

Gaztambide, D. J. (2021). Do black lives matter in psychoanalysis? Frantz Fanon as our most disputatious ancestor. *Psychoanalytic Psychology, 38*(3), 177–184. https://doi.org/10.1037/pap0000365

Gerber, A. S., Huber, G. A., Doherty, D., Dowling, C. M., & Ha, S. E. (2010). Personality and political attitudes: Relationships across issue domains and political contexts. *American Political Science Review, 104*(1), 111–133. https://doi.org/10.1017/s0003055410000031

Gerber, A. S., Huber, G. A., Raso, C., & Ha, S. E. (2009). *Personality and political behavior.* Available at SSRN 1412829.

Gershon, R., & Fridman, A. (2022). Individuals prefer to harm their own group rather than help an opposing group. *Proceedings of the National Academy of Sciences of the United States of America, 119*(49). https://doi.org/10.1073/pnas.2215633119

Hoffman, I. Z. (1983). The patient as interpreter of the analyst's experience. *Contemporary Psychoanalysis, 19*(3), 389–422. https://doi.org/10.1080/00107530.1983. 10746615

Iyengar, S., & Krupenkin, M. (2018). Partisanship as social identity; implications for the study of party polarization. *The Forum, 16*(1), 23–45. https://doi.org/10.1515/for-2018-0003

Jost, J. T., Glaser, J., Kruglanski, A. W., & Sulloway, F. J. (2003). Political conservatism motivated social cognition. *Psychological Bulletin, 129*(3), 339–375. https://doi.org/10.1037/0033-2909.129.3.339

Jouet, M. (2017). Millions standing against their own economic interest. In *University of California Press eBooks*. University of California Press. https://doi.org/10.1525/california/9780520293298.003.0007

Klein, E. (2021). *Why we're polarized*. Avid Reader Press/Simon & Schuster.

Pinsker, J. (2022, February 15). The friend and family relationships the Trump Era Broke. *The Atlantic*. https://www.theatlantic.com/family/archive/2021/03/trump-friend-family-relationships/618457/

Saad, B. L. (2021, November 20). U.S. still leans conservative, but liberals keep recent gains. *Gallup.com*. https://news.gallup.com/poll/245813/leans-conservative-liberals-keep-recent-gains.aspx

Samuels, A. (2004). Politics and/of/in/for psychoanalysis. *Psychoanalytic Perspectives, 2*(1), 39–47. https://doi.org/10.1080/1551806X.2004.10472894

Sherif, M. (1956). Experiments in group conflict. *Scientific American, 195*(5), 54–58. https://doi.org/10.1038/scientificamerican1156-54

Silander, N. C., Geczy, B., Marks, O., & Mather, R. R. (2020). Implications of ideological bias in social psychology on clinical practice. *Clinical Psychology-science and Practice, 27*(2). https://doi.org/10.1111/cpsp.12312

Solomonov, N., & Barber, J. P. (2018). Patients' perspectives on political self-disclosure, the therapeutic alliance, and the infiltration of politics into the therapy room in the Trump era. *Journal of Clinical Psychology, 74*(5), 779–787. https://doi.org/10.1002/jclp.22609

Starr, K. (2018). Caught in the crossfire: Political intersections, collisions, and confrontations. *Psychoanalysis, Self and Context, 13*(4), 389–397. https://doi.org/10.1080/24720038.2018.1499306

Tublin, S. (2017). Partisanship in the psychoanalytic community: Navigating the conflicting roles of citizen and analyst amid Trump-era polarization. *Contemporary Psychoanalysis*. https://doi.org/10.1080/00107530.2017.1384671

Tummala-Narra, P., Claudius, M., Letendre, P. J., Sarbu, E., Terán, V. G., & Villalba, W. (2018). Psychoanalytic psychologists' conceptualizations of cultural competence in psychotherapy. *Psychoanalytic Psychology, 35*(1), 46–59. https://doi.org/10.1037/pap0000150

Walle, A. H. (2023). *True believers and the great replacement: Understanding Anomie and Alienation*. Taylor & Francis.

Weisman, J., Igielnik, R., & McFadden, A. (2023, December 20). Poll finds wide disapproval of Biden on Gaza, and little room to shift gears. *International New York Times*.

Whitesides, J. (2017, February 7). From disputes to a breakup: Wounds still raw after U.S. election. *U.S.* https://www.reuters.com/article/us-usa-trump-relationships-insight/from-disputes-to-a-breakup-wounds-still-raw-after-u-s-election-idUSKBN15M13L

Part V

Going-on-Being in the Countertransference

16 Going-on-Being When the Going Gets Rough

An Impasse in the Negative Transference/Countertransference

Heidi Knoll

Just moments before starting a session with my patient Sally, my veterinarian called me to say she could only make a home visit in the next hour to euthanize my beloved 14-year-old dog who was experiencing acute significant pain. As I started the session, I felt shaken; it was difficult for me to access my analytic mind. With eyes watering and voice quivering, I started the session in discomfort knowing that my emotions were visible to my patient. After chiding myself internally that I should be able to hold it together and be present with the patient, it became very clear to me that I could not continue the session. Soon thereafter, I let the patient know I had an emergency situation to deal with and could not continue the session. She asked if it was related to my dog. I told her it was. I wondered how she knew but did not explore it at the time. I was flustered and uncomfortable about the degree to which I felt 'off my game'. I felt extremely awkward about this intrusion into *my* analytic stance and yet knew there was nothing I could do other than to stop the session.

In this chapter, I will be discussing how difficult it was for both myself and my patient to 'go-on-being' in the face of my abruptly ending the session. In subsequent sessions Sally became highly resistant to exploring her reactions.

A relational 'knot' of countertransference and a projective identification response to the patient contributed to each of us feeling disrupted over the course of a series of subsequent sessions. I did not feel like the sturdy or 'tough' analyst who was able to maintain my analytic stance in the face of my patient's anger toward me. In my 35 years of practice, this is the first time that I had experienced such a dysregulated state during a session. I have worked with self-harming adolescents, suicidal and eating disorder patients whose physical and psychological states were in in acute jeopardy and not felt daunted at the prospect of facing moments of dysregulation in a session while maintaining my analytic focus.

Much has been written about induced countertransference but less has been written about the dynamics resulting from moments in sessions when our life outside the consulting room intrudes unexpectedly. Andrew Morrison (1996), Eric Mendelsohn (1996) and others have written poignantly about working in the context of a protracted period of impending serious medical

DOI: 10.4324/9781003607120-22

situations and death. Barbara Gerson's (1996) book *The Therapist as a Person* addresses other kinds of intrusions into analytic space. These contributions all emphasize the increased tendency for intense countertransference reactions. What has not been addressed as much is 'spur of the moment' situations when the analytic space is unwittingly intruded upon.

Jody Messler Davies (2004) addresses the relational knots which can occur when a clinician is trying to respond therapeutically to a patient who is voicing their anger at the therapist. She describes the difficult challenge of being in the moment and out of it at the same time and allowing for an intensity of psychic experience while sustaining the patient's and analyst's capacities to reflect on that experience.

These are complicated enough moments to bear and work through; staying in touch with the different selves of both the patient and the analyst is a 'tall order'. I examine how my personal situation collided with my patient's experience and history. Collision is a strong word; it suggests the degree I felt 'knocked off' my analytic position in the unexpected and emotional moment at the outset of a session and the exploration of that session in subsequent sessions. In the subsequent session, the patient's reaction to my abrupt cancellation of the session was 'off putting' and distressing to me. It contributed to my missing some important transference-based material. That made me feel worse; I felt even more concerned that my analytic stance was compromised. My countertransference was based on my own discomfort and sadness at the outset of the session. I had unwittingly been more human than my usual analytic stance, and that had made me uncomfortable. However, it became clear there was more than that going on and then the going got tough for a while. A transference reaction related to the patient's history was occurring before me, but I was not able to recognize it as such due to the intensity of the many factors contributing to my countertransference. In the context of her resistance to pursuing her feelings about my abrupt cancellation I felt the difficulty of withstanding her angry transference reactions.

I ascertained further understanding of my patient's dynamics in the process of examining her reactions. A key factor was the patient's angry resistance to naming and processing what had been evoked for her. 'Going-on-being' became difficult for both of us. I ended the session prematurely when I realized I would not be able to maintain my analytic stance.

I contacted Sally later and rescheduled her appointment for two days later that week. I was feeling more composed as I entered the office that day. Although still in the early stages of grief over the loss of my dog, I was feeling more intact, and more like my analytic self. The patient looked awkward when I greeted her in the waiting room. She began the session as she usually did, silent for about three minutes while she gathered her thoughts. I often have this experience with this patient as I wait, feeling almost invisible as she goes through this ritual each session. As she began talking, I was listening for derivatives or a direct reference to the session two days earlier. She said nothing directly about the aborted session. Instead, she began by talking about a recently irritating interaction with her neighbor. Indignant at the neighbor's request to situate her garbage cans elsewhere on her property, she railed against the neighbor for being intrusive and unreasonable. The derivative was quite clear and I commented that she had been asked to leave the session earlier in the week (to move her 'stuff out of the way'). I wondered if she had felt similarly; she had been asked to leave her stuff on hold because of my emergency situation. She paused and looked taken aback. And then, angrily stated, "This isn't about you." She continued talking about her anger at the neighbor's unreasonable demands. I attempted again to connect the derivative to the current situation between her and me. "Like with your neighbor I am wondering if you were angry with me for canceling the session". She resisted my inquiry again. Or so it seemed to me. She continued, "I would not have had to deal with this if you didn't have a home office. I would not have had to see your dog. Why do therapists do this?" As she is saying this, I am dumbstruck, surprised at her indignant reaction. I found myself in a non-neutral moment filled with strong countertransference feelings. I felt vulnerable, hurt and frustrated by her angry response. While I was aware going into this session of the obvious significance for this patient of my "abandonment" earlier in the week, I found myself angry about her resistance to explore it with me.

The situation felt uncomfortable and complicated. I was filled with these strong feelings, and my analytic mindset was shaky. This was a co-constructed moment for certain. Yet, I recognized my troubles should not be in the room and my patient perceived any exploration of what had occurred as further focus on me rather than on her. I took note that my countertransference superego was in a dialogue with my more centered analytic self. I wanted to respond to the patient and take my own vulnerability out of the equation. I felt guilty that my personal situation had intruded into the analytic space and had caused her distress. No matter how hard I tried, the patient's aggressive tone contributed to my deadlocked countertransference. I wanted to be able to achieve what Jody Messler Davies (2004) described as to be in the moment and out of it at the same time.

The pertinent background information is relevant to the understanding of these clinical moments.

History

Sally, an only child, had been raised by a narcissistic mother who divorced when the patient was 4. Her father moved out of the country to the Far East and was not very involved in raising Sally. During my patient's early school years her mother subsequently moved with my patient multiple times, often in the middle of the school year to different cities to pursue romantic relationships. The patient remembers several times when she returned home from school to find a moving truck at her home with no advance notice.

Treatment History

The events described occurred about a year into Sally's return to treatment with me after a hiatus of several years. Initially, she had been in treatment with me for five years regarding her contentious relationship with her adolescent son, the youngest of her three children. Sally recognized she was overly reactive to her son's disorganization and his moves towards increased autonomy. When her son left to go to college Sally terminated her treatment, eager to focus on developing a small business.

Sally contacted me two years later in the context of becoming very depressed after relinquishing a dog she had fostered and subsequently adopted. She had begun fostering this dog soon after the death of a long-time family pet and her youngest child leaving for college. She described having been totally devoted to re-training the dog's aggressive behavior for several months. Despite many attempts over a significant period, including specialized trainers and medications to modify the dog's behavior, the problematic behavior continued. It escalated to the point where the dog would become aggressive towards family members. Interestingly, she never expressed anger about the dog.

After much agonizing she decided to return the dog to the foster organization. She found herself tearful, having difficulty sleeping and preoccupied about the dog's well-being for weeks post-relinquishment. Sally felt overwhelmed by the magnitude of sadness she felt at relinquishing the dog she had adopted. Although she recognized she had gone above and beyond with her dog, she felt relinquishing the dog was a defeat. Themes of guilt and doubt pervaded the material in the early sessions.

Returning now to work, I was stymied following the session when Sally was angry and avoidant when I inquired about her reactions to the abruptly canceled session and to her question whether my emergency was related to my dog. She wanted none of it. It seemed highly likely Sally would have many feelings about my dog getting my attention and displacing her from the session. She may have been critical of the way I cared for my dog. The tenor of our interactions became almost argumentative when I opened space for her to examine her reactions. I inched forward with the exploration, and she resisted. Unpacking this with the patient was slow and was characterized by minimal forward motion interspersed with continued angry avoidance. I felt like my hands were tied. And I felt like the child trying to convince their parent that what they wanted was reasonable – like the second dessert or the umpteenth toy at the toy store. However, as I gained some distance, it became a bit clearer to me that there was an enactment going on. I was feeling anger at her resistance to exploring her reactions but unable to address that with her. She has always felt very inhibited to address her disappointment and anger at her mother. She had lived through a childhood of loneliness and a sense that any equilibrium would get disrupted at a moment's notice. That part of her history certainly suggested that the abrupt cancellation would have felt very triggering for her. But what was her resistance to exploring that in response to my providing the space to explore those feelings? My attempts to explore that were experienced by the patient as unnecessary, as being self-serving. I had become the mother who was trying to 'convince' her that this exploration would be useful, not like her mother who would beg Sally not to express upset when Mother informed her of yet another move.

But I continued to pursue it. Who was she fighting with internally? A conflict between the absent object who imposes on her and the wish and fear to have an impact on the object?

It seemed so obvious to me. I asked myself, why was it so threatening to her to explore this? I had privileged my dog over her; my needs prevailed and interrupted hers. She felt abandoned and unseen, yanked away from a place of safety so similar to what she felt numerous times with her mother's decisions to move for her own needs, often in the middle of a school year without consideration of her daughter's needs. I was disconcerted by her anger and her reluctance to recognize or even to consider how her anger evoked previous situations in her life. (Remember her indignation that if my office were in an office park we would not be in this situation and that the abruptly canceled session/interruption/abandonment was because my dog was to be euthanized.) She was unable to address the strong affect around any issues related to her dog that got stirred for her in the context of the canceled session and the reason for it. I had experienced her reactions to my attempts to explore her resistance and anger as very narcissistic. In Sally's view I became the narcissistic object pursuing her relentlessly to explore her feelings. Internally her wish to preserve the attachment to her mother prohibited her from being able to articulate her upset directly about the canceled session. She was experiencing my attempts for her to be in touch and articulate her feelings as she had as a child in response to her mother's narcissism as an onslaught of feelings she had to try to protect herself from. I had become the selfish object – pushing my 'agenda' of exploration on her. And she responded by verbalizing her anger.

As my patient and I processed this, albeit with significant resistance, what emerged was a realization that her expressed anger was rooted in a deep terror of relationships and interactions where she feels vulnerable. She spoke about the intense discomfort she had felt seeing my tears when I prematurely ended her appointment. It became apparent I was the bad object causing her pain and vulnerability, both by my cancellation of the session and by my pursuit of encouraging her to explore her feelings about it. In addition, she feared being in touch with the vulnerability she felt when she felt let down or abandoned. She knew she was chronically enraged at her mother but had never been able to address this with her mother for fear she would be viewed by the mother as selfish. That historic dynamic hit me like a ton of bricks as I realized that *I* had felt she was being selfish in her reactions to a situation that was difficult for both of us. She hated that characterization of herself. Yet, she had enacted it with me. She perceived me as being 'selfish' for asking her to explore what I knew were very strong feelings in her. I initially read that perception as resistance but came to understand she was standing up to me/'her mother' who had a strong personal agenda. Saying no was a way of verbalizing her distress, and symbolically saying No to her mother. My encouragement to explore her feelings about the canceled session felt like acquiescing to her mother once again.

Generally, I enjoy working with this patient but during the sessions when we were unpacking her feelings about the canceled session, I felt impatient and found it hard to have compassion for her. Was I so determined to address her resistance as a way to calm my feelings of disappointment with myself that I could not contain my raw feelings on the day I received the news about my dog? What does it mean to our patients when they see emotional vulnerability in us? At those moments in sessions when we are jolted out of our seats in a collision with a patient's negative transference maybe the first and best thing to do is to **not** 'do' anything.

References

Davies, J. M. (2004). Whose bad objects are we anyway?: Repetition and our elusive love affair with evil. *Psychoanalytic Dialogues, 14,* 711–732.

Gerson, B. (Ed.). (1996). *The therapist as a person: Life crises, life choices, life experiences, and their effects on treatment.* Analytic Press, Inc.

Mendelsohn, E. M. (1996). More human than otherwise: Working through a time of preoccupation and mourning. In B. Gerson (Ed.), *The therapist as a person: Life crises, life choices, life experiences, and their effects on treatment* (pp. 21–40). Analytic Press, Inc.

Morrison, A. P. (1996). Trauma and disruption in the life of the analyst: Enforced disclosure and disequilibrium in "the analytic instrument." In B. Gerson (Ed.), *The therapist as a person: Life crises, life choices, life experiences, and their effects on treatment* (pp. 41–54). Analytic Press, Inc.

17 When There Is No Room to Play

Mehr-Afarin Kohan

Zoha arrives 15 minutes late and sits down without taking off her coat. She is wearing her usual all black attire, her hair is covered, and her face is pale and downcast. Her husband is waiting in the car and once again, she is in a rush to leave. She seems at a loss about how these sessions are supposed to go. My questions do not take us far either.

On better days, Zoha talks about her suffering in Afghanistan, which at times gets sidetracked into tales about a near apocalypse and resurrection of *Mahdi* – the redeemer of Islam that will rid the world of evil. She goes into details about the signs of *Ghiamat* – the judgment day – and how she knows that it is near. All the signs are there for her, the many bloodsheds, the draughts, the injustices, the broken families, drugs and sex. In fact, she says, "Mahdi has been spotted riding on his white horse in the mountains."

At other times, Zoha describes the beauties of their family garden before the Soviet-Afghan war in the 1980s. She was a very young child at that time and this lost paradise holds the saintly image of its gardener, her father, who was killed before she reached 7. Her story follows years of significant deprivation and trauma as a child, and it becomes less dreamy and more real as it loses color. A depressed bereaving mother that stays in bed, tiny limbs that turn black in the cold winters sewing Burka, long dark nights sleeping on an empty stomach. She is forced to drop out of school and go to work as an adolescent. She takes care of her younger siblings and makes sacrifices for them.

Zoha's adolescence takes place at the time of Taliban and is saturated with unimaginable trauma that continues to haunt her in waking life and sleep. She is chased, beaten, burnt by acid and humiliated. She remembers gory details of what she witnessed at sites of bombings. She is exposed to beheadings and other atrocities committed by the Taliban, whom she fears and hates. As an attractive young woman, she is also chased in a different way. But she never finds love, she says, and marries out of obligation to her husband and flees Afghanistan with him as a young adult.

Her married life is unfortunately not much better. Zoha is once again at the mercy of an abusive man who batters her until she loses consciousness, spits on her and calls her names. She feels "old and ugly." She bears children and loves them but has a hard time finding joy and hope in them. When the family

DOI: 10.4324/9781003607120-23

moves to Canada, the physical abuse subsides for fear of the authorities, but verbal and psychological abuse remains a daily occurrence.

Zoha experiences significant depression and trauma-related symptoms when she comes to see me. She struggles with frequent flashbacks and nightmares and lives in constant fear. There is no joy in her life, no restful sleep, no desire for food, no hope for the future. She is isolated because she is too afraid to leave the house by herself. She has panic attacks in ESL classes and has to run away. She gets flashbacks of bombings in crowded places, hence cannot take public transit. She is therefore dependent on her husband for rides to our sessions and this soon becomes a main source of argument between them.

The life narrative that I am presenting here is more *my* creation than Zoha's. Over the course of a two-year weekly psychotherapy, I struggled to wrap my head around a collage of stories told sporadically interspersed with religious tales and nostalgic accounts of her past. Zoha told her stories in a stereotypical manner (i.e. the same memories and images were repeated over and over), often not chronological and sometimes incoherent. At times I found myself wondering if her intense focus on Ghiamat and resurrection of Mahdi was bordering on delusions, and whether her piety was literally in anticipation of his arrival. This was in combination with a general sense of emptiness, not only in real absences from therapy and immature departures, but also in her form of narration (e.g. silences, not bringing material to sessions) and her black attire. I came to see her as a perpetual mourner of her past. There was no room for color in a world saturated with trauma, devoid of a potential space for imagination and dreaming.

Myth as Dream

Freud and Jung both viewed myths as narrative accounts that carry unconscious contents of the mind and childhood fantasies (Segal, 2003). In this sense, myths brought into analysis can be treated as manifest contents of dreams and interpreted in a similar fashion with the goal of bringing unconscious material into consciousness (Bonnafé-Villechenoux, 2008).

For a long time, my approach to Zoha's mythical stories was similarly to listen to them as metaphors/dreams representing her wishes, her object relations, her view of herself and the world, as well as what was happening in the relational matrix between us (i.e. her role as a mourner and my role as a rescuer). I offered interpretations about how her past experiences, including her father's death, indeed resembled a kind of apocalypse, how her suffering seemed insurmountable, leaving her with a constant need for a savior, how she was in constant mourning for what she had lost, including her home country (the family garden), and how she hoped for justice in an overly unjust world.

Even though Zoha did not disagree with my interpretations, they were often met with dismissive or perplexed looks. She seemed confused about the process of therapy and the suggestions I was making regarding the potential meaning of her words. She often did not further elaborate on my interpretations;

they did not seem to land anywhere, and her narratives did not evolve in any way in the following sessions. I found it impossible to establish a therapeutic process and began to feel hopeless after not seeing any change in her situation. But the first glimpse of hope for the possibility of transformation came with a different sort of intervention that I made in a desperate attempt to encourage her to become more independent of her husband.

At that time, the verbal abuse had escalated at home and there were some instances of him spitting on her face. Her daughter accompanied her to one session because her husband refused to give her a ride. Zoha appeared upset, distant and helpless. It was in this highly charged moment that I had a reverie about the story of Prophet Muhammad's *Hegira*.

Now it is important to note that I am secular and have only rudimentary knowledge of Islam from what I learned in school as a child. So, to have a reverie about a religious story was highly unusual and unique for me. Here is how I remembered the story: Prophet Muhammad and his followers are faced with significant hardship and harassment in Mecca by the pagan tribe and decide to secretly relocate to another city rather than engage in a losing battle. *Hegira*, meaning "migration," is the story of their journey from Mecca to Medina, where a city is established for Muslims to live in peace.

Certain that Zoha knew this story, I said: "You've done the best you could in your marriage, but like the prophet did at the time of the Hegira, there's a time to fight and there's a time to leave in order to survive." Whispering "May peace be upon him!" Zoha's gaze lifted from the floor to meet my eyes. I was unsure of what this intervention had done at that time, but I still vividly remember the look she gave me.

I was taken by surprise when Zoha announced in the next session that she had decided not to ask her husband for rides any longer and would take public transit with her daughter instead. She kept that promise until the beginning of the pandemic. She also talked about wanting to get her driver's license and actually tried the driving test four times, alas without success due to anxiety. I was seeing the first glimpses of change and hope.

Perhaps the meaning of the story resonated with Zoha, not only in terms of becoming independent from her husband, but also her journey of immigration from Afghanistan. Perhaps I was offering a more healing narrative to her; the agency of immigrating versus the passivity of waiting for a savior or leaving a traumatic past behind to move towards a more peaceful future. But is there more to this intervention than just suggesting an alternative narrative or meaning?

Translating Versus Playing

Ferro (2006) describes his idea of *"transformational co-narration"* as a way for the patient and therapist to be in the room where they engage in co-constructing a drama together with increasing degrees of complexity. For him, this approach takes the place of interpretation. Ferro gives special consideration to Row C of Bion's Grid, where he places myths and dreams.

He suggests that "being with the patient in Row C means refraining from operations of interpretative translation, or transliteration from one dialect to another" (p. 29). For him, interpretation of myths or dreams by the therapist can actually be considered an attack on the patient's creativity. What is important to Ferro (and other Bionian field theorists) is the creation of meaning by furthering the narrative in the field (Stern, 2015).

From this perspective, the personal convictions of the analyst become irrelevant as long as they are able to get fully immersed in the patient's experience. A moment of truth, or *analytic truth*, is created when the patient feels that the analyst's statement resonates with her experience (Summers, 2020). There is no objective truth against which the patient's words, no matter how mythical, psychotic or metaphysical they are, are interpreted or labeled as such.

An example provided by Michel Foucault is demonstrative. He cites the case of a psychotic individual who believed he was dead and was actually starving to death. As part of the treatment, he quotes:

> a group of people who had made themselves pale and were dressed like the dead, entered [the patient's] room, set up a table, brought food, and began to eat and drink before the bed. The starving "dead man" looked at them; they were astonished that he stayed in bed; they persuaded him that dead people eat at least as much as living ones. [The patient] readily accommodated himself to this idea.
>
> (Foucault, 1965, p. 189)

Foucault maintains that in treating such cases, it is necessary to "continue the *delirious discourse*" (p. 188). This illustrates an intervention that does not involve a translation of the patient's discourse but rather a playful and creative engagement. For this playful engagement to work, however, it has to occur within what Winnicott (2005) defines as a transitional space. This is the intermediate area between reality and illusion where the question about what is conceived subjectively and the objective world is *not* to be formulated.

Perhaps similar to the actors in the case of the "dead man," I immersed myself in and continued Zoha's discourse by referencing another religious tale familiar to her in a way that did not betray the illusion of play. What matters is not just *what* I said, but *how* I said it (i.e. in a way that was believable). For a moment, I entered the world of my patient as different as it was from mine, much like the actors who painted their faces pale but then probably hung their costumes and went home.

Room to Play

What I have talked about so far is the difference between interpretation as a vehicle for meaning making and play as a vehicle for furthering the narrative in the field. Our understanding of what happened in the dynamic between me and Zoha, however, is incomplete without attention to the relational factors.

Stern (2015) makes excellent comparisons between Bionian field theorists such as Ferro and the relational analysts in their approach to internal versus external worlds. I will not be repeating his ideas except for the following. He writes, "To understand everything the patient says as a dream makes the external world into nothing more than a means of expression and deprives trauma of a meaningful place in the genesis of human problems" (p. 95). Relationalists are concerned with the continuous dialectical interaction between internal and external worlds and ask how the drama created between the patient and the analyst could be shaped by factors relevant to the outside world. They might ask, where did this sudden shift to religious talk come from within me? What kind of enactments could have been taking place between Zoha and me, and how could it have possibly impacted the relational field? How could the actual differences between us influence our dynamic?

Stern (2015) makes the case that relational freedom is limited by unconscious defenses against eruption of dissociated "not-me" states into the room, of either patient or analyst. If the relational matrix is such that one participant is inducing an intolerable "not-me" state in the other, rigidity or "deadlock" may be introduced into the field, leading to "stereotyped interactions," where the participants' responses to one another become constrained (p. 112). Stern talks about these "not-me" states as "an identity that, because of my particular history, I cannot accept being" (p. 214). An individual cannot tolerate being that person and therefore unconsciously resists against it.

In this dynamic, each participant's experience of the other becomes static, obstructing ongoing engagement between the two of them. Consequently, working through these dissociated self-states is required in order to increase the "possibilities for relatedness," which in turn lead to transformations in the field (p. 112).

In this sense, it was not only Zoha's stories that were stereotypical, but also *my* responses to them for reasons that only became apparent to me two years into the therapy. The fact is Zoha's religious narratives were extremely familiar to me but in a very different context. Growing up in the post-revolutionary Iran, I was bombarded and forced to comply with Islamic rhetoric at school and the society at large, which felt very oppressive to me as I was raised in a family of secular leftist activists, persecuted by the Islamic government. I had also experienced harassment and humiliation (due to "anti-Islamic conduct"), at a smaller scale but similar to what Zoha had endured at the hands of Taliban extremists.

I believe my past experiences made it very difficult for me to immerse myself in Zoha's religious view of the world. This was a way of being that I could not accept or tolerate. I was unconsciously committed to maintaining my own secular stance and not letting myself be impacted by what my patient was bringing in. But in guarding against this "not-me" self-state, I was in essence making Zoha's contributions irrelevant to our work together, not giving space to her "way-of-being" (Stern, 2019, p. 102). Basically, I was dismissing it as "religious babble" and translating it into another language that was more tolerable to me through my analytic interpretations.

Moreover, Zoha's stories and religious adherence unintentionally triggered my own dissociated past trauma, disrupting *my* going-on-being and, subsequently, ability to play. I was unconsciously guarding myself against the material she brought into the sessions because it was too close to my own painful experiences. I distanced myself from true engagement with her and hid behind my words and interpretations, leaving no room for play.

Relational psychoanalysts tend to see language as a kind of action, rather than a neutral activity of interpreting psychic material. What the analyst chooses to focus on, the words that are used and how something is said, all communicate an implicit meaning to the patient that may or may not be in line with the explicit message. The unconscious forces within us determine what could be reflected upon in the analytic field and what must remain unarticulated (Stern, 2019). These unconscious forces include the ghosts of our individual past, but also our collective unconscious (Rozmarin, 2017).

Zoha's piety, attire (i.e. being covered head to toe) and the victim position brought up many intolerable self-states within me. In defending against any identification with her, I was indeed not recognizing, or even rejecting, important parts of her. Ironically, this was a repetition of what she had experienced all her life, in Afghanistan and in her married life – someone who was irrelevant and did not matter. And someone who needed to be saved. I had positioned myself as "the savior" for Zoha. A position that was much more tolerable for me than identifying with her as a victim.

It was in the context of trying to "save" her from her abusive husband that I became aware of the submission that *I* had unconsciously demanded of her all this time. A submission to *my* version of the truth and my secular worldview, in which her stories were considered myths or statements to be translated.

In re-evaluating our relationship, and re-considering the power dynamics between us, something fundamental had changed within me in how I viewed my patient, and this had created new possibilities for relatedness (Stern, 2015). I had opened myself up to let her in along with her religious narratives/myths. I had overcome an obstacle that had previously made it impossible for me to talk about "the prophet Muhammad" or "Hegira."[1] I had pushed what Donãs (2018) courageously calls "the little left-wing *micro-fascist-within*" to step aside for a moment to free up room for Zoha's truth, and to give her a share of the authorship of the relational field.

From a Foucauldian perspective, by engaging with Zoha within her own discourse, I took a step in creating an experience of empowerment for an individual who had been undermined and silenced most of her life. It is this experience of being recognized, an experience that is at the core of the establishment of a vital sense of self, that is also at the heart of empowerment (Benjamin, 2004). Once a space is established in which the patient is not being oppressed by the analyst's truth, possibilities for living as a full person open up.

In reality, there was no way for me to save Zoha from her husband, or the Taliban, or her past trauma. I could provide guidance and support if she asked, but true liberation for her lay in her becoming her own savior.

Ending

The best ending for this chapter was offered to me by my patient's toddler, who accompanied her to our sessions on occasion. I often gave him Play-Do to keep him occupied. One day, as we spoke, he mixed all the dough together and made something.

"What did you make?" I asked at the end of the session.

"That's *me*," he said shyly as he held up his creation. It was a stick figure with a large round belly and long arms and legs. I was struck by the belly, a collage of purple, blue and green that seemed to hold much of the content of our sessions; the beatings, the frozen fingers, the dead, but also the colors of Zoha's lost garden. And I was also touched by how this convoluted figure, with its prominent limbs, claimed its existence in the room with the boy's, "That's me."

Note

1 Of course, this required a working through of my own past trauma in Iran, which was concurrently happening at that time in a separate context, allowing me to access dissociated self-states within me.

References

Benjamin, J. (2004). Beyond doer and done to. *Psychoanalytic Quarterly*, *73*(1), 5–46.

Bonnafé-Villechenoux, M. (2008). On the fringe of the oedipal narrative, the fairy tale. *Psychoanalytic Quarterly*, *77*(3), 1009–1011.

Donās, V. A. (2018). The undream: When the clinical (becomes?) political. *Psychoanalytic Dialogues*, *28*, 528–534.

Ferro, A. (2006). *Psychoanalysis as therapy and storytelling* (P. Slotkin, Trans.). Routledge.

Foucault, M. (1965). *Madness and civilization*. Vintage Books.

Rozmarin, E. (2017). Immigration, belonging, and the tension between centre and margin in psychoanalysis. *Psychoanalytic Dialogues*, *27*(4), 470–479.

Segal, R. A. (2003). Jung's very twentieth-century view of myth. *Journal of Analytical Psychology*, *48*, 593–617.

Winnicott, D. W. (2005). *Playing and reality*. Routledge.

Stern, D. (2015). *Relational freedom*. Routledge.

Stern, D. (2019). *The infinity of the unsaid*. Routledge.

Summers, F. (2020). From resistance to analytic truth. *Psychoanalytic Dialogue*, *30*, 73–83.

18 Going-on-Being as a Couple During Environmental Trauma

Anastasia Tsamparli

The sociocultural adversities of the last decades have revealed new ways of suffering that have endangered our identities and have promoted the fragility of our links. When the scale of an environmental trauma is that of a disaster (e.g. recession, pandemic, immigration) then it provokes unthinkable pain and is experienced as an attack on our psychic, social, political identities, destroying thus our symbolic systems and our ability to think. Undoubtedly, the need to reflect on the impact of this socio-cultural malaise on individuals, couples, and families is an urgent task in psychoanalysis. The concept of environmental trauma covers a range of meanings, but above all it "is a concept that links an external event with its specific consequences for the inner psychic reality" (Bohleber, 2010, p. 98).

There are two ways to understand these specific consequences in couples: the first, based on reconstructive logic, sees the current trauma as a re-edition of the old (Dicks, 1967). In this hypothesis, the notion of repetition, fixation, etc. is evoked. The second underlines the elements of novelty, of the "unforeseen", stemming from the dynamic relationship of the couple to the multifactorial present (Puget, 2010; Eiguer, 2009). According to this approach, environmental trauma has consequences for the psychic life of the couple, but their nature can only be partially explained by the established organization of the couple in the past (Eiguer, 2009). The present, that is what follows the experience of trauma, is equally important. This approach applies a main theoretical assumption of Pichon Riviere's link theory, according to which, "All unconscious mental life – that is, the domain of unconscious phantasy – must be seen as the interaction of internal objects (the internal group) in a continuous dialectical interrelationship with the objects of the external world" (Pichon Rivière, 1965/1971, p. 172).

From the moment environmental trauma sets in the life of a couple, it becomes a determining force, a point of reference for the couple and in that sense, it can be conceived as a third, "the uninvited guest" (Fisher, 1999) whose presence splits the sense of time, creating thus a different temporal conception of the relationship. Nothing seems to be the same, and partners feel anxious and lost. It is as if the environmental trauma alienates the couple from their history as they become unable to assimilate the new traumatic

DOI: 10.4324/9781003607120-24

experience. So, partners experience their relationship before and after the trauma as different. Before the trauma the functional couple's intimacy provided an "empathic protective shield" (Bohleber, 2010) as each partner provided holding for one another. After, the shared psychic space of the couple gets organized around anxiety about safety, unpredictability, and the uncertainty it entails. The fantasy of a good enough couple giving birth to a baby (Ruszczynski, 1993) which underlies a constructive intimacy may become that of an eminent catastrophe that may threaten the couple's resilience. If the fundamental holding object relationship of the couple breaks down then inner loneliness, a sense of vulnerability and hopelessness sets in (Bohleber, 2010). The link finds new ways of expression such as somatization, conflict, and open aggression among others. The environmental trauma puts the couple's link at its mercy. It imposes a re-negotiation of the couple's structure, of the way they share their space and engage one another in the relationship. For instance, partners may resort to fraternal mutual transferences evolving around antagonism and fights over fairness and injustice. That way new questions are put forward: how much of me, how much of you, how much is mine, how much is yours? Being in the link is now experienced as a risk of "rejection of one's desires in favor of those of the other, in short, the rejection of one's self" (Eiguer, 2009).

As tension between partners rises, the fundamental mechanisms that have had a structuring role in the link (fantasies, myths, ideals), the previously held constructive "denegatif pacts" (Kaes, 2007), assumptions, habits, roles, and expectations are no longer applicable, and the most cherished attachments are called into question. Although tension between partners' individual desires is constantly present in every couple relationship, when environmental trauma sets in, the tension present may be too toxic for the partners to contain. The partner who was able to serve as a support for the other before the trauma is less available and tends to withdraw, anxiously seeking to regain his or her own balance. As a result, the weaknesses of each partner, which may have been compensated for by the other's ability to provide support, security, and solicitude, are compromised (Eiguier, 2009). That way, each partner discovers unfamiliar aspects of the other. Partners experience disillusion and the other's failure to respond must be mourned to restore a new workable illusion. If not, the feelings of trust, safety, and the sense of belonging to the link are compromised. Mutual recognition within which separateness and connection may be recognized and the narcissistic recomfort of "been seen" by the other cannot take place. Battles over sameness/similarity and difference may unfold around the fantasy of assimilation or exclusion of the other, a "my reality or yours" game, characteristic of twoness (Benjamin, 1990). So, the previously cherished other becomes a stranger as his/her alterity extinguishes and as a consequence his/her differentiation. Otherness is experienced as an attack that is defended to by control and "imposition" (Puget, 2010), as the only way to get safety. This control may take place in two ways: either by dominating the discourse or by withdrawing from it completely (Ruszczynski, 1991). Partners may resort to a world of complementary power relations back and forth in an endless cycle, fueled by omnipotence. Conversely, during these stressful times partners may reactively distance themselves from each other to protect themselves from real or imagined hurt (Ruszczynski, 1991). So, faced with environmental trauma the couple needs all its past and present resources to integrate the traumatic experience into a meaningful narrative and assure the survival of their link. If they don't, then the uncontained psychic material functions as a "crypt" (Abraham & Torok, 1976) waiting to be given meaning. The aim of couple therapy is mainly to help the couple regain the elasticity and spaciousness of their marital container within which the psychic contents of "crypts" created by the trauma may be exposed, metabolized, and given meaning.

Clinical Illustration

The Couple B

Mr. and Mrs. B are respectively 45 and 38 years old and have a son of 5 years old. Mr. B calls for an appointment saying that it's terribly urgent. They arrive for the first session and seem overwhelmed by anxiety. They talk about their fights, anger, and loneliness. They both agree that their relationship deteriorated after the bankruptcy of Mr. B's company arising out of the economy being in recession. Mr. B expresses desperation as his wife has put forward an ultimatum: "You change, or we divorce". This perspective seems to frighten him, and he feels shattered. He says: "I just don't recognize my wife, anymore. She is not the woman I married. How can she discard 16 years of happiness with such an ultimatum? How can she behave as if I were her enemy?" Mrs. B expresses her anger by accusing Mr. B of having become irresponsible and selfish. She claims that he must change and be again the considerate husband he used to be. They both seem to share the feelings of not recognizing the one they married. They both recall how their relationship used to be before Mr. B's bankruptcy. It is as if bankruptcy opened a new time perspective for them: the relationship before and after its appearance. Mr. B talks about Mrs. B's anger linking the present to the past:

> before bankruptcy, she also got very upset and angry or had panic attacks whenever something went wrong but that was no problem because when she got upset I would listen to her and that calmed her down. In fact, she also listened to my problems. But I was the one in the comforting role in our relationship. I am not anymore. It is as if the balance in our relationship has been lost.

Mrs. B describes her difficulties in managing uncertainties and confirms that

> it is all over . . . what we had together is lost. I miss him telling me: ok, don't worry . . . it will pass . . . or it worries you now but it will pass . . .

we will work it out, find a solution, you will see. Now, I no longer feel comfortable saying anything to him because he starts shouting and criticizes me. It is as if after bankruptcy we became two irritable people instead of one. Now we are like two stones that bump into each other.

Bankruptcy brought to light new aspects of each of them while it abolished others. For instance, before bankruptcy Mrs. B experienced their high economic status as a "secure base" and admired Mr. B's success as a businessman and a breadwinner of the family. She describes him as a "silent force" dedicated to the family's needs and in doing so, she associates to the terror of poverty in her family of origin and to her father's financial irresponsibility which threatened the family's safety. Mrs. B describes a childhood of continuous uncertainty towards which she reacted with panic attacks, psychosomatic symptomatology, and controlling behavior. In the family constellation she was the mother's supporter, her savior against father's reckless behavior. Mr. B, respectively, says that he really enjoyed her admiration and trust in him in the past. He associates to his rejecting and emotionally unavailable mother. He expresses his resentment to his mother who seemed to favor his sister, a brilliant student, while he was not doing well at school due to his dyslexia problem. In the family constellation he was in the position of the inadequate one, someone from whom one could expect nothing. So, they both share a persecuting parent: Mr. B his mother and Mrs. B her father.

Since the bankruptcy Mrs. B is the breadwinner of the family while Mr. B stays at home, trying to find a job. This redistribution of roles put forward a new model of sharing to which they had difficulty adapting. For instance, Mr. B complains about Mrs. B not sharing with him the management of the family budget anymore. He has discovered an authoritarian, controlling side of her and feels rejected. Mrs. B complains about his negligence regarding household chores as well as her own needs. She feels neglected, left alone to face her anxiety. The fact that Mrs. B took up the breadwinner role seems to have reawakened the feelings of negligence and injustice she experienced in her family of origin, where she was in the role of parental child. In the session it became apparent that she finds whatever Mr. B does not "good enough". Due to her projective identification she only "sees" what her husband does not do and ignores his efforts to respond to his new role. Mr. B equally feels loneliness and lack of support. He says:

she complains that I neglect the chores she asks me to do. She just doesn't care about how I feel, how much I worry about not finding a job. I have been looking for a job for some time now, but nothing has come up. It is a jungle out there. It is not easy when you are so close to your 50s. She just doesn't see that finding a job is my biggest worry.

The discovery of new aspects of the other engenders feelings of strangeness, a change in the sense of identity of the other who is partly experienced as a stranger. Mrs. B says "you are not the person I knew who had feelings for me. All I hear is that I don't handle things right. The one I knew isn't there for me, anymore". It is as if after bankruptcy the containing function of their link failed and the fragilities of each partner which may have been compensated for by the presence of the other, reappear. Before bankruptcy, Mrs. B found a container for her rage (linked to her terror of uncertainty experienced in childhood) and Mr. B enjoyed the narcissistic relief of her admiration for him (which counterbalanced the rejection experienced in his family of origin). The trauma they are faced with now has weakened them: they both are less available and tend to withdraw, anxiously seeking to regain their own balance. They both feel lonely and at the same time they feel too narcissistically vulnerable to use their families as networks of support. Mr. B has not talked to his parents about the bankruptcy. He says:

> I will not tell them because I know what they will think: he blew it all. He made a mess of it, again. I do not want them to feel that their point of view was confirmed and to feel that they've been vindicated.

Mrs. B equally says, "my family feels like a kindergarten. They are a bunch of children needing support. I have been supporting them for so long in the past, so what's the point of asking their help now?" For Mr. and Mrs. B, the families of origin cannot function as a "holding" environment. There is no network of support to protect them from their anxiety during these hard times. The unbearable anxiety they feel rekindles the distrust experienced in the past and at the same time invalidates confidence in each other in the present. Under these changes destabilization and fears of annihilation due to uncertainty invaded their coupledom. Their link acquired a persecutory quality; its previous containing function now fails. They feel lonely in the face of an unbearable tension triggered by the fear that they might not be able to control the consequences of bankruptcy and recover. So, each became for the other a stranger they could no longer trust and continue to be attached to. The distress they experience due to losses (loss of Mr. B's financial and professional status, loss of narcissistic comfort, loss of holding and safety) remains uncontained and in that sense, what was lost cannot be mourned.

The Sessions

During many sessions in the raw, a fight-like situation around depreciating each other and not-acknowledging the other as a desiring subject prevailed. Each put forward their own viewpoint, as being the only right one, characteristic of twoness. The atmosphere of these initial sessions made it very difficult for me to be in a "creative couple state of mind". I strongly felt their pressure on me to take sides, to restore justice, to recognize the truth of each. My clarifications or interpretations at times were politely accepted and then ignored, while at other times they were met with silence, and I felt puzzled and wondering whether my interventions were experienced as threatening to each's truth. It felt as if each needed me to share his/her point of view. This went on for many sessions and I felt like I was in a labyrinth with no way out. At a certain point I realized I felt angry at being ignored and doubtful whether there was anything I could (or even wanted) to do to help them in any way. At certain moments I had the fantasy of their leaving therapy, and it became clear to me that I felt relieved by this idea. It was at one of those difficult moments that Mrs. B's ultimatum to Mr. B came to my mind: you change, or we divorce. That helped me realize that in my countertransference it was as if I were experiencing a similar ultimatum: "you respond to my interventions as I expect you to, or you go". So, at that point of therapy the transference/countertransference relationship seemed to be organized around the unconscious belief (Britton, 1989) that each expected the other to agree or be rejected. It was as if none of us could think, making space for the other's point of view. This helped me realize that I was unable to remain differentiated, maintain a distance between myself and them, the same way they did between them. This allowed me access to the couple's inner world which was organized around the binary structure of twoness in which conflict could not be dealt with as one reality or the other was alternatively acknowledged (Ogden, 2004). In their world psychic contents instead of being articulated in the transitional space between subjects are transmitted through them (Losso, 2006).

As therapy progressed, a transitional space began to open. As a result, the tension of the sessions gradually diminished. Angry accusations became calm complaints. One of the turning points which signaled the couple's capacity to "dream their thoughts" was when Mrs. B brought a dream, for the first time after a year in therapy. Mrs. B's dream:

> I was walking somewhere, alone. I ended up in an old white house. There were old men there, talking. As I walked, I saw animal excrement and vomit all over the place. I wondered how come they talk instead of cleaning. Then I heard the voice of a girl shouting at them: why don't you clean up? How can you be so indifferent to this filthy mess? The men went on talking ignoring the girl.

Following the associations of the dream we were able gain further insight into the symbolic meaning of bankruptcy in both their respective histories, the organization of the couple's link as well as the therapeutic relationship. The "excrement's mess" became a key metaphor for: Mrs. B's anger towards her father for his reckless overspending, her mother's inability to protect her, and the role she was assigned as "the family's cleaning woman who had to clean up their mess". The current bankruptcy had rekindled her uncertainty and anger, now projected to Mr. B who did not protect her from bankruptcy which, she claims, he "should have foreseen". Now she must work hard to clean up his mess. This rekindled Mr. B's painful view of himself as being the "useless one" in the family of origin. At this point, I began to understand the anger and humiliation I often felt in my countertransference (*an unpro-cessed countertransference*). I felt useless too for not being able to clean up their mess. This realization helped me regain my capacity to think about the couple and opened the way to the creation of a transitional third space in the context of which the painful disturbing psychic contents of the couple could be turned into thinkable material that could be analyzed (Losso, 2006).

Conclusion

Environmental trauma can be conceptualized as an invasion that violates the internal world of the partners and establishes conflict into their link. Some of the implications of the intrusion of trauma in the dynamics of the couple are the following: it alters the chronicity of the link by establishing a time before and after the trauma, a rupture between a safe past and an uncertain future. Therefore, environmental trauma introduces uncertainty in the link which impedes an essential function of partnership: that of dreaming together about their future. Second, it renders unavailable aspects of the partners' per-sonalities while it rekindles others (mainly those linked to intergenerational trauma). As a result, the "other" is now experienced as unfamiliar (Mr. B says to Mrs. B: you are not the woman I knew anymore!). This impaired percep-tion manifests itself in a feeling of strangeness and anxiety. This may lead to a disruption of the sense of identity and perception of the other, producing embarrassment, destabilization, and the non-acknowledgement of the other as a desiring subject. Working with these traumatized couples is challenging for the therapist as she is faced with strong emotional charges (β-elements) that remain unmetabolized and are constantly evacuated through violent pro-jective identifications. A main challenge for the therapist is to keep effective her containing function by maintaining her internal setting; that is to hold a "couple's state of mind" (Morgan, 2001) in the context of which she can be "subjectively involved with both individuals, but also, at the same time, being able to stand outside the relationship and observe the couple" (Morgan, 2001, p. 17). That way she will be able to "hold" and transform the unbear-able emotions of the couple.

References

Abraham, N., & Torok, M. (1976). *Cryptomanie. Le verbier de l'homme aux loups*. Flammarion.

Benjamin, J. (1990). An outline of intersubjectivity the development of recognition. *Psychoanalytic Psychology, 7*(Suppl.), 33–46.

Bohleber, W. (2010). *Destructiveness, intersubjectivity, and trauma*. Karnac.

Britton, R. (1989). The missing link: Parental sexuality in the oedipus complex. In J. Steiner (Ed.), *The Oedipus Complex today: Clinical implications* (pp. 83–101). Karnac.

Dicks, H. (1967). *Marital tensions: Clinical studies towards a psychological theory of interaction*. Basic Books.

Eiguer, A. (2009). La crise du couple: Trois hypothèses théorico-cliniques alternatives. *Cahiers critiques de thérapie familiale et de pratiques de réseaux, 1*(42), 113.

Fisher, J. V. (1999). *The uninvited quest.* Karnac.

Kaes, R. (2007). *Linking, alliances and shared space.* The International psychoanalytic Association.

Losso, R. (2006). Intrapsychic, interpsychic and transpsychic communication. In J. S. Scharff & D. E. Scharff (Eds.), *New Paradigms for treating relationships* (pp. 33–42). Jason Aronson.

Morgan, M. (2001). First contacts: The therapist's "coupe state of mind" as a factor in the containment of couples seen for initial consultations. In F. Grier (Ed.), *Brief encounters with couples* (pp. 17–32). Karnac.

Ogden, T. H. (2004). The analytic third: Implications for psychoanalytic theory and technique. *Psychoanalytic Quarterly, 73*, 167–195.

Pichon Rivière, E. (1971). *Freud: Punto de partida de la psicología social [Freud: As the starting point of social psychology]* (pp. 169–173). Ediciones Galerna S.R.L. (Original work published 1965)

Puget, J. (2010). The subjectivity of certainty and the subjectivity of uncertainty. *Psychoanalytic Dialogues, 20*, 4–20.

Ruszczynski, S. (1991). Unemployment and marriage–the psychological meaning of work, *Journal of Social Work Practice: Psychotherapeutic Approaches in Health, Welfare and the Community, 5*(1), 19–30. https://doi.org/10.1080/02650539108413453

Ruszczynski, S. (1993). Thinking about and working with couples. In S. Ruszczynski (Ed.), *Psychotherapy with couples: Theory and Practice at the Tavistock Institute of Marital Studies* (p. 31–47). Karnac.

19 Taking Sides

Managing Strong Countertransference Feelings in Couples Therapy

Melinda Blitzer

"Countertransference is the *sine qua non* of all human relationships. The manner in which the couple's therapist deals with countertransferential feelings can have a powerful impact as either a force for healing or a force for destruction."
(Lander & Nahon, 1995, p. 79)

Couples' therapists face a myriad of unique challenges that differ from those encountered in individual therapy and are frequently called upon to navigate treacherous waters. Countertransference is often more intense with couples than with individuals, and we may feel like we are sitting on a powder keg of emotions: our own and those of our patients. Reasons for this include the presence of a maelstrom of transference and countertransference relationships (Goldner, 2004, Mendelsohn, 2009), confusing psychological defenses, regressive and non-regressive couple object relations (separate from each individual member's object relations) (Mendelsohn, 2017) and the fact that many of these processes occur mostly outside of consciousness. Classical psychoanalysis emphasized the importance of neutrality, but it is easy to get caught in the vortex of powerful emotions where maintaining equilibrium becomes difficult. What if we dislike one or both partners? How might we utilize our powerful negative feelings into productive work?

Since couples are comprised of two individuals who have differing needs and feelings, the therapist may face intense clinical and emotional challenges when the desires and interests of the two partners conflict. For example, if a spouse becomes verbally or physically abusive to their partner, the therapist will likely feel anger, disdain, and an overwhelming desire to take sides, set limits by steadfastly naming the behavior "out of bounds," and protect the recipient of the abuse. "Couples therapists must rise above these reactions, however, and attend to the complex complementary and concordant countertransference reactions pertaining to both the abuser and the abused" (Francis, 1997, p. 218). In addition, Bagnini (2012) warns that couples therapists may micro-manage couples' emotions because they are unable to manage their own anxieties triggered by the two partners.

DOI: 10.4324/9781003607120-25

Furthermore, covert challenges may arise. For example, a therapist might feel pulled into an enactment of reacting like one partner's condemning parent, lose empathy, and ultimately take a side. As Mendelsohn (2017) states, "As we move from the primary love objects of our family of origin and fall in love, the intimate life partner takes on many of the object-relational conflicts of earlier development" (Mendelsohn, 2017, p. 223). Complicating matters even further, although three people participate in the couples therapy, there exist a multitude of shifting transference relationships: the relationship between partners, each partner and the therapist, and each partner's relationship to their partner's relationship to the therapist. In addition, the therapist develops transference to each partner as well as to the couple. This can be triggered by the therapist's own parents, as I will illustrate shortly.

The therapist's transference and blind spots may lead them into enactments instead of maintaining a separate emotional stance. Consequently, the therapist may act out by reacting to their patients as though they were significant objects from their past. For example, when I was in grade school, my parents, who had a contentious marriage, decided to separate. And although their separation only lasted one night, I felt my world crumble. The loss of security and stability was profound. This early experience stimulated a symbiotic pull that created a strong desire for me to save their, and eventually my patients', relationship. As I will illustrate here, however, it is possible to create a more positive outcome if the clinician understands how these past experiences color how we treat couples. This self-awareness can help us engage couples in a new way to advance the work.

Judith Seigel (1997) points out that the "therapist's countertransference [also] becomes a [wonderful] tool that allows the therapist to experience important aspects of the spouses' inner worlds and of their relationship, for the issues externalized onto the therapist are those that invariably cause the couple the most conflict and tension" (Seigel, 1997, p. 11). Therefore, it is advantageous for the therapist to recognize her own intense reactions and explore the ways they emerge from the couple's relationship.

Here I present a case where I experienced a strong amalgam of countertransference responses to Audrey and Leo, a challenging couple with whom I worked for over four years. Some of my responses reveal what I felt, but also how I used those feelings to formulate an understanding of their relationship. That awareness ultimately enabled me to cultivate a more effective therapeutic approach.

Audrey and Leo

Audrey and Leo began four years of couples therapy amidst marital turmoil. They sought treatment to deal with a double betrayal. They had been married for over 12 years and Audrey had just learned that Leo had made a pass at her sister Emily. Behind Audrey's back, Emily had flirted with Leo through texts.

When the couple arrived for their first session, and in many subsequent sessions, Audrey was visibly distraught. Leo was panicked, felt hopeless, riddled with guilt, and unable to comfort Audrey. She felt as if her world was "crumbling." She had been simultaneously betrayed by her husband and sister. How could they ever spend holidays together again? How could she remain in such a marriage?

A middle-aged, blended family, this couple's relationship had always been turbulent. But now their pain and suffering had reached a climax, and they were forced to face some hard truths about themselves, each other, and their unraveling relationship.

Audrey was a strong, hard-working woman who cared deeply about her family and yearned for a happy life, and I felt powerfully connected to these values. But she ignored red flags early on, especially regarding Leo's long history of emotional and financial irresponsibility. After his first wife died, he left his twin toddlers in his mother's care for weeks at a time while spending the money he was awarded through his wife's life insurance policy to play on a traveling baseball team.

Despite her knowledge about Leo's past, Audrey was surprised at his deceptive behavior. "I never thought he would or could ever do anything like this to me," she exclaimed. As is often the case with a trauma victim, her resilience was limited, and she was unwilling to accept the trauma in her marriage. I could relate to and understood her angry blaming of him and sense of hopelessness.

It was painful for me to witness Audrey's agony, and it stirred a sense of helplessness in me that echoed feelings from my childhood. At times I felt overpowered by my relentlessly rivalrous brother and my mother, who often took his side and had a loud, rigid temper. At times, I felt despondent and without an effective ally. Audrey had been severely traumatized as a young girl, when her stepfather molested her over a three-year period. Her passive mother felt financially and emotionally trapped in her marriage and lacked the courage to leave, or to compel her husband to end the abuse. Audrey struggled to disidentify with her mother and frequently mentioned that she did not wish to repeat her mother's mistakes by remaining with a betrayer. Audrey could not accept Leo's behavior, but like her mother, she also could not bring herself to leave him.

The couple maintained the status quo for over four years. Due to her past and present traumas, Audrey felt indignant in the face of Leo's betrayal and refused to examine the role she might have played in their relationship. She was stuck on the idea that someone else was supposed to make her happy and was waiting, hoping, for Leo to reform, and transform into the person she wished him to be: a remedy for her past. To avoid shame, Leo placated Audrey and rebelled against her contempt by being secretive, largely about financial issues. He was afraid of her hostile reactions and being blamed for everything that was faulty in the marriage. He could not metabolize anger or defend himself. Nevertheless, Leo was more receptive to my feedback because he felt I would not hold him in utter contempt as Audrey did. I was the sturdy, empathic female figure missing from his life which made him feel safe and allowed me to confront him.

I attempted to break through Leo's penchant for secrecy and fear of retaliation. "Try to understand, Leo, that the important things you keep from Audrey feel like a betrayal to her and trigger her rage and anxiety. Every time you withhold information, it is a lost opportunity for building trust." Whenever Audrey uncovered the truth about Leo's secrets, she would explode with indignation and threaten divorce. Leo often retorted, "I know, Dr. Blitzer. But I feel so overwhelmed. It's hard to discuss anything with Audrey; she's always yelling at me." "I understand why you'd want to avoid being yelled at," (Leo's father had low frustration tolerance and would shout at him and his mother) I replied, "but you can't keep hiding, no matter what Audrey's reaction might be. Do you want Audrey to trust you? Does this matter?" As usual, I felt Leo was placating me rather than listening to what I had to say to avoid getting yelled at by pulling me into the role of the nagging wife.

As their dynamics unfolded, it became clear that Audrey assumed the moral high ground and turned Leo into the "bad guy." She felt that Leo, like her father, mother, and sister, did not consider her needs. I identified with Audrey's anger because Leo's provocative behavior (secretiveness, lack of loyalty and integrity) could be quite infuriating. He had little insight into his behavior and could not explain his betrayal. I also identified with Audrey's experience of not feeling supported because my parents had failed to protect me against my brother's aggressive behavior, such as pushing me off the bench so he could practice piano or blasting his stereo while I studied.

As the treatment progressed, battling over Leo's betrayal morphed into bickering over mundane aspects of daily family life. Leo complained that Audrey constantly picked on and criticized him, similar to how his unhappy, ungrateful father behaved towards his mother and with Leo. He would yell, and sometimes become physically abusive, if Leo didn't do as he was told or if he talked back. His father threw his weight around and Leo was intimidated by him. Like his father, Audrey was impossible to please, and likewise, Leo had no interest in doing things to please her. In fact, he often deliberately provoked her. They were in a gridlock. Neither of them was willing to see the other's perspective and make needed adjustments to improve their relationship.

Audrey only expressed her complaints, raw rage, and contempt, instead of changing her behavior and being open to my feedback and interventions. She owned the spotlight because of her angry, critical tirades and chronic devaluing. She typically said to Leo,

> I don't know how I can be with someone like you anymore. You won't eat the food I make, take out the garbage, or clean up the mess in your closet. You dress like a schlep, too, wearing T-shirts all the time. I want to be with a man who's more cultured and worldly.

Leo would retort with, "What about what *you* do, Audrey? You're always screaming at someone or complaining. You bring everyone down and won't look at your own behavior." She was tortured and bereft because she felt he should be different.

Over time, I grew more and more frustrated with Audrey's finger pointing at Leo and her lack of insight. I could identify with her victimhood but also had a rejecting attitude towards her anger and lack of agency. I knew what it felt like to be victimized by one's own family, neglected and devalued. Yet her tendency was to see things in black and white terms and, as time went on, I began to identify more with Leo. Working with Audrey was like trying to penetrate a mound of concrete. She was impossible to influence and believed if she admitted her own wrongdoings, she would let Leo off the hook, and perhaps her stepfather as well. In hindsight, it might have been more helpful to explore what kept her in the marriage (her compulsion to repeat being in a victim role) and to help her articulate her core values.

At times, I felt empathic towards Leo and his sense of helplessness that he could not comfort Audrey or meet her boundless demands. He was more upbeat and easygoing and had a more pleasant personality – at least on the surface. What I grew to understand over time, however, was that he was also sadistic and could be a "slippery fish." He made me angry and frustrated by the lip service he paid to serious subjects, and his unreliability and unwillingness to follow through on agreed upon tasks and behaviors in his marriage.

Overall, Leo whitewashed and sugarcoated his behavior and Audrey denigrated it. I linked Leo's destructiveness to his childhood, which had also been traumatic. His father was domineering and verbally abusive toward him and his mother, who passively withstood his father's tyranny and struggled with depression. He was raised in a machismo culture and was bullied physically and emotionally by other boys in the neighborhood. Sadly, no one intervened to protect him. He later served in the military during Desert Storm, an experience he had difficulty discussing and thus its impact on him remained a mystery to me, and to Audrey too. His life experiences and lack of healthy role models made it difficult for him to express his anger appropriately and effectively. As a result, he tended to act out rather than understand his negative feelings.

I did my best to combine empathy with direct feedback.

Audrey, if you don't want this conflict in your marriage, what will it take to change it? There are things you also need to do differently to live with less conflict. Can we talk about that? If you don't want to work harder, then are you willing to live like this?

She responded, "Why should I have to work to make up for Leo's shortcomings? He is the one who damaged us, not me." My comments activated her grudge. She experienced him as toxic. And I became her mother and another betrayer because I challenged her. This made confronting her complicated.

I attempted to address her defensive stance to construct a more holistic overview of the couple's problems. "Ok, so you don't believe in interactions?" I asked, "I'm trying to bring this to your attention because you need to feel more control over the dynamics in your relationships and understand that what you say and how you say it has a detrimental impact on your marriage." She could not accept my message.

Upon reflection, I realized that I was enacting my own countertransference by engaging in a power struggle with Audrey. I recognized that I had a maternal transference to her, since my mother had also been highly critical, negative, emotionally heavy, and vocal about her unhappiness. When my mother was angry, it was impossible to break through the ramparts of her defenses. Essentially, Audrey and my mother were two of a kind: anti-libidinal women who were unable to be playful. Both women viewed the world as black or white, which limited their abilities to respond to life's challenges with flexibility and creativity. But I convinced myself, and tried to convince her, that if I could just get through to her, it would empower her and be a relief to me. I wanted to "fix" her, something I had never accomplished with my mother.

With both women, I felt turned off and angry about their intractable negativity. Their jaded perspectives made me feel less able to be free and lighthearted. Yet I knew I was no longer a helpless child at my mother's mercy. I recognized my own feelings of helplessness being triggered and often wanted to give up in the work. Sometimes, I even sighed in the session to demonstrate my fed-upness, hoping it might spark a reaction in Audrey and loosen her hold on her chronic beliefs which kept her marriage in a gridlock position. Maybe getting her to be angry at me would help her to focus less on Leo. I was determined not to give up. I wanted to find a way to "enlighten" and "lighten" her – and me.

In Leo and Audrey's marriage, an Oedipal triangle emerged when he became interested in her sister; boundaries were crossed, which complicated their already troubled marriage. The triangulation in their relationship and in the treatment became clearer over time. Audrey felt betrayed by everyone, including me. I became the mother who protected the bad guy. Leo's covertness was like my father's (he was also indirect and secretive), creating another triad in the treatment room with me. And so, I came to realize that, in many ways, I was dealing with my parents and my parents' marriage!

After several years of ups and downs, gridlock, and resistance, I eventually grew weary. They did too. I knew Audrey and Leo got some gratification from watching me work hard to try to change them. They were trying to thwart each other and render me useless. I think it gave them a sense of power as they often felt powerless to influence or change each other and their circumstances. Perhaps they were envious of me as well because I didn't have to live with them and their suffering. They were both combative and had sadomasochistic tendencies that they played out with one another. Audrey tried to create a courtroom environment and Leo went along with it. He felt guilty and could martyr himself by pushing Audrey's buttons and then complain about how harshly she reacted to him.

Finally, there came a turning point in our work, and in my approach. I realized that my objectivity had broken down and my intense need to change them came from my need to change my parents, instead of helping this couple motivate to change themselves. My frustration peaked, and I felt I no longer had anything to lose. I needed to help this couple see themselves by creating a new space for them to understand how they were each contributing to their marital problems, instead of allowing them to continue blaming one another. I think I scared them, and they realized they would be left to their own devices if they did not change their tac.

I decided to try something new and give up the fight. I no longer wanted to work so hard. One day, I just sat back, and I said nothing for at least 10 minutes. They bickered and pointed fingers, as they always did, and it bored me to tears. Finally, they took notice of my silence. Audrey inquired, "Aren't you going to say something today?" I replied, "Every week you guys come in here miserable and every week I think I can help you, and every week it goes south. Today, I think I'm just going to sit back and watch you interact with one another." I tried to use a different approach to see if it could create movement in their relationship and in the therapy. And then I began to use my creativity instead of staying stuck in the muck with my negative feelings. I asserted my entitlement to live my own life, so to speak. Separating myself from Audrey and Leo by stepping into a role of observer and commentator, rather than arbitrator and referee, enabled me to extricate myself from their dysfunctional system and regain my analytic stance.

Conclusion

I learned a lot from my work with this couple: It was easy for me to recognize when I had been moving into a split and taking sides. Eventually, my countertransference helped me to change my approach. In a sense, the analytic space had collapsed on me, and earlier, my identifications with this couple prevented me from finding a productive path.

As previously mentioned, the therapist's intense emotional reactions may result in enactments in which the therapist, because of their own issues and blind spots, may become entangled in the couple's dynamics rather than maintaining equanimity. This can lead to a more positive therapeutic outcome if the clinician eventually understands the dynamics that took place and makes use of the event to advance the treatment.

Liberating myself from the enactment of trying to change them by force, instead of helping them to change themselves, enabled me to shift the dynamic in the room by separating from this couple's drudgery. I had to disengage, not just to be outside of the couple, but also to give myself space. I was overly involved and overly active. By disengaging from the enactments, I modeled a way for them to interact differently: hopefully, more independent, and separate.

Audrey eventually gained more clarity about what to do to move forward in her life. One day, a few months before we ended treatment, she announced that she was more convinced than ever that she wanted to end their marriage and she wanted Leo to move out. She sounded relieved and began the process of withdrawing from the treatment. Leo was extremely wounded and defensive. Although he agreed to the separation, he was reluctant to follow through. Money was tight and financial constraints were a mutually stated reason for staying together. They tried to separate once during our work, but their young children became so distraught, it broke their hearts to think about dividing the family. The couple continued therapy for several more months, but they both wanted to terminate. Leo was "tired of Audrey villainizing him during every session," and Audrey was "emotionally spent" and wanted to focus on other things in her life. Ultimately, we all realized that there was no open road for us. They refused to be helped, if that meant Audrey had to give up her grudge, and Leo had to reform – and this was as far as we were able to go. On a positive note, they resolved some of their ambivalence by getting rid of me, another third! Perhaps they were ready to be on their own.

In the end, I helped Audrey and Leo disengage from the intractable path they were on, and I stopped trying to change my parents' marriage. My intervention helped them to see how destructive their behavior was. I realized I was over functioning instead of facilitating development of the case. I stopped advocating for them to change and instead I decided to be more involved with "seeing" who they were, rather than making something fit. This corresponds to what I wanted to help them do – see each other rather than mold each other into the partner they wanted. In a sense, I ended up having the same problem they did – wanting them to be different. My comments freed me up and helped to destabilize our entrenched dynamics. In hindsight, I should have given up the struggle and held up a mirror sooner.

The couple stayed together despite their powerful, hostile attachment, due to financial and emotional need. Their sadomasochistic dynamics were part of the libidinal glue that held them together and fueled their relationship. Leo enjoyed deceiving her as a way to direct his anger and Audrey kept allowing him to fool her. Neither of them thought the other was enough but their dissatisfaction wasn't worth ending the marriage and they settled on the terms of the relationship. The couple found stability in instability and the thought of meeting the demands of everyday life living independently was too frightening for both of them. Ultimately, they established a new equilibrium, where they began to think and behave with more individuation. Owning a boat was Audrey's lifelong dream and since Leo's credit was poor, she bought one for the family using her own savings for the down payment. Leo began sublimating some of his frustrations by taking Pickleball lessons and joining a league. Although Leo and Audrey still fought, he was no longer as reactive to Audrey's bouts of anger.

In conclusion, when we find ourselves taking sides, it's a signal to examine the powerful emotions being triggered. It should be an internal process that we analyze and use to help our patients and ourselves. For me, this involved getting in touch with some of my childhood traumas and developing an open-minded curiosity about what was occurring with Audrey, Leo, and me.

I learned a great deal about myself in "failing" to cure this couple. The process connected me, in full force, to my perceived infantile omnipotence which had once convinced me that I could fix my parents and live in a loving world. So, in my pain, I also felt relief that I could survive failure and be satisfied sharing the limitations of life with my patients. Accepting this failure also provided a bit of wisdom. Although I was only partially relieved of my guilt for not living up to my omnipotent ideal of curing the respective hurts and conflicts of these two families (mine and this one), I realized that my patients were not my parents. Just as I could not fix my parents, certain aspects of this couple's problems were unfixable. In therapy, we must accept incompleteness and the limits of what we know.

References

Bagnini, C. (2012). *Keeping couples in treatment: Working from surface to depth.* Aronson.

Francis, C. (1997). Countertransference with abusive couples. In J. Seigel (Ed.), *Countertransference in couples therapy* (1st ed., pp. 218–237). W.W. Norton and Company.

Goldner, V. (2004). When love hurts: Treating abusive relationships. *Psychoanalytic Inquiry, 24,* 346–372.

Lander, N., & Nahon, D. (1995). Danger or opportunity: Countertransference in couples therapy from an integrity therapy perspective. *Journal of Couples Therapy, 5*(3), 79–92.

Mendelsohn, R. (2017). *A three-factor model of couples therapy: Projective identification, couple object relations and omnipotent control.* Lexington Books.

Mendelsohn, R. (2009). The projective identifications of everyday life. *The Psychoanalytic Review, 96*(6), 871–894.

Seigel, J. (1997). *Countertransference in couples therapy* (1st ed.). W.W. Norton and Company.

Conclusion

In the last year of his life, Donald Winnicott wrote: "May I be alive when I die!" (1971/1989). With these words, Winnicott emphasized the importance of maintaining the life impulses even during times when agonies prevail. Going-on-being, as a concept, captures the sense that mere survival is not enough for a good life. This regulatory state of going-on-being can be stalled or intruded upon by the exigencies of everyday life. Going-on-being speaks to the act of holding aliveness in the face of overwhelming trauma which threatens our very self-cohesion. It depends upon psychic work and emotional labour to reestablish an ongoing state of continuity where the impingements of life can be lived through and faced, leaving the self receptive to the possibility and hope once more.

Human beings are born underdeveloped and completely dependent on the care of the (m)other to survive and flourish in early life. This biological fact leaves the infant quite susceptible to any psychosocial insult and its resulting anxieties. Freud (1926) described this human infant as primarily seeking tension-reduction and thus fearful of the loss of the (m)other. Later, in development, the child develops anxieties related to the loss of love, and loss of approval from the other. Melanie Klein (1946) described the infant as experiencing desperate anxieties relating to fragmentation and annihilation of the self, and the fear of having destroyed the loved one. Winnicott (1963) extended Klein's work and focused on the mother-infant dyad and said that without maternal care, there would be no such thing as a baby. It is the caregiver's holding, soothing and exquisite attunement to the mental states of the baby that allow the baby to have the experience of going-on-being. The unavoidable impingements of the caretaker's separation and their misattunements to the baby's states interfere with the baby's continuing state of going-on-being resulting in overwhelming anxieties. Developmentally throughout life, we continue to be confronted with various impingements on our state of wellbeing where we struggle to cope and regain balance again.

Our already fragile states of going-on-being have been disrupted by the Sturm and Drang of our current times. Added to the threats to the self from ill health, life cycle losses and developmental challenges, we have experienced

DOI: 10.4324/9781003607120-26

the cascading consequences of the Covid pandemic coupled with the vicis-situdes of the current social and political changes. They have exacted their toll, bringing our mortality front and centre. This world trauma has brought a sequence of impingements to everyday life. What brings patients to our clinic are the attending unmanageable anxieties wrought by the disruptions to their ongoing state of going-on-being.

This leads us to inquire, what are the conditions, qualities and processes that allow us to regain and maintain our going-on-being? The authors in this volume address this very concern. Three main themes emerge from these chapters: the importance of the ability to accept and mourn our losses; the ability to language our pain so that we can symbolize and find meaning in our suffering; and the necessary requirement of the presence of the other in the process.

The importance of the act of mourning is a central concept that runs throughout this volume. It is integral to the clinical work witnessed in these chapters as the authors accompany their patients through their dark times. We cannot avoid suffering; our strength as human beings lies in accepting life's many losses and limitations, including the ability to acknowledge death, and mourning our losses to find meaning together. It is in this way that we cope and go on to develop resilience which allows us to accept uncertainty and find the freedom to move from concrete despair to the expansiveness of hope.

A major impingement to mourning is the prevalence of our communal denial of death. Freud (1915) left us with this challenge when he wrote, "We are unable to maintain our former attitude towards death and have not yet found a new one" (p. 292). In our denial of death and our refusal to mourn our losses, "we must not complain, then, if now and again they [our illusions] come into collision with some portion of reality and are shattered against it" (p. 280). Thereby, Freud left us as individuals and nations with a provocation to go forth and acknowledge our vulnerabilities together which allows for mourning.

Several of the authors in this volume have spoken about the importance of helping patients represent their places of suffering. Through the creative process of re-presenting our experience, we begin to think about and work through our pain. As time allows, we can begin to symbolize affect, and it is then that grieving can begin. It is in developing these very symbolic capaci-ties that we can grieve together in the face of overwhelming loss in order to go-on-being again.

The harshest realities of our lives are easiest to bear when seen through the eyes of a fellow human being. For Winnicott (1963), the ability to go-on-being emerges from the relationship with the first 'other' in the world. This volume contributes to the theme of the importance of the other in the regulation of going-on-being throughout our life cycle. The psychoanalytic process facilitates finding the words to make meaning together, through the softening effects of symbol and metaphor, within the context of a holding, containing, environment. The 'other' remains essential throughout our lives and it is through our shared humanity that we re-find our equilibrium and are guided back to the state of going-on-being.

There is a sense of deep abiding hopefulness that emerges in these chapters. We are all psychic survivors of the painful process of losing and re-establishing going-on-being. Yet, as difficult as these destabilizations can be, new possibilities to go on living and flourishing can be fashioned from our shattered hopes and dreams. As Charles Dickens (1861) wrote in *Great Expectations*: "I have been bent and broken, but – I hope – into a better shape".

References

Dickens, C. (1861). *Great expectations*. Chapman and Hall.
Freud, S. (1915). Thoughts for the times on war and death. *Standard Edition, 14*, 273–300. Hogarth Press.
Freud, S. (1926). Inhibitions, symptoms and anxieties. In *Standard Edition, 20*, 77–178. Hogarth Press.
Klein, M. (1946). Notes on some schizoid mechanisms. *International Journal of Psychoanalysis. 27*, 99–110.
Winnicott, D. W. (1963). Dependence in infant care in child care, and in the psycho-analytic setting. *International Journal of Psychoanalysis*, (44), 339–344.
Winnicott, D. W. (1989). A reflection. In C. Winnicott, R. Shepherd, & M. Davis (Eds.), *Psychoanalytic explorations*. Karnac. (Original work published 1971)

Index

active stance 4, 70–71
agency 38–45
aging 38–45
agonies, archaic 49, 60–61; background
    50; beginning 50–52; biological
    transformation 58–59; cameo
    phallus 54–55; discontinuity
    52–53; music in the air 57–58; oral
    and anal worlds 53–54; paranoia
    versus autistic-discontiguity 55–57;
    processing birth trauma 59–60;
    transformation 58–59
anal worlds 53–54
anti-space 68–70
archaic agonies 49, 60–61; background
    50; beginning 50–52; biological
    transformation 58–59; cameo
    phallus 54–55; discontinuity
    52–53; music in the air 57–58; oral
    and anal worlds 53–54; paranoia
    versus autistic-discontiguity 55–57;
    processing birth trauma 59–60;
    transformation 58–59
autistic contiguous 55–57, 74–81

Bachelard, Gaston 22, 27–29
Becker, E. 85–86, 90
beliefs see political beliefs
beta 8, 70, 76, 109
biological sciences 107–108
biological transformation 58–59
Bion, Wilfred 2, 67–68, 144, 177–179
birth trauma 59–60
body, the: clinical approach 112–113;
    clinical illustrations 110–112;
    contributions from biological
    sciences 107–108; moving from the
    concrete to the symbolic 108–109;
    psychoanalytic approaches to
    psychosomatic functioning 106–107

case studies see clinical vignettes/case
    studies
catastrophic trauma 127–134; see also
    trauma
Chambers, J. E. 85, 90
Chat GPT 102–103
children 49, 60–61; background
    50; beginning 50–52; biological
    transformation 58–59; cameo
    phallus 54–55; discontinuity
    52–53; music in the air 57–58; oral
    and anal worlds 53–54; paranoia
    versus autistic-discontiguity 55–57;
    processing birth trauma 59–60;
    transformation 58–59
clinical vignettes/case studies: the body
    110–113; death awareness 87–89;
    environmental trauma 184–188;
    immigrants 148–154; managing
    countertransference feelings
    191–196; mourning 15–18; negative
    transference/countertransference
    171–174; political beliefs 159–160;
    rage 75–80
cognitive styles 162–163
Cole, Gilbert 24
Cole, Teju 143
community, psychotherapy 160
concrete, the: clinical approach
    112–113; clinical illustrations
    110–112; contributions from
    biological sciences 107–108; moving
    from the concrete to the symbolic
    108–109; psychoanalytic approaches
    to psychosomatic functioning
    106–107
conservative patients 159–160
contiguity see autistic contiguous
countertransference 7–8, 89, 162–164,
    169–174; and environmental trauma

182–188; managing strong feelings in couples therapy 190–198; and play 175–181
couples: countertransference 8; and environmental trauma 182–188; managing strong countertransference feelings in couples therapy 190–198
Covid-19 pandemic 22–30, 31–37
cultures 146–148, 154–155; clinical material 148–154
cure: refusal to be cured 63–71

death 1, 4–5, 28–29, 35, 200; and representation 100–103, 107, 116–117, 120–122; the role of psychic organizers in death awareness 82–91; and threats to self 56–61
defenses 121
dehumanization 127–134
design *see* interior design
Dickens, Charles 129, 201
disclosure, political 160–161
discontiguity: autistic-discontiguity 55–57
discontinuity 52–53
downsizing 38–45
dream, myth as 177

early trauma 49, 60–61; background 50; beginning 50–52; biological transformation 58–59; cameo phallus 54–55; discontinuity 52–53; music in the air 57–58; oral and anal worlds 53–54; paranoia versus autistic-discontiguity 55–57; processing birth trauma 59–60; transformation 58–59; *see also* trauma
Einstein, Albert 55, 128, 134
environmental trauma 182–184; clinical illustration 184–188; *see also* trauma

failure, systemic 70–71
family constellation 117
Ferro, A. 177–179
freedom 29; clinical vignette 15–18; and mourning 13–21
Foley, James 143
Freud, Sigmund 1–3, 13–20, 4–65, 74, 84–85, 106–107, 132–134, 199–200
Fromm, G. M. 68–69, 71
Frommer, M. S. 86

going-on-being 1–2, 8–9, 51–54, 77, 80–81, 199–201; aging, agency, and downsizing 38–45; the body 106–113; catastrophic trauma 127–134; countertransference 7–8, 169–174, 175–181, 182–189, 190–198; Covid-19 31–37; environmental trauma 182–188; freedom and mourning 13–21; Latinx immigrants 146–155; negative transference/countertransference 169–174; rage and autistic-contiguity 74–75; representation 5–6, 97–105, 106–115, 116–124; resilience 97–104; social-political upheaval 6–7, 127–136, 137–145, 146–155, 156–166; threats to the self 4–5, 49–62, 63–73, 74–81, 82–94
Gottlieb, R. M. 63, 65, 68
Greek mythology *see* myth
group meetings 139–140

higher education 146–148, 154–155; clinical material 148–154

ideology 156–158, 160–163
individual patients 7–8
interior design 23–25, 29
interoception 108
interpretation 98–99, 176–180
interpretive inferences 120–121

Josephs, B. 64–65

knowing: refusing to know 67–68
Kohut, H. 44, 64–65, 68, 75, 85

Latinx immigrants 146–148, 154–155; clinical material 148–154
location 24
loss 2–4; aging, agency, and downsizing 38–46; Covid-19 pandemic 31–37; death as 85; freedom and mourning 13–21; pre- and post-Covid office landscape 22–30

meaning 120–121; of objects 38–42
melancholia 2–3, 13–15
Memento Mori 5, 82
mind 25; clinical approach 112–113; clinical illustrations 110–112; contributions from biological sciences 107–108; moving from the concrete to the symbolic 108–109;

psychoanalytic approaches to
psychosomatic functioning 106–107
mourning 1–3, 6–8, 34–36, 200;
    clinical vignette 15–18; and freedom
    13–21
music 57–58
myth: as dream 175–177; refusal to be
    cured 63–71; and resilience 97–105

narrative 148, 154, 176–180
negative transference/
    countertransference 169–174
Nepantla 146–148, 154–155; clinical
    material 148–154
Neruda, Pablo 2
neutrality 26–27; and political beliefs
    156–166; robust 27

objects: and meaning 38–42
October 7 137–144
office space 22–30
Ogden, Thomas 2, 74–75
"Once" 28
Oracle of Delphi 98–100
oral worlds 53–54
Ornstein, P. 65

pandemic *see* Covid-19 pandemic
Pandora's Box 100–101
paranoia 55–57
phallus 54–55
Philoctetes, myth of 63–71
play 178–181
polarization 158–159
political beliefs 156–157, 163–165;
    cognitive styles 162–163;
    conservative patients 159–160;
    ideologies 161–162; origins of
    modern-day polarization 158–159;
    political engagement 162; political
    talk 157; psychotherapy community
    160; shift towards political disclosure
    160–161
politics: political disclosure 160–161;
    political engagement 162; political
    talk 157; *see* political beliefs;
    social-political upheaval
potential space 31–37
preverbal phase of treatment 117–119
progress in therapy 121–123
projective identification 67, 169, 185
psychic organizers 82–91
psychosis-inducing trauma 116–123

psychosomatic 106–109, 185
psychotherapy community 160

rage 74–81
reality, death as 86
refusal to be cured 63–71
relational, death as 85–86
relationship *see* therapeutic relationship
representation 5–6; and the body
    106–115; and psychosis-inducing
    trauma 116–124; and resilience
    97–105
resilience 88–89, 97–105
return 28, 29–30
Rosenfeld, H. 64–65, 68

safe space 137–144
scholarship students 146–148, 154–155;
    clinical material 148–154
self, threats to 4–5; children suffering
    from early trauma 49–62; death
    awareness 82–94; refusal to be cured
    63–73
Sisyphus 101–102
social-political upheaval 6–7;
    dehumanization 127–136; Latinx
    immigrants 146–155; October 7
    137–145; political beliefs 156–165
somatic compromise 108–109
space, potential 31–37
stamps 42–45
students: Latinx immigrants 146–155;
    and October 7 137–144
symbolic, the: clinical approach
    112–113; clinical illustrations
    110–112; contributions from
    biological sciences 107–108; moving
    from the concrete to the symbolic
    108–109; psychoanalytic approaches
    to psychosomatic functioning
    106–107
systemic failure 70–71

taking sides 190–198
therapeutic relationship 156–157,
    163–165; cognitive styles 162–163;
    conservative patients 159–160;
    ideologies 161–162; origins of
    modern-day polarization 158–159;
    political engagement 162; political
    talk 157; psychotherapy community
    160; shift towards political disclosure
    160–161

threats to self 4–5; children suffering from early trauma 49–62; death awareness 82–94; refusal to be cured 63–73
transferences 19–20, 24, 112–113, 128, 162–164, 169–174, 190–191
transformation 58; biological 58–59
translating 177–178
trauma: background 50; beginning 50–52; biological transformation 58–59; cameo phallus 54–55; and dehumanization 127–134; discontinuity 52–53; environmental 182–188; music in the air 57–58; oral and anal worlds 53–54; processing birth trauma 59–60;

psychosis-inducing 116–123; transformation 58–59; treating children suffering from early trauma 49–61

uncertainty 31–37
unsafe world 137–145

void 68–70

Winnicott, Donald 1–2, 38–40, 49–52, 57–58, 61, 66–71, 74–77, 127–129, 199–200
Wittgenstein 116

Yalom, I. 84–85

For Product Safety Concerns and Information please contact our EU
representative GPSR@taylorandfrancis.com
Taylor & Francis Verlag GmbH, Kaufingerstraße 24, 80331 München, Germany

www.ingramcontent.com/pod-product-compliance
Lightning Source LLC
Chambersburg PA
CBHW071413290326
41932CB00047B/2815